How to
Design & Implement
A
RESULTS-
ORIENTED
VARIABLE
PAY
SYSTEM

John G. Belcher, Jr.

amacom

American Management Association

New York • Atlanta • Boston • Chicago • Kansas City • San Francisco • Washington, D.C.
Brussels • Mexico City • Tokyo • Toronto

Library of Congress Cataloging-in-Publication Data

Belcher, John G.
     How to design & implement a results-oriented variable pay system/
John G. Belcher.
          p.   cm.
     Includes bibliographical references and index.
     ISBN 0-8144-0296-8 (hardcover)
     1. Wage payment systems—United States.   2. Incentives in
industry—United States.   3. Compensation management—United States.
I. Title.
HD4927.U6B45   1996
658.3'225—dc20   96-4737
                                                                        CIP

Printing number

10   9   8   7   6   5

Contents

List of Figures

List of Tables

1

Pay and the Competitive Environment

Traditional approaches to compensation do not meet today's business needs and are failing American industry. As the recognition of failure grows, U.S. companies are rapidly adopting alternative reward systems in an attempt to deal with the challenges of an increasingly competitive marketplace.

What's Wrong With Traditional Reward Systems?

As international competition intensified in the 1980s and 1990s, many American companies found themselves unable to compete in a global economy. Millions of jobs and entire industries were lost to foreign competition. It became apparent that the established management model—tall hierarchies, tight control, and autocratic management—was no longer effective.

Change has become an imperative, and progressive managers began to challenge entrenched business systems and practices. Continuous improvement became the mantra, with the emphasis first on productivity and later on quality. Managers began to think in terms of processes rather than functions. The concept of internal customers and internal suppliers began to take hold. Organizations were flattened and decisions were pushed down to the lowest possible level. Frederick Taylor's principle of division of labor gave way to work teams and participative management. Costs were slashed and employees were asked to take on responsibilities formerly reserved for management. Employees became associates, and supervisors became team leaders. The sacred cows of traditional management were taken out and executed one by one. Even the executive dining room began to disappear from the scene.

The compensation practices of American business were an outgrowth of outdated management theories and were therefore outdated as well. Existing pay systems were not aligned with the new management and organizational strategies. Companies weren't reinforcing the behaviors that were now deemed to be necessary to achieve business success.

Fortunately, pay systems are beginning to adapt to the new realities, but the pace of change is slow. Where compensation practices have not kept pace with change, they are impeding a transformation that is critical to the viability of the enterprise in a global economy.

The established approaches to compensation fail to support today's business strategies for a variety of reasons:

- *Traditional reward systems compensate, but do not reward.* While systems exist that theoretically reward performance, the reality is quite different. Merit increases, as they are typically administered for salaried employees, have little to do with merit. There is only slight differentiation among low and high performers, and merit pay therefore amounts to little more than an across-the-board increase. This is partly because the purpose of merit pay in most companies is not limited to rewarding performance; it is also used to adjust the overall salary structure for changes in the labor market and for increases in inflation. As a result, a substantial portion of the potential "merit" increase must, almost by necessity, be awarded to all employees.

The failings of merit pay are also partly due to the inherent difficulties in objectively measuring performance and the reticence on the part of many supervisors to honestly differentiate among their subordinates. For the typical hourly employee, there is generally not even a pretense of pay for performance. These employees are paid at the same rate regardless of their contribution to the success of the business. There is simply nothing to motivate employees to take the initiative to improve the performance of their work area. Schuster and Zingheim, authors of *The New Pay*, said it well: "Traditional pay, although professing to reward performance, is actually based on tenure, entitlement, and internal equity."[1]

- *Traditional reward systems do not reinforce teamwork.* Pay for performance, to the extent that it exists at all, is awarded to individuals. Not surprisingly, this encourages behaviors on the part of employees who maximize their personal stature and benefit, often at the expense of their peers or others in the organization. The result is a lack of cooperation and collaboration between individuals and groups, the withholding of information that might benefit others, and suboptimization of performance in an interdependent organization.

- *Traditional reward systems do not support strategic business priorities.* An organization's reward system is a powerful force, not only because it motivates improvement but also because it sends a powerful message about what is important to the business. Traditional compensation practices fail to harness this force because they do not communicate business priorities and do not reinforce the behaviors that are important to the success of the business.

- *Traditional reward systems are inflexible and are not reflective of business results.* Under traditional practices, organizations pay people the same regardless of the performance or profitability of the business. Compensation, therefore, is essentially a fixed cost.

Not only is compensation a fixed cost, but in many industries it is fixed at a very high level relative to competition. This predicament is an outgrowth of years of large increases in pay when business was good or inflation was high. While an enterprise can afford high pay levels during the good times, it cannot afford them when tough new competitors with lower pay levels enter the arena.

Traditional reward systems have outlived their usefulness. They are not aligned with today's business priorities and are incongruent with today's organizational strategies. As Rosabeth Moss Kanter, professor of business administration at the Harvard Business School, succinctly puts it, "Old ideas about pay are bankrupt."[2] This incongruity, of course, cannot last. Either our compensation systems must change or the business vision of many of our enterprises will not be fully realized.

To meet this challenge, American companies are rapidly adopting alternative reward systems. While these alternative reward systems come in a variety of forms, variable pay—for which we will develop a working definition shortly—is probably the most broadly applicable and meets many of the current reward system needs.

Specifically, variable pay serves two very important purposes: It aligns the pay system with the business and human resources strategies, and it makes compensation at least partly contingent upon the performance of the organization.

Aligning Compensation With Contemporary Management Practices

For most of the twentieth century, management practices relative to work design were driven by the principles of "Scientific Management," as espoused by Frederick Taylor and further developed by his disciples Frank Gilbreth and Henry Gantt, around the turn of the century. The objective of Scientific Management was to maximize the efficiency of the work process through the analysis of manual work operations and the grouping of those operations into individual jobs. A given process was therefore broken down into its component tasks, with each worker specializing in one set of tasks.

This paradigm was right for its time. Our markets were growing rapidly, and Scientific Management facilitated the development of mass-production technologies to meet the ever-growing demand for high-volume, standardized products. Labor was plentiful and education levels were low. What business needed from the employee was a "pair of hands."

Management emphasis on control was a natural accompaniment to Scientific Management. Mass production required that the activities of hordes of workers be coordinated and that every job be done right. Since workers were hired for their hands, not for their brains, they could not be expected to exercise the requisite degree of control. Entities external to the productive process, collectively known as Staff, were required to ensure that proper controls were in place. Hence, hierarchies grew and bureaucracies flourished.

The advent of international competition in the 1960s and 1970s, however, invalidated this approach to the design of work. Entire industries in the United States found that their costs were too high and their quality too low. Customers demanded products and services better suited to their needs, delivered when they wanted them, with no defects. Companies had to change their fundamental management practices, and then, because markets and technologies changed with blinding speed, they had to change again. Change became a constant for American industry.

The bureaucratic systems that industry had created were wholly unsuited to an environment of rapid change. Layers of management and entrenched staff slowed decision making to a crawl and therefore impeded change. Companies were anything but nimble; on the contrary, they were virtually paralyzed. Supervisors, brought up to believe that output was all that mattered, did not adapt to the realities of a marketplace that demanded quality, service, and responsiveness. Employees, oblivious to the competitive challenges (management didn't deem it necessary to inform them) and having no control over their workplace, resisted change as well.

Scientific Management has gradually given way to a very different approach to work design in the 1980s and 1990s. It became clear that an organization could adapt quickly to environmental changes only if every employee understood the importance of these changes and was empowered and motivated to meet the resulting challenges to the viability of the business. The stifling bureaucracy had to be cleared away so that decisions could be made at the lowest possible level by those who had the best information. And business leaders began to recognize that the working-level employee indeed had the best information relative to the dynamics of the work area.

American business also learned that employees in an interdependent organization are more effective at adapting their work processes and improving performance when they thoroughly understand how all the jobs fit together and when they capitalize on the synergy inherent in group processes.

The implication of these revelations was that people should be organized into teams and empowered to make decisions rather than work mindlessly as a collection of individuals. The bureaucracy was thus superseded by the team concept, and a vast cultural change was under way. According to a 1994 *Business Week* special report on the changing nature of work,

> *The last decade, perhaps more than any other time since the advent of mass production, has witnessed a profound redefinition of the way we work. . . . In companies that are flattening hierarchies and, bit by bit, decentralizing decision-making, workers are gaining greater control over what they do; self-direction has superseded the doctrine that workers do only what they're told.*[3]

As this change unfolded across the corporate landscape, a new problem became apparent: The current organizational systems were not compatible with the new management philosophy.

Developing Organizational Systems Compatible With a New Management Philosophy

A variety of organizational systems influence people's behaviors and shape an organization's culture:

▪ *Selection systems* establish criteria for the hiring decision, which in turn impacts the type of employee that populates the organization. It is difficult to create a participative, high-performance culture when an organization hires people who lack initiative and prefer not to be involved in decision making.

▪ *Training systems* determine the skills and competencies of the workforce. It is unrealistic to expect employees to continuously improve the performance of their work area when they lack basic business or technical skills.

▪ *Information-sharing practices* directly impact the employee's knowledge and understanding of the business and the competitive challenges. Uninformed employees cannot be expected to make decisions that are in the best interests of the business. Furthermore, employees who lack information will misunderstand, and mistrust, management decisions that affect them.

- *Appraisal systems* define the employee characteristics or behaviors that are reinforced. If businesses fail to evaluate people on their ability to adapt to a participative environment and their willingness to work with a team, management should not expect them to concentrate on developing these attributes.

- *Promotional practices* establish who advances to positions of power and authority. If people are promoted solely because of their technical skills, businesses cannot expect to have managers with a high level of commitment to participative management.

- *Control systems* set boundaries around employee practices through policies, procedures, and approval authorities. It is difficult to empower employees when their latitude to make decisions is severely limited through tight controls.

This list is not complete, of course, until we add *reward systems.* How businesses compensate people, in fact, may have the greatest influence of all on the organizational culture. Reward systems motivate; employees will do those things that bring them added recompense. Reward systems direct employees' efforts by reinforcing the behaviors that produce the rewards. Reward systems communicate by conveying management's priorities, and clearly have a powerful influence on the organization's culture.

These systems, unfortunately, were developed in most companies during the era of Scientific Management. Businesses didn't need team-oriented employees who would take on responsibilities for continuous improvement, so why consider those characteristics in the selection process? There was no reason to develop employee skills beyond those needed to execute the narrowly defined jobs, so why waste resources on training in business and team skills? Management didn't want employees to make decisions, so why provide them with business information? Businesses didn't expect supervisors and managers to empower their employees, so why incorporate that behavior into the appraisal and promotional criteria? And businesses didn't want employees to work in teams, to question the way their job had been scientifically designed, or to take on responsibilities that had always been reserved for management, so why reward them for such deviant behavior?

To achieve alignment of their compensation systems with a high-involvement, high-commitment strategy, many corporations today are rethinking their compensation philosophy. This need to align compensation with the business and organizational strategies is one of two driving forces for the implementation of variable pay.

The Importance of Reward System Alignment

What are the consequences when an organization's systems are not aligned with its human resources strategy and work design? Misalignment wreaks havoc in the organization by sending conflicting signals to the workforce. Management lacks credibility when it says it wants to change the culture from autocratic to participative. Pressures build within the organization, as management asks employees to do one thing but the organization's systems reinforce very different behaviors. Should a rational individual do what management asks, or play it safe and do what has worked in the past and will bring added pay and promotional opportunities? Eventually, something has got to give. Unfortunately, what usually gives is the change initiative, which, being fragile and threatening to the status quo, is overpowered by the hard reality of organizational systems.

The contributors to the literature on organizational change are unanimous with regard to the importance of reward-system alignment:

> *Running through all serious scholarly work on large-scale organizational change is the notion that you have to change old reward systems to support new practices.*[4]

> *The emerging paradigm of the field is based on a strategic orientation where issues of "internal equity" and "external equity" are viewed as secondary to the firm's need to use pay as an essential integrating and signaling mechanism to achieve overarching business objectives.*[5]

> *When organizations reorganize and ask individuals to pursue new strategic objectives, failing to change the reward system can hamper the change. All too often organizations expect dramatic changes in behavior because of an announced reorganization, when in fact the reward system is communicating to individuals that change is undesirable.*[6]

> *Compensation is a critical piece of an overall human resources strategy. Because compensation is both visible and important to employees, a compensation program designed to communicate and reward strategic goals increases the probability that employees not only will understand what those goals are but also will achieve them.*[7]

And Ed Lawler, director of the Center for Effective Organizations, defines in simple and unambiguous terms the consequences of a lack of alignment:

Unless most systems in an organization are changed to be congruent with participative management practices, ultimately participative management programs will not be effective.[8]

Contingent Compensation

The second driving force for the implementation of variable pay in American industry is the need to make a portion of the employee's compensation contingent on the performance of the company.

Traditionally, base pay is the only form of compensation for most employees (the exception, of course, being bonus compensation for the senior executives). The first problem with base pay is that it is fixed. The second problem is that, barring unusual circumstances, it always goes up. And since it is (by definition) fixed, compensation stays up. Compounding the problem is the tendency of many companies in the past to peg compensation at relatively high levels versus the market (the 60th or 75th percentile, for example). The idea is to attract and retain good employees.

While companies were busy attracting and retaining employees, however, foreign competitors with substantially lower wage rates and comparable (or better) productivity and quality crept slowly onto the scene. Many of these attractive and retentive companies discovered, much to their chagrin, that their labor costs had rendered them uncompetitive in the world economy. The rest is history: layoffs, bankruptcies, entire industries lost to other countries. Those employees that were attracted and retained soon found themselves out of jobs.

The reality of a competitive environment is clear and stark. Corporations can afford to pay employees higher-than-market levels of compensation when their businesses are performing at high levels relative to the competition, but they cannot afford those high levels of compensation when the opposite situation prevails. Paying employees high compensation when the business is under severe competitive stresses is a ticket to bankruptcy.

The obvious response to this predicament is variable pay. When pay is in part variable with the performance of the business, compensation costs flex and adjust to the company's competitive and financial circumstances. Automatic cost reduction is obtained when times are tough, improving the viability of the business.

And variable pay delivers a subtle benefit for the organization's employees: It improves employment security. When all compensation is fixed, the only way a company can adjust its labor costs to the competitive realities is to lay off employees. The cost relief provided by declining variable pay, on the other hand, lessens the pressures to reduce the workforce.

This issue of employment stability is not a trivial one for the company, as well. A company seeking to change its organizational culture cannot afford to ignore the issue of job security, which goes hand in hand with the high-involvement, high-commitment organization. It is difficult to convince employees that management values them and seeks to develop a partnership with them when their jobs evaporate at the first sign of trouble. There are also considerable costs associated with layoffs and the subsequent rehiring when business improves. These include severance pay, training of new hires, lost productivity, and the deleterious effects of low employee commitment owing to resentment and insecurity.

When one considers the use of variable pay as part of the compensation system, the implications for base pay almost immediately come to mind. Should the implementation of variable pay be accompanied by a reduction in base pay? Do companies with variable-pay systems generally have base pay levels that are below competitive levels? Once variable pay is in place, will there be no more increases in base pay?

A substantial majority of companies participating in recent surveys on pay practices (typically 75 to 85 percent)[9] report that variable pay is an "add-on" to a competitive base pay. In other words, there is no pay at risk for employees; there is only upside potential. In view of the importance of organizational buy-in to variable pay, this is the most desirable situation. Variable pay truly represents a win-win opportunity for the company and its employees.

The reality, however, is that conditions are not always conducive to this ideal outcome. Many companies face a situation in which their base pay levels are well above market levels because of either the dynamics of past union negotiations or an "attract and retain" compensation philosophy. Maintaining this above-market position, particularly in the face of international competition, may not be a viable alternative.

The drastic solution to this problem, of course, is to cut pay back to competitive levels and institute variable pay to ensure that above-market compensation is paid only when business performance justifies it. While this course is followed in some cases (primarily when the survival of the business is at stake), it is not a realistic alternative for those organizations seeking to build high-involvement work systems.

The pragmatic approach for most companies with above-market pay is to reduce the rate of increase (or, in more serious situations, eliminate increases) in base pay until compensation levels are more in line with the market. Many of the companies that declared in the above-mentioned surveys that variable pay is an "add-on" are, in fact, following this course of action. While pay is not at risk in the sense that employees may suffer an outright reduction in their compensation, it is at risk in the sense that employees may earn less in the future than they would have had the company continued to increase fixed pay on the same basis as in the past. Schuster and Zingheim refer to this strategy as "potential base pay at risk."[10]

Undoubtedly, employees would rather not place future pay increases at risk, and companies with both above-average productivity and pay at market levels probably can avoid that course of action. For others, however, there may be little choice if their businesses are to remain viable in the long run. And for the employees, there is a tradeoff for that risk: more secure jobs and the prospect of even higher remuneration, through variable pay, than would be possible under a system of base pay alone. For a company in a highly competitive business environment, substantial increases in base pay are simply not an option.

A Working Definition of Variable Pay

Having explored the rationale for variable pay, it is now time to develop a working definition to guide subsequent discussion.

At its simplest, the term *variable pay* could be applied to any compensation system in which pay is not fixed. This definition is overly simplistic, however, and would encompass approaches that do not meet the key objective of aligning pay with business strategy. Variable pay is defined for our purposes as:

> *An alternative compensation system that ties pay to business outcomes and supports a participative management process. Cash payouts are based on a predetermined measure or measures of group or organizational performance.*

Certain words and phrases in this definition require extra emphasis. Variable pay is an *alternative* pay system, which implies a departure from the principles and assumptions underlying traditional approaches to pay. The *tie to business outcomes* serves to create a level of contingent compensation that improves the competitiveness and viability of the business. The performance to which pay is tied is that of a *group or organization* rather than individuals. This provision fosters teamwork and commitment to common goals. Variable pay supports a *participative management process* by aligning pay with a team-oriented, high-involvement human resources strategy. This objective clearly positions variable pay as a change vehicle. Bonus payments are made in *cash*, on a lump-sum basis; deferred-payout retirement programs and systems that increase base pay are, therefore, eliminated from further consideration. Finally, the payout is based on a *predetermined formula*, which effectively excludes discretionary bonus systems.

A word that is noteworthy by its absence from our definition is *incentive*. While variable pay unquestionably has some incentive aspects, it is dangerous to view this system as nothing more than an incentive program. Incentives, almost by definition, are designed to directly bring about improvement by inducing employees to work faster or harder. Our definition, on the other hand, states that variable pay serves to support a participative management process, and it is this process of empowerment that brings about the improvement in performance. Working faster is not the issue; working smarter is.

Unfortunately, traditional organizations do not allow their employees to work smarter, and there are many barriers to changing this paradigm, such as supervisory resistance, lack of skills, lack of teamwork, mistrust of management, and misaligned organizational systems. Variable pay, by itself, will not overcome these barriers; in fact, it will likely aggravate the negative effects of these dysfunctional characteristics. Lacking involvement, employees will have little influence on work processes, and the variable pay system is, thus, not likely to achieve its full potential. Since the effectiveness of variable pay is contingent, to no small degree, on the existence of a participative improvement process, this brings us back, then, to our view of variable pay as a vehicle to support change by aligning the compensation system with a human resources strategy. If companies adopt variable pay only because they "need an incentive," they will probably fail to establish the participative improvement process that is so critical for success.

We divide variable pay systems into three categories, based on the nature of the formula that is used to determine the reward:

1. *Cash profit sharing.* Those systems in which the payout is a function of some measure of profits or profitability. The determining measure may be fully accounted profits, operating profits, return on assets, return on investment, or a variety of other possibilities. Absolute profits may be shared from the first dollar or from a threshold level, and the profitability measure may apply to a company, division, plant, or any other organizational entity.

2. *Gain sharing.* Those systems in which the payout represents a share of the financial gains associated with improvements in group or organizational performance measures. Commonly used measures include costs, productivity, material and supplies utilization, quality (both internal and external), timeliness or responsiveness, safety, uptime/downtime, environmental compliance, attendance, and customer satisfaction. The base level of performance for these measures may represent current performance, past performance, or some improvement over current or past performance.

3. *Goal sharing.* Those systems in which a predetermined amount is paid for the achievement of group or organizational goals. The variables around which goals are typically set are the same as those for gain sharing plans. Some plans have a single goal for each variable, while others employ multiple goal levels for each variable, with progressively higher payouts.

As we will see later, combinations of the above categories are possible. For example, profits could fund a variable pay pool, with the amount actually paid out from the pool based on the number of organizational goals achieved.

Unfortunately, the term *variable pay* has been widely misused in the literature, often including pay systems that are not variable at all. In many cases, it is used synonymously with the term *alternative pay*, which gives license to include almost anything that is nontraditional in nature. It is important, therefore, to note that certain types of compensation systems do not meet our definition of variable pay:

- *Skill-based pay* is a system in which base compensation is determined by the number of jobs in which the individual has demonstrated proficiency rather than based on any particular job classification. Employees are thus reinforced for obtaining multiple job or business skills and are better able to take on self-management responsibilities with their team members.

While skill-based pay offers great potential as an alternative pay system for team-based organizations, it does not qualify as variable pay for two reasons: It is a base pay system (and is therefore fixed rather than variable) and it is an individual (rather than group) compensation system. The same comments also apply to a variation of skill-based pay known as *competency-based pay.*

- *Individual incentives,* such as piecework systems, are variable but obviously fail to meet the group reward test. In addition, most individual incentives are traditional, rather than alternative, reward systems in that they are designed to support the Scientific Management paradigm.

Piecework systems, in fact, are rapidly losing favor in American industry because they fail to support quality and responsiveness initiatives and are incongruent with team-based work systems.

- *Discretionary bonuses* are variable in nature but are not tied to a predetermined measure of group or organizational performance. Therefore, they fail to communicate business priorities and probably have little impact on behavior.

- *Merit bonuses* are a form of variable compensation and represent an

Table 1-1. Prevalence of variable pay programs.

Type of Program	Percentage of Companies Using:
• Organizationwide incentive	33%
• Current profit sharing	21
• Small-group incentive	18
• Gain sharing	11

Source: *Variable Pay: Nontraditional Programs for Motivation and Reward*
(New York: The Conference Board, 1993).

improvement over the traditional practice of adding the merit increase to base pay. When paid as a lump sum, merit pay is no longer an annuity, to be paid to the employee for the rest of his career, but must be earned every year.

This approach also can serve as contingent compensation if the overall level of merit bonuses is partly a function of business performance. As an individual reward, however, the merit bonus fails to meet our working definition of variable pay.

• *Deferred profit sharing* does not provide for current cash payouts. These systems are generally designed to deliver retirement benefits rather than reinforce performance improvement, and therefore serve a different purpose.

The Prevalence of Variable Pay

Variable pay is no longer an unusual system, practiced by only a few innovative organizations. The prevalence of various forms of variable pay as we have defined it, based on a 1993 study by The Conference Board, is shown in Table 1-1. For clarification, the term *organizationwide incentive* is defined by The Conference Board as a variable payment, usually based on the organization's earnings, which may also include an evaluation of individual or group performance. Using our taxonomy, this approach would be a combination of two of the categories, such as cash profit sharing and goal sharing. While the percentages shown in Table 1-1 are not totally additive (for example, some companies have more than one of these systems in use), it is clear that variable pay has deeply penetrated American industry.

Variable Pay as a Change Strategy

Surveys in recent years inevitably support the conclusion that variable pay is most effective when used as part of a broader organizational change strategy:

> *While many organizations see group incentives as a way to introduce variability into their pay programs, interest in the variable pay objective was surprisingly low, relative to their objectives. This suggests that organizations are coming to recognize precisely what group incentives are: a means of reinvigorating the corporation and managing change, rather than just an attempt at developing a different (or perhaps less costly) way of paying people or shifting risk to employees.[11]*

> *The gainsharing plan is more an expression and enhancement of a particular organizational culture than it is a compensation arrangement. Rather than the payment being the primary focus, it is almost a by-product of the proper functioning of the organization's culture.[12]*

This orientation toward variable pay as a change vehicle is reflected in the list of objectives established for variable pay by a business unit of a major corporation:

- To create an awareness that each employee is part of a team and is accountable to team members for improving total team effectiveness
- To share business success with all team members in return for their contribution of knowledge, skills, commitment, and effort
- To better ensure job security by improving business success
- To increase employee participation, thereby improving the quality of the work environment
- To improve job satisfaction by enabling employees to use all of their capabilities
- To enable employees to identify with business goals as their personal goals
- To support the evolution of the team concept
- To increase total compensation
- To enhance communications
- To enhance customer focus
- To improve the company's financial performance

The forces that are moving American industry toward greater employee empowerment and team-based work systems will likely continue unabated for the foreseeable future. With many of the world's nations just beginning to realize the benefits of industrialization and a free-market economy, the competitive challenges can only increase. Only those companies that can successfully engage their employees in meeting these challenges will survive these turbulent times ahead.

As the pace of organizational transformation accelerates, it will become clear to more and more organizations that traditional pay systems represent a major impediment that cannot be abided. Compensation practices will have to be brought into alignment with organizational strategies. In sum, variable pay is a system whose time has come.

References

1. Jay R. Schuster and Patricia K. Zingheim, *The New Pay* (New York: Lexington Books, 1992).
2. Rosabeth Moss Kanter, *When Giants Learn to Dance* (New York: Simon and Schuster, 1989).
3. "The New World of Work," *Business Week,* October 17, 1994.
4. Robert E. Cole, "Large-Scale Change and the Quality Revolution," in Allen M. Mohrman, Jr., et al., *Large-Scale Organizational Change* (San Francisco: Jossey-Bass, 1990).
5. Luis R. Gomez Mejia and David B. Balkin, *Compensation, Organizational Strategy, and Firm Performance* (Cincinnati: South-Western Publishing Co., 1992).
6. Edward E. Lawler III, *Strategic Pay* (San Francisco: Jossey-Bass, 1990).
7. George T. Milkovich and Renae F. Broderick, "Developing a Compensation Strategy," in Milton L. Rock and Lance A. Bolger, *The Compensation Handbook* (New York: McGraw-Hill, 1991).
8. Edward E. Lawler III, *High-Involvement Management* (San Francisco: Jossey-Bass, 1991).
9. Jerry L. McAdams and Elizabeth J. Hawk, *Organizational Performance and Rewards* (Scottsdale, Ariz.: American Compensation Association, 1994). Also, *Variable Pay: New Performance Rewards* (New York: The Conference Board, 1990).
10. Schuster and Zingheim, *The New Pay,* p. 203.
11. "Achieving Results Through Sharing," survey report by Towers Perrin, 1990.
12. *Variable Pay.*

2

The First Steps

To restate a major point made in Chapter 1, variable pay is a nontraditional way of rewarding people for nontraditional behaviors that support the business strategy. Variable pay, therefore, represents change for most organizations.

Any organizational change initiative will face a variety of impediments, such as inadequate leadership for change, entrenched organizational systems, a lack of skills to adapt, inertia, low organizational awareness of the need to change, and outright resistance to change. The success of any such initiative is, therefore, dependent in no small part on the quality of the preparation and the efficacy of the first steps.

Before the process of system design and implementation can begin, a number of preparatory steps must be taken. The very first step (as it would be for any change effort) is for management and other stakeholders to learn all they can about variable pay. They should understand its purpose and objectives. They should learn about the experiences of other organizations. They should become conversant with the broad array of design options, along with the pros and cons of each. They should learn as much as possible about the pitfalls and causes of failure. The usual resources are available for this education: the literature, seminars, site visits, consultations with experts.

Having gained a basic understanding of variable pay, management should next determine whether variable pay makes business sense for its organization.

Fit With the Business and Organizational Strategy

Like any organizational system, compensation should support and reinforce the business vision and organizational strategy. If it does not do so, it will be ineffective at best and counterproductive at worst. To assess the congruency and fit of variable pay, management must ask itself some hard questions.

1. *What are our organization's values?* Values drive decision making in an organization; if management believes that people are an asset to be developed, its decisions will be very different than if the opposite belief prevails. Many companies today have an explicit statement of values, and this may serve as one indication of management's convictions. Management's behaviors, however, provide the clearest indication of management's values. If people are not treated with dignity and respect, all the lofty wording in a values statement will ring hollow and variable pay will be viewed by employees as just another effort to manipulate people.

2. *What is our human resources strategy?* In some cases, the more appropriate question may be, do we have a human resources strategy? The real power of variable pay, as discussed in the previous chapter, lies in its ability to support a strategy of employee empowerment and partnership. Where no such strategy exists, variable pay will provide contingent compensation, but it is not likely to produce significant improvements in performance. It may, in fact, produce resentment among employees because they are unable to realize the added compensation that variable pay promises.

3. *Are we really committed to creating a high-involvement culture?* It may be difficult to find an organization today that does not profess to be committed to employee involvement. There is often a great gap, however, between verbal endorsement and execution. Management may think it wants to empower its employees, but when it comes right down to abandoning the comfortable, tried-and-true practices, management may opt for the low-risk approach of maintaining the status quo. With little real involvement, variable pay will not likely meet expectations.

4. *Are we prepared to commit the resources necessary to support this change?* It is unrealistic to expect to achieve significant organizational change on a shoestring. A commitment of financial resources is required for training, restructuring systems, and obtaining consulting assistance. An even bigger concern may be the commitment of management time, which always seems to be in extremely limited supply. If management is not willing to allocate adequate resources to this effort, it is doubtful that the commitment is there to successfully pull off a variable pay plan.

5. *How much do we really want our employees to know about the business?* Information sharing goes hand in hand with employee involvement and commitment to the business. Management cannot expect employees to behave like partners in the business and take the initiative to improve the organization's performance if they do not understand the mission, priori-

ties, and challenges of the business. The attitudes that employees would not understand business information or could not be trusted with competitive information are symptomatic of a lack of belief that people really are important to the success of the business. Given the tremendous competitive challenges faced by most businesses today, the risk associated with failing to provide business information to employees may be far greater than the risk of people making inappropriate use of that information.

6. *Do we really want a more collaborative relationship with the union?* Unions are a fact of life for many companies, and they have a major impact on organizational functioning. Management has a choice: It can fight the union every step of the way on general principles, or it can seek to develop a positive, cooperative relationship. The first choice is inimical to variable pay because the effort will be viewed with great suspicion by the union and its members, and the resulting resistance will likely render the entire effort unworkable.

It is very important that management not react to these questions in a knee-jerk fashion ("Of course, we want our employees to be involved!"). There is too much lip service given to the values of teamwork and employee empowerment, and too little manifestation of these values in the day-to-day functioning of an organization. It is often useful, in fact, to obtain data from the workforce with respect to employees' perceptions of management's values and commitment to change. If employees do not believe they are valued by those in authority, management needs to do some soul-searching and examine its behaviors.

Who Participates?

If management concludes that variable pay is a good fit with its business strategy, it now faces its first important design decision: Who will participate in this new compensation system? This first decision is also one of the most important, for it will send a powerful message about the company's compensation philosophy and its commitment to a team-oriented culture.

There often is an inclination to designate only the hourly or nonexempt employees as the participants in a variable pay plan. The focus of the organization's employee-involvement effort is typically on this segment of the workforce, and the incongruity of the traditional pay system is most apparent here. Management may even convince itself that it already has a pay-for-performance system, in the form of a merit increase program, for salaried employees.

When the variable pay program is an outcome of a collective bargaining process, there may be an even stronger argument for limiting its application to the hourly workforce. Variable pay is often negotiated as a tradeoff for a smaller-than-normal increase in base pay for bargaining-unit employees, and, as such, would seem inappropriate where salaried pay increases are determined by a different set of criteria.

A decision to limit the application of a variable pay plan to hourly employees may be an unfortunate one, however, for it flies in the face of the team orientation that management is seeking to develop. Systems that differentiate between salaried and hourly employees give rise to conflicting goals and help preserve the "us-versus-them" mind-set that drives behaviors in traditionally managed organizations. For those companies that are serious about creating a high-involvement, high-commitment culture, any system that draws distinctions between classes of employees is anathema.

In addition, new stresses may be created in the organization, as the excluded salaried employees come to resent the fact that hourly workers now have the opportunity to earn additional compensation. Their enthusiasm for supporting ideas for improvement, at a minimum, will be dampened. The logical decision in most cases, then, is to include all employees in the variable pay plan. Management can then have a degree of confidence that all employees are working toward, and being rewarded for, achievement of common objectives.

Existing pay systems may represent an additional complicating factor for some companies. In recent years, a number of large corporations have created contingent compensation systems for their salaried employees in order to slow the rate of increase in fixed compensation costs. These systems generally tie salaried bonuses to a measure of corporate profitability. The problem arises when these companies subsequently implement a variable pay system for hourly or union employees at the plant or business unit level. While management may recognize the benefits of including salaried employees in the new plan, it often concludes that this course of action would be inappropriate because it would represent "double dipping."

Allowing an existing pay system to dictate a decision on variable pay is unfortunate for more reasons than one. Not only does the company miss an opportunity to advance the team orientation at the unit level, it also forgoes the opportunity to more effectively reinforce continuous improvement behaviors among the salaried ranks. It is unlikely that bonuses tied to corporate profits in a large company will materially change the behavior of salaried employees below the executive level. With pay tied to the performance of a single operating unit, on the other hand, management can expect to enjoy the behavior-modification effects that accompany a system tying pay to measures that employees can impact and can understand.

One major corporation with a salaried bonus program considered this issue at length before embarking on its first plant gain-sharing program. Its decision was to retain the salaried bonus for those employees at plants with gain-sharing programs, but to allow the affected employees to earn the gain-sharing bonus to the extent that it exceeded the salaried bonus for the year. The company was thus able to tie salaried compensation to site performance while retaining the link to corporate results.

Another corporation in a similar situation reached a different conclusion. Since the salaried bonus was instituted as a partial replacement for the traditional merit increase program, it was not viewed as incremental pay and double-dipping was therefore not an issue. Salaried employees in this company received bonuses from plant-level variable pay plans in addition to the companywide salaried bonus.

It should be noted that there is one small group of employees that is almost always ineligible for bonuses from a unit-level variable pay system: those senior managers who are participants in an executive bonus system. A variety of reasons are advanced for this exclusion. First, senior managers might make decisions that are not in the best interests of the company in order to increase their variable pay bonuses; second, senior managers should be focusing on strategic issues rather than on measures that are relevant to working-level employees; and third, senior managers should not "double-dip." None of these arguments is particularly compelling, but the exclusion of top management has become an established practice in American industry.

Defining Group Boundaries

The next major decision that management must make relates to group boundaries. Should bonuses be based on the performance of the entire corporation, on an operating unit (such as a division or plant), or on a work team? This decision, like the previous one, is not trivial, as it will have great bearing on the character of the system and its impact on employee behavior. At the same time, it may not be an easy decision, owing to the tradeoffs involved.

The most significant tradeoff is between the two objectives of variable pay: contingent compensation and alignment with the human resources strategy. The decision that maximizes a system's effectiveness in achieving one objective will likely preclude its achieving maximum effectiveness in the other.

For example, if contingent compensation is the primary objective, the variable pay system should produce total compensation costs that vary with the company's bottom-line performance. Profitability is probably the best determinant of a company's ability to pay high compensation, and times of low or nonexistent profitability are precisely when the company needs cost relief to ensure its ability to pay its bills, attract capital, and fund investments in the future. Obtaining such short-term cost relief may even be critical to its survival.

If a variable pay system is structured around the performance of individual sites, or teams within these sites, compensation costs will not be tied precisely to the company's profitability. A company with poor profitability may well have a certain number of high-performing units or teams, and the company would be obligated to compensate these groups accordingly. The cost relief obtained during periods of economic distress would thus be correspondingly less than would have been obtained under a companywide formula.

A single-minded pursuit of the contingent compensation objective would, therefore, lead one to conclude that there should be one variable pay system, covering everybody in the company, based on overall company profitability. A simple, companywide profit-sharing program would have great appeal here. Unfortunately, the advantage of such a companywide formula for contingent compensation purposes quickly becomes a disadvantage when pursuing the objective of aligning compensation with an employee empowerment strategy.

Employees generally have a great deal of difficulty relating their behaviors on the job to the profitability of the company. First, there is the problem of sheer numbers. An individual who is one of thousands of employees cannot be expected to feel that he has any real impact on company profitability. Second, profitability is heavily impacted by forces that are totally out of the average employee's control. Pricing, raw material costs, product mix, inventory changes, even arcane accounting adjustments can overwhelm any performance improvements to which the employee may have contributed.

The individual, in variable pay jargon, would be said in this situation to have a low *line of sight.* He or she will not be able to relate individual performance on the job to the bonus earned through the profit-sharing program. Management should not, therefore, expect any meaningful behavior change to occur. For this reason, profit sharing is probably not a good choice when the primary objective of variable pay is to align compensation with a high-involvement strategy. Behavior change, after all, is the major desired outcome of alignment.

In pursuit of this objective, management might expect maximum behavior change to occur when variable pay is structured around individual work teams. Each employee's bonus would then be a function of the performance of his or her team. The measures would be meaningful to employees, and they would likely feel that they have a significant impact on those measures. This approach, often called *small-group incentives* or *team incentives*, would appear to be the best alternative when the primary objective of a variable pay plan is alignment of the reward system.

Unfortunately for the alignment camp, the decision to utilize a small-group structure is not as simple as it may seem, for along with the benefits come some serious complications and risks:

1. *The phenomenon of suboptimization.* When people are rewarded for the performance of their department or team, they will naturally focus their efforts internally in order to improve the team measures. They are less likely to concern themselves with their impact on other groups within the organization. If the activities of departments or teams are totally independent of each other, this may not represent a serious consideration. Where there is interdependency, however, the outcome of this behavior can be poor interfaces between groups and a deterioration of the performance of the larger organization.

2. *Perceptions of inequity.* A potentially very serious complication arises from the variation in performance across teams. By its very nature, team incentives result in some groups receiving larger bonuses than others. Teams that receive little or no bonus will almost certainly find fault with the system. They may conclude, for example, that their formula represented a greater challenge than those of other teams. Or they may feel that their performance prior to the implementation of variable pay was higher than that of other teams, resulting in less opportunity for improvement. Inevitably, then, there will be perceptions of inequity. For those groups that consistently receive low payouts, the consequences are predictable: discouragement, demotivation, and, ultimately, loss of interest in and commitment to the variable pay system.

3. *Excessive payments by the company.* It is not difficult to conceive of a situation where some teams improve their measures while the performance of others declines. The net effect for the company could well be little or no improvement (or even an overall decline) in performance. Yet bonuses would have to paid to the successful teams, and the company's compensation costs would therefore increase.

4. *Administrative complications.* There are a number of administrative complications associated with small-group incentives. The system would likely be more difficult to design in the first place, as measures would need to be developed for each team and great care would have to be taken to avoid building real inequities into the system. Once the plan is in place,

there would be several complications relative to the transfer of employees from one group to another. For example, how would the bonus be determined for an employee who worked in two different teams during the bonus period? How would management convince an employee to transfer from a high-earning to a low-earning group? And record-keeping requirements, of course, would be significantly greater for a small-group system.

In view of these complications, the important question is, are the benefits of the small-group approach worth the risks? This question is impossible to answer with certainty in most cases, but there are circumstances where the answer is likely to be in the affirmative. For example, in a very large organizational unit, with several thousand employees, the obvious line-of-sight problem certainly increases the attractiveness of team incentives. By the same token, an organization with relatively independent—as opposed to interdependent—groups does not face as high a risk of suboptimization.

Where there is a relatively self-contained organization, such as a plant, with a few hundred employees or less, a sitewide variable pay plan probably makes more sense. While some line-of-sight benefits will be sacrificed, that is probably a good tradeoff for avoiding some major problems that could undermine, and even nullify, the effectiveness of the plan.

It should be noted that there is a middle ground between the organizationwide formula and the small-group approach. There are a variety of plan designs that combine a sitewide formula with a small-group feature. One approach is simply to have two formulas: one that measures the overall organizational performance, and another that measures team results. Employees would thus receive bonuses from two sources. One plant in the defense industry even has three formulas. The first consists of productivity measures for individual departmental teams; the second measures the combined productivity and overall cost and quality performance of each of the two buildings on the site that houses these teams; and the third formula includes the combined performance of the two manufacturing buildings plus the administrative and overhead costs associated with managing the site.[1] Such tiered formulas are discussed further in Chapter 6.

An alternative way to combine the organizationwide and small-group approaches is to fund a variable pay pool based on the organization's performance, but require that individual work groups or teams achieve certain goals in order to receive their full share of that pool. In one plant, for example, a gain-sharing bonus pool is funded by reductions in the unit cost of the plant's production. In order to get its full share of that pool, each department must meet quality and safety goals. This alternative seems to be particularly prevalent in the health-care industry. Several hospitals have plans in which departments must qualify for their share of a bonus pool that is funded by savings in costs versus budget. This qualification is typically attained by holding departmental costs within budgeted levels and achieving some sort of quality or service goal.

Through these hybrid approaches, an organization can gain some of the line-of-sight benefits of a team incentive while diminishing the associated risks. Perceptions of inequity may be lessened, and any suboptimizing behaviors would negatively impact the offending employees' total bonus potential. In any event, the group-boundary decision should be made prior to launching a variable pay process, as little work can be done on developing a formula without knowing the composition of the variable pay groups.

Piloting the Variable Pay Plan

In a multisite organization, management faces another important decision before it can proceed to design a variable pay system. Should variable pay be installed throughout the company immediately, or should it be piloted in one or more sites? In most cases, management should opt for the latter, for two reasons.

The first reason relates to an organization's lack of experience in designing and implementing a variable pay program. These systems are complicated to design, and the probability is high that the first effort will not be perfect. The implementation process, in addition, is demanding and critical to success. Piloting the plan in one location or organizational unit will provide valuable experience that can be applied later, as the program is diffused throughout the organization.

The second reason for piloting the variable pay plan is that there is likely to be considerable difference in the readiness of various units to support and successfully execute a nontraditional form of compensation. Low readiness is a major cause of failure in the ability of variable pay plans to meet the objectives established for them (see the following section). If a large company were to implement variable pay in all of its locations simultaneously, there would very likely be a number of disappointments, if not outright failures. Piloting, on the other hand, allows the organization to proceed where readiness is greatest and to work on raising the readiness of other locations prior to implementation.

A related question that often arises is whether variable pay should be piloted in one group within a single site. This course of action is probably not advisable unless the site in question is very large and composed of relatively autonomous units. In an interdependent organization, it is difficult to judge the effectiveness of a variable pay plan in isolation from the influences of other groups. Performance improvement (or the lack thereof) in the pilot group may be due to actions of other departments or teams. It also creates additional stresses in the organization, as those departments or teams not chosen as the pilot may resent not having the opportunity to earn additional compensation.

Evaluating Organizational Readiness

Before beginning to design a variable pay plan, management needs to give some consideration to the readiness of the organization. If the sole objective of variable pay is to create a layer of contingent compensation, readiness may not seem a major issue. If, on the other hand, management seeks to reinforce employee involvement and continuous improvement through variable pay, readiness is anything but a trivial issue. As was noted in the previous section, low readiness is a major cause of failure in implementing variable pay programs.

For the company with multiple operating units, the major, if not sole, criterion for selecting the pilot site or sites should be readiness. If the initial effort fails, the effect will be reduced management and organizational interest in variable pay and a lack of sponsorship for implementing the plan elsewhere in the organization. Management is well advised, therefore, to begin where the likelihood of success is greatest. This advice sometimes runs counter to a management inclination to implement variable pay where there are major performance problems. Believing that variable pay will solve these problems, however, is wishful thinking. The very existence of serious organizational or management problems will work against the development of an effective improvement process that is key to the success of a variable pay system.

Where there is only one organizational candidate (or one obvious choice) for variable pay, an assessment of readiness is still useful, as it will highlight areas of organizational functioning that could represent impediments to success. Armed with this knowledge, management can then take steps to deal with these issues prior to, or at least coincident with, implementation of the variable pay plan.

Management Commitment to Change

The first, and most important, readiness criterion is management commitment to change. Since variable pay aligns compensation with a high-involvement strategy, there clearly must be some level of commitment among the organization's senior management to execute such a strategy. The variable pay system does not, by itself, produce improvements in performance. Variable pay rewards improvements produced by other processes that engage employees in performance improvement activities. If management is not committed to these involvement processes and willing to overcome the impediments to their success, variable pay will probably fail to meet expectations.

On the surface, management commitment may not seem to be a problem in many organizations. It would be hard to find a manager today who does not profess to be a supporter of employee involvement and teamwork. Unfortunately, however, the willingness to attack and overcome the barriers to organizational change often fails to match the rhetoric.

How does one know if management is truly committed to change? One way is to examine management behaviors. Has organizational change been accorded an explicit priority? Has management significantly increased the level of information sharing? Is there a plan to implement change? Is employee involvement on the agenda for all staff meetings? Have time and resources been committed for training employees and supervisors in the necessary skills? Are there initiatives under way to redesign organizational systems that are not congruent with a high-involvement culture? Are managers adapting their own behaviors and modeling participative management? Never has the phrase "Actions speak louder than words" been more appropriate than when evaluating management's true intentions.

Another way to gauge management's commitment to change is to ask the hourly employees and first-line supervisors. They are affected by management decisions and actions every day and are therefore qualified to assess where management's true priorities and commitments lie. Assessment tools, such as surveys, interviews, and focus groups, can be very useful here.

Employee Involvement

Another readiness issue is the present state of employee involvement. As suggested above, the involvement process is the engine that drives the improvements that fund payouts from the variable pay system. Variable pay is, therefore, most likely to meet expectations where there exists an established involvement or team process that provides a degree of empowerment to employees. Indeed, if the organization has no involvement vehicles, such as problem-solving teams or work teams, through which employees can implement their ideas, there may be little they can do to improve the performance of their work areas.

This should not be taken to mean that a sophisticated, self-directed team process must be in place prior to the implementation of variable pay. On the contrary, it may be impossible to create an advanced involvement process without some form of alternative reward system. It does suggest, however, that it may be premature to implement a variable pay system where the employee involvement process is in its infancy or has not yet even begun.

Information-Sharing Practices

The effectiveness of present information-sharing practices represents another readiness issue. If the workforce has not been provided with business and performance information on a regular basis, employees will not appreciate the business issues and cannot be expected to behave as if they are partners in the business. Lacking knowledge of the business, employees will also have difficulty understanding the purpose and mechanics of the variable pay system. Finally, a lack of information sharing invariably breeds low trust, which is in itself a readiness issue.

Employee Trust

Where trust is low, the variable pay system will have little credibility. Employees will question management's intentions, perhaps viewing the initiative as nothing more than a ploy to avoid paying a fair wage. They will also fear that management will manipulate the system to deprive them of bonuses that they have legitimately earned. And in a union environment, union leadership may fear that management will use the existence of variable pay as a lever at the bargaining table.

Extent of Teamwork

The degree of teamwork should also be considered when evaluating readiness. Teamwork is deficient in traditional organizations for a variety of reasons. Management fails to share information on business goals and how the various organizational units contribute to those goals. Poor communication results in a lack of understanding of other groups' needs. Traditional reward systems encourage turf protection and behaviors that lead to suboptimization of performance. Adversarial labor relations foster a "us-versus-them" attitude. Lack of teamwork in an interdependent organization represents a serious impediment to success with a variable pay program, as significant improvement opportunities requiring cooperation will not be realized.

Employment Stability

Another readiness issue is employment stability. It may be difficult to create a high-performance culture where job security is low. Employees are likely to be less receptive to productivity-improvement initiatives if the expected outcome is loss of jobs. It is also unrealistic to expect the workforce to feel and act as if they are partners in the business when people fear for their jobs. In recognition of this fact, many companies today are developing employment stability strategies to lessen these barriers and increase employee commitment to the business.

Receptivity to Change

An important readiness concern that is often overlooked is supervisory receptivity to change. The first-line supervisor is a key player in this process, for he or she has a significant impact on the behaviors of hourly or nonexempt employees. First-line supervisors can, if they so choose, undermine the whole change process. A certain amount of supervisory resistance to employee involvement, and by extension to variable pay, is predictable and understandable. At minimum, there will be a major change in role of supervisors; rather than give orders, they are now told to be coaches and facilitators. This may well be viewed by supervisors as a loss of power and authority. And it doesn't take much imagination to carry this change to its logical conclusion: elimination of supervisors altogether.

Management often has a blind spot here; it assumes that supervisors will support the change effort if told to do so. Management may schedule some skills training for supervisors, but do little else to address their needs and build their commitment to the process.

Almost as important as management commitment is union support for change. If the union does not at least acquiesce in the implementation of a variable pay plan, it is not feasible to launch such a program in the first place. But acquiescence is really not enough; readiness is considerably enhanced when the union leadership actively supports, or even sponsors, the initiative. The union wields considerable influence in most organizations, and a lack of enthusiasm for variable pay on the part of union leadership will likely have a dampening effect on the level of employee buy-in to the program.

The Business Situation

Finally, the organization's business situation should be taken into account when evaluating readiness for variable pay. The most desirable situation is one in which the business is relatively stable or growing. In a declining business situation, it may be difficult for employees to improve certain variables, such as productivity, which are influenced by volume changes. In addition, management may be forced to implement some unpleasant measures, such as workforce reductions. As noted earlier, job insecurity does not contribute to a sense of well-being and commitment to the business on the part of employees.

Another concern in this category is any pending business or organizational changes of a significant nature. Acquisitions, reorganizations, restructurings, expansions, or the addition or deletion of major product lines may distract people from a focus on performance improvement and may also invalidate the variable pay measures. It is wise under these circumstances to defer launching a variable pay plan until some degree of stability has returned.

The reality in many industries, on the other hand, is that one major change follows another, and stability is a state that is not likely to be experienced in the foreseeable future. In that situation, one can only proceed when otherwise ready and be prepared to modify the variable pay system as events warrant.

Some Examples of Readiness Assessment Processes

While the readiness criteria described above represent the key issues, this is not an exhaustive list. One Fortune 500 company, in fact, evaluates eighteen criteria, as shown in Table 2-1.

Another major corporation has a very well-developed and rigorous readiness-assessment process that each site must undergo before receiving clearance from the corporation to design and implement a variable pay plan. The assessment is a three-phase process and is administered by a variable pay steering committee at the corporate headquarters.

In the first phase, a questionnaire is completed by site management. This instrument probes management's strategies relative to many of the areas already identified as readiness issues. The second phase, assuming that management's responses pass muster with the steering committee, involves administration of a written survey to the employee population. The survey contains thirty-five questions, and it addresses the same issues as those in the management questionnaire. The third and final phase employs focus groups to obtain more detailed and qualitative information on the readiness issues.

The corporate steering committee then meets with site management to review the assessment results and provide counsel relative to any organizational issues that represent impediments to the successful execution of a variable pay process. Based on its findings, the corporate group either approves the site's proceeding to the design stage or requires that specific deficiencies be dealt with before approval is granted. To date, this company has implemented eleven variable pay plans without failure.

It should be noted that readiness is not an absolute, nor is it suscep-

Table 2-1. Readiness criteria for Fortune 500 company.

Cultural	
• Business understanding	• Decision making
• Productivity	• Trust
• Participation	• Training
• Group or team approach	• Communications
• Status	• Job distinctions
• Employee relations	• Employment security
• Fairness	

Business	
• Business maturity	• Cyclicality
• Business viability	• Competitive standing
• Technology	

Source: Michael A. Bennett, "Gainsharing—Company Uses Technique to Enhance Safety, Cost-Cutting, Customer Service," *ACA News*, March 1994. Reprinted from *ACA News*, March 1994, with permission from the American Compensation Association (ACA), 14040 N. Northsight Blvd., Scottsdale, Arizona U.S.A. 85260; telephone 602/951-9191; fax 602/483-8352

tible to precise quantification. Ultimately, readiness is a judgment call. For example, it is not necessary that an organization score high on all the readiness criteria in order to have a reasonable capacity to support a variable pay program. What is important is that there be movement in the right direction, along with a commitment on the part of management to continue that movement.

Timing

There has been long-standing debate regarding the appropriate timing for implementation of an alternative reward system during the evolution of a change process. Some years ago, the consensus among change experts was that transformation to high-involvement, team-oriented work systems should be well along before changing the reward system. Without effective involvement vehicles in place, the theory went, employees would not be empowered to bring about the kind of improvements that would yield them significant rewards through the variable pay system.

Contemporary thinking on this issue is much less rigid. Using variable pay to lead, rather than follow, an organizational change has many advocates today.[2] One study, in fact, concluded that 52 percent of the variable pay programs were implemented to lead, rather than follow, an organizational change process.[3] The argument for implementing variable pay early in the change process centers on the powerful communications capability of reward systems. Management's announcement of its desire to transform the organizational culture from autocratic to participative is invariably met with a great deal of skepticism on the part of employees. By implementing a variable pay system, however, management is "putting its money where its mouth is," sending a strong message about its commitment to change.

Launching a variable pay system early in the evolution of a change process is a legitimate option if the readiness assessment produces no major red flags, such as a high level of distrust or a poor union-management relationship. It probably should not, however, be the first step in the change process, as it would likely cause confusion and would be impaired by the lack of any systems to evaluate and implement employee ideas. At a minimum, management should increase the sharing of business information and implement some elementary idea-handling schemes to unfreeze the organization prior to launching variable pay.

Contract Issues

The final issue that must be addressed before proceeding to the design process applies specifically to unionized organizations. The issue is the relationship of variable pay to the collective bargaining process.

The first reaction by many is that variable pay must be negotiated at the bargaining table. It is, after all, a compensation system, and compensation is a bargainable issue. However, the best approach in most cases is to design and administer the variable pay system outside the bounds of collective bargaining. There are two reasons for this. First, collective bargaining is, by design, an adversarial process. It is most effective when dealing with issues where management and the union have conflicting objectives. Each party comes to the table with the objective of obtaining the best possible outcome for those it represents. Through the give-and-take of bargaining, a result is obtained that is acceptable to both parties. In doing so, management and the union accept less than satisfactory results on some issues in order to gain the desired objective on other issues.

Variable pay, however, must be a win-win proposition if it is to be successful. The objective of a variable pay design effort should be to produce the best possible system, so that maximum performance improvement, and therefore maximum bonuses, are achieved. This outcome is possible only if the system meets the needs of the business while simultaneously being perceived by employees as a fair opportunity for them to earn increased compensation. The worst possible outcome would be a system design that favors one side or the other because of the dynamics of the collective bargaining process.

The second reason to keep variable pay out of the bargaining process is a practical one. Most industries face a dynamic and turbulent business environment, and the variable pay system will almost certainly have to change over time if it is to continue to meet the needs of the business. If details of the plan were written into the union contract, the contract would have to be reopened every time there was a need to modify the variable play plan. This degree of inflexibility would be a threat to the viability of the program in a rapidly changing business environment.

If the system is not negotiated at the bargaining table, how should it be designed to ensure that it meets the business needs and is, at the same time, fair and equitable for the employees? The answer is that the plan should be developed through a collaborative labor-management design process. The nature of this process will be discussed in detail in Chapter 3.

The foregoing discussion should not be construed to mean, however, that there should be no contract language whatsoever relating to the variable pay system. It is common practice to write enabling language into the contract to ensure that the collaborative design process and the resulting system are sanctioned by the labor agreement. An example of enabling language at its simplest appears in an addendum to one contract:

To recognize the contributions of our employees, the company will establish a gain sharing program. The gain sharing plan will be developed to share future savings generated with our employees through running a more efficient and productive plant.

An example of more detailed language, as spelled out in a separate memorandum of agreement signed by the company and the union, is shown in Figure 2-1. This document contains most of the features typically found in such agreements.

The memorandum states, for example, that the variable pay plan will be developed jointly by labor and management using consensus decision making. As such, the plan is not subject to the contract's grievance and arbitration procedures. Note also that either party can terminate the plan with sixty days' notice. This provision ensures that labor and management will work together to resolve any problems or inequities that may arise. This particular memorandum also makes a powerful statement in support

Figure 2-1. Variable pay memorandum of agreement.

The Company and the Union hereby agree to the following conditions regarding a gain-sharing program:

1. A Design and Steering Committee consisting of salaried and hourly employees will be established. It will develop consensus recommendations for the gain-sharing process to be consistent with the guidelines established by the Company. Final approval of any and all terms and conditions of the program, including subsequent needed modifications and the decision on whether to proceed, must be acceptable to both the Company and the Union.

2. The Company and the Union agree that those issues that have historically been resolved between the parties through the mechanisms provided by the National Labor Relations Act and the parties' collective bargaining agreement remain subject to such resolutions; the parties further agree, however, that issues relating to the Company's gain-sharing program shall be considered to be beyond the jurisdiction of the Act and the parties' grievance resolution mechanisms contained in the collective bargaining agreement.

3. The Company and the Union may terminate the gain-sharing program by providing written notice of such intent at least sixty (60) days in advance of the desired termination date.

4. This Agreement shall survive beyond the expiration of current and future collective bargaining agreements subject to Item #3 above.

5. No one shall be laid off as a consequence of this program.

6. Operational problems or employee complaints will be addressed and resolved by the Design and/or Steering Committee.

7. If at any time either party has a major concern relating to the gain-sharing program, either party can request a meeting to discuss the issue. If, after a meeting, either party still has concerns, that party can initiate Item #3 of this Agreement, which provides sixty (60) days' notice for termination of the program. The parties then have sixty (60) days to work out the concern or the plan is terminated.

of a partnership orientation by providing that no employee will lose his or her job as a result of the variable pay program.

There is an unfortunate tendency on the part of management to wait until these issues must be addressed before approaching the union about its participation in a variable pay program. This is a vestige of the traditional mind-set: Management must develop its own plan and ensure that all contingencies have been thought out before approaching its adversary, the union. The union's reaction in this situation is predictable: skepticism and suspicion. If management has planned this initiative in secret, the reasoning goes, it surely cannot be in the best interests of the union to embrace the program.

A change-oriented company, on the other hand, will recognize that a partnership is not possible if one of the partners is left out of the planning process. Ideally, the union should be approached at the beginning of the process, when management is in an exploratory and learning mode. There is no reason why the union cannot learn about variable pay jointly with management, and participate in all the planning steps described in this chapter.

The Ducks Are in Line

At this point, the preparatory steps for variable pay have been completed:

1. Management has evaluated the fit of variable pay with the company's business and organizational strategies.
2. Decisions relative to program participants and group boundaries have been made, based on a thorough consideration of the alternatives.
3. A decision has been made relative to the appropriateness of piloting variable pay.
4. The readiness of the target organization has been evaluated, and steps have been taken to address readiness shortfalls.
5. The union has been brought into the process, and both parties have agreed on the relationship of variable pay to the union contract.

Having laid the proper groundwork, the company is now ready to advance to the next phase, where some of the greatest challenges will be encountered: the design process.

References

1. John G. Belcher, Jr., *Gain Sharing: The New Path to Profits and Productivity* (Houston: Gulf Publishing Company, 1991).

2. Anne M. Saunier and Elizabeth J. Hawk, "Realizing the Potential of Teams Through Team-Based Rewards," *Compensation & Benefits Review,* July-August 1994. See also Jay R. Schuster and Patricia K. Zingheim, *The New Pay* (New York: Lexington Books, 1992); Edward E. Lawler III, *Strategic Pay* (San Francisco: Jossey-Bass, 1990).
3. Jerry L. McAdams and Elizabeth J. Hawk, *Organizational Performance and Rewards* (Scottsdale, Ariz.: American Compensation Association, 1994).

3

The Design Process

The final decision that must be made before the variable pay design process can begin relates to the nature of the design process itself. How, in other words, will design decisions be made?

Management can always fall back on traditional approaches to designing a compensation system. A consultant can be hired to do the job, or management can delegate the task to in-house experts (assuming there are any). But why create an incongruence by using a traditional approach to the design of a nontraditional reward system? Would it not be better to model the participative philosophy that variable pay is designed to support?

There is a excellent opportunity to model this philosophy by engaging the employees in the design process. For example, a cross-functional design team, including both hourly and management employees, provides many obvious benefits. By involving people from different functional groups and various organizational levels, management can incorporate a variety of perspectives into the design of its system. You are much more likely, as a result, to produce a system that not only meets the business needs but also will be viewed as equitable by the participating employees. Those different perspectives will likely produce many creative ideas that will enhance the effectiveness of the system. Perhaps most important, the product produced by the design team will benefit from a degree of organizational ownership that would not be possible with a consultant-designed or management-designed system.

There is still a role here for an in-house expert or external consultant, if technical help is needed. That role is to facilitate and counsel the design team to ensure that all viable options are considered, the pitfalls are avoided, and a system of sound design is created. The task of developing a variable pay plan is a difficult and complex one, and expert assistance can be invaluable for a group that has little or no previous experience in designing these systems. Engaging employees in the design of a compensation system would have been a radical idea fifteen to twenty years ago. Today, however, use of a design team is rapidly becoming the norm in the development of alternative pay systems.

Selecting the Design Team

Considerable thought should be given to the composition of a variable pay design team. An obvious criterion is that the membership represent a cross-section of the organization. All major functional groups should be represented, as should various levels in the hierarchy. While hourly or nonexempt employees, technical specialists, and a member of middle management are obvious selections, a common oversight is the first-line supervisor. As a key player in any organizational change process (and potentially a readiness issue, as discussed in Chapter 2), the supervisor's perspective should not be excluded from the design process.

Beyond the general objective of obtaining a demographic cross-section of the workforce, certain functional skills should be present on the team. An individual with a quantitative orientation is an obvious need. This person should have access to, and thoroughly understand, performance and accounting data. He or she will play an invaluable role as the team sorts through and selects the various measures that will constitute the formula. An individual who has a good understanding of the organization's productive process, whether it be manufacturing a product or delivering a service, should also be on the team. This individual will be of great assistance to team members in evaluating the validity, accuracy, and appropriateness of various measures that may be considered. The human resources function is usually represented on these teams as well, since the product of the team's effort is, after all, a compensation system.

There is one class of employee that should not, in most cases, be on the design team. That is senior management. Senior managers tend to be dominating personalities, and that characteristic does not contribute to an effective team process. Even if executives are able to hold their natural inclinations in check, there remain additional concerns. Lower-level employees often do not feel comfortable expressing their opinions or raising concerns about management practices in the presence of an authority figure. In addition, the group will likely defer to the senior member for guidance when facing a difficult decision, rather than work through the problem themselves.

But do you *not* run a major risk if senior management is omitted from the design team? Might not the team produce a product that does not meet the business needs or is otherwise unacceptable to the decision makers? There are two ways to lessen, if not virtually eliminate, that risk. The first is to establish clear management guidelines or parameters for the system design; this subject will be addressed in the following section. The second is to ensure that there are interim reviews of the design team's progress by senior management, so that input and critiques are provided on an ongoing and timely basis. These interim reviews are, in fact, an important element in the design process, and will be discussed further later in this chapter. The ultimate fail-safe mechanism, of course, is the final management approval that must be obtained before the variable pay system can be implemented.

Design team members should also possess certain personal characteristics. First, they should be team-oriented. The effectiveness of this group will be dependent, in no small part, on the ability of the members to reach consensus decisions and function effectively as a team. The rigid, domineering, control-oriented personality has no place on a variable pay design team. Second, team members should be aggressive enough to make their opinions known and to take an active role in resolving team process issues. Third, they should be thoughtful and receptive to new ideas. Finally, they should be tenacious, for the process of designing a variable pay system is generally demanding and often frustrating.

Team members should also be informal leaders among their peers. Organizational buy-in to the variable pay system is important and will be greatly facilitated by having design team members that are respected by their coworkers.

In a unionized situation, the question of participation by union leaders invariably arises. While it is certainly appropriate to have at least one union leader serve on the design team, union representation on the team should not be drawn exclusively from the leadership ranks. This is partly for the same reason that you would not want the salaried representatives to consist entirely of senior managers; a design team of senior management and union leadership would represent anything but a cross section of the organization. More important, the team meetings may look like, feel like, and ultimately come to be like, bargaining sessions. As suggested in Chapter 2, variable pay is best approached as a collaborative labor-management process, rather than as a bargaining issue.

In some cases, senior management and union leaders form a steering committee to oversee and approve the work of the design team. This approach allows more rank-and-file employees to be involved while providing the leadership on both sides with an opportunity to actively support the process through a joint vehicle of their own. Where this structure is adopted, the design team reports to the steering committee on a periodic basis, and the steering committee represents the final approval authority for the plan.

In terms of size, design teams typically have between six and twelve members. There is a clear tradeoff here; while a larger team is desirable in order to involve as many people and organizational groups as possible, a smaller team will generally be less cumbersome and more efficient at performing the task. As a practical matter, teams of fewer than six people will probably not have the desired cross section (unless the organization is quite small), and teams with a membership greater than twelve will probably be unwieldy.

In some cases, nonetheless, management's desire for broad representation on the team has led a few companies to organize design teams with as many as twenty-five members. If this is to be workable, the team should be divided into subcommittees so that decisions are made in smaller groups. The subcommittees could then report their conclusions periodically to the full committee. One organization that adopted this approach divided the work among three subcommittees, as follows:

1. *The Formula Committee* developed the variable pay measures and baselines.
2. *The Rules Committee* addressed the payout frequency, the distribution method, the capital investment adjustment provision, and the eligibility rules.
3. *The Communications Committee* prepared and disseminated regular reports to the workforce, scheduled management review meetings, and developed the communication plan to support the launch of the system.

There are a variety of possible selection processes for the design team. Management and union leadership can develop selection criteria (preferably collaboratively rather than independently) and then jointly select those people that best meet those criteria. These people would then be approached and asked to serve on the design team. This selection process would, presumably, produce an ideal team composition. This alternative has two disadvantages, however: The members selected may not be enthusiastic about serving (and their enthusiasm is guaranteed to decline further through the long, demanding design process), and an opportunity for employee involvement in the selection process has been lost.

An alternative is to call for volunteers. You now are ensured of having team members who want to be involved, but you lose a degree of control over the quality of the design team membership. It is to be hoped that enough people will volunteer to provide a sizable pool from which team members can be chosen, based on the defined selection criteria.

The most involving approach is to allow the employees themselves to choose the design team members, typically by allowing each department or major group to elect its own representative. While this option may seem risky to management, which has now lost all control of the selection process, experience has shown that a surprisingly strong team usually results. We empower people, after all, on the assumption that they can and will make good decisions if given the opportunity.

Establishing Guidelines and Procedures

The design team, once organized, will require some guidance. The members' knowledge of variable pay principles will likely range from limited to nonexistent, and their comprehension of the business needs may be limited as well. If they are to succeed in producing a well-designed system, they will need several things:

- Design parameters that set boundaries and define management's expectations
- Developmental activities, such as education in variable pay design principles and team development exercises
- A step-by-step plan to guide their deliberations

Developing Management Parameters

The system produced by the design team must meet the needs of the business and provide a return to the company. If these objectives are not met, management support will fade and the plan will wither and die. As was suggested earlier, the risk of the design team's producing an unacceptable system will be considerably lessened if senior management provides the team with a set of design parameters or guidelines.

Design parameters are plan features or options that management considers to be essential if the variable pay system is to meet the needs of the business. These parameters place some boundaries around the design process by specifying minimum critical specifications. In a multisite organization that envisions separate variable pay plans in each of its locations, management parameters serve another important purpose as well. They ensure that the various plans will have some degree of consistency and will lessen the possibility of serious inequities between the plans.

Areas around which management parameters are often developed include the following:

- *Plan participants.* To meet the business need of having a team-oriented organization, management may deem it necessary that all employees participate in the program. Or, owing to the existence of other variable pay plans, management may require that certain groups be excluded.

- *Performance variables incorporated in the system.* It is entirely reasonable for management to mandate that key variables be included in the formula. If, as an example, management's top priority is customer satisfaction, it would be appropriate to require that some indicator of the organization's performance in that arena be included in the formula.

- *Rewarding continuous improvement.* A system with a fixed base against which performance is measured indefinitely may not be viable in a highly competitive business environment. If this the case, a requirement might be that the baseline or goals change on an annual basis.

- *Sharing ratio.* To ensure equity across multiple variable pay plans, a common sharing percentage between the company and employees may be required.

- *Distribution method.* Owing to legal and administrative complications, a specific approach to distributing bonuses to individual employees may be required. (See Chapter 11 for a discussion of the legal requirements.)

- *Impact of profitability.* Management may feel it necessary to protect the company against the possibility of high payouts in times of low or negative profitability. There are a variety of design options, which will be reviewed in later chapters, to ensure this outcome.

- *Capital investment adjustments.* A provision to adjust the system when major capital investments are made may be required to avoid distorting capital investment decisions (see Chapter 12).

An example of a simple set of management requirements, established for a steel manufacturing facility, is presented in Figure 3-1.

A more elaborate set of parameters was established by a leading company in the building products industry. Anticipating the eventual implementation of variable pay plans in a large number of plants, management established a corporate task force to develop a set of guidelines that would ensure that all the plans were aligned with corporate business objectives, while at the same time guaranteeing a degree of consistency among the plans. The guidelines are presented in Figure 3-2.

Preparing the Design Team

The initial activities of the design team are critical and will play an important role in the quality of its product. The team members are likely to

Figure 3-1. Management parameters for steel plant.

- All employees below the level of vice president will participate.

- The formula will measure performance and reward employees by a combination of plantwide and departmental measures.

- Both productivity and quality indicators will be used.

- 80 percent of planned profitability must be achieved in order for there to be a payout.

- The baseline must change on a routine basis.

---

be ill equipped to design a variable pay system. They may lack knowledge of business issues and priorities, probably know little or nothing about variable pay, and may have never worked together as a team before.

The first order of business is to educate the team on the purpose of variable pay and the principles of variable pay system design. The education should emphasize the role of variable pay in supporting organizational change and the importance of creating a customized system to meet the needs of the business. A broad array of design options and features should be presented to ensure that the team members are knowledgeable about various alternatives. A suggested agenda for a design team educational program is presented in Table 3-1.

The second order of business should be some team-development exercises. Where there has been a history of traditional management practices and adversarial union-management relationships, members of the design team will likely bring very different perspectives to the table. There may well, in fact, be a variety of unspoken and possibly conflicting agendas present. It is also unlikely that this particular group of people will have ever worked together before. In a large or multisite organization, they may not even know each other.

If the team effort is to have a successful and satisfying outcome, the members must understand the dynamics of team functioning, develop a sense of common goals, and gain skills in consensus decision making. Given the importance of the task, it would not be wise to skimp on the provision of resources for team-development activities.

It can also be useful for the design team to write for itself a mission statement so that the members have a clear understanding of what they are attempting to accomplish. It will also give the team members an opportunity to practice consensus decision making before tackling the design of the system itself. One team's mission, for example, was:

Figure 3-2.   Management guidelines for building products company.

- *Site participation:* Include all employees, except those in the management incentive plan, to be consistent with the company philosophy that supports a team environment.

- *Existing incentive plans:* Traditional incentives are no longer acceptable; the plant must develop a plan to eliminate incentives.

- *Information sharing:* Share publicly disclosed financial information, data for plant performance measures, and other business information that will improve the employees' ability to contribute to the operation's effectiveness.

- *Union collaboration:* The union is to be a partner in the process from the start.

- *Formula structure:* Use a family of measures (multiple measures) to provide the greatest flexibility and allow for the explicit use of non-cost factors, such as quality, delivery performance, and safety.

- *Performance measures:* There should be a minimum of three and a maximum of six measures. Each plant is required to include the "process effectiveness" measure in the formula. Additional measures may be selected from a recommended list, or others may be used.

- *Company/employee share:* A 50/50 share should be used to ensure a consistent corporatewide sharing percentage and minimize perceived inequities at other sites.

- *Baselines:* The baseline should be based on historical averages and should change, preferably on a twelve-quarter, rolling-average basis.

- *Frequency of payout:* Quarterly, consistent with the reporting of company results and to smooth out peaks and valleys of performance.

- *Smoothing mechanism:* A deficit reserve must be used to offset volatile measures and to ensure that overall payouts are not greater than total gains.

- *Capital appropriations:* For all appropriations over $1 million, adjust the affected baselines after one full quarter of effective operation of the modified or new process.

- *Maximum payout:* A cap is not needed, as the plan is self-funding.

- *Split among employees:* Distribute bonuses as a percentage of the employee's income to simplify administrative procedure and ensure consistency across all plants.

- *Maintenance of system:* A Steering Committee must be established to periodically review the system and recommend design changes to the plant manager.

Table 3-1. Design team education agenda.

Overview of Variable Pay

- Transforming the organizational culture to meet the challenges of today's competitive environment
- Why reward systems must change to support the transformation

- Definition and key features of variable pay

Design of Variable Pay System

- Who the participants are?
- Cost formulas
- The family of measures formula approach
- Goal-sharing formulas
- Tying bonuses to financial results
- Establishing baselines

- The sharing ratio
- Frequency of payout
- Distribution methods
- Smoothing mechanisms
- Capital investment adjustments
- Defining eligibility

The Design Process

- How design teams function.

- Consensus decision making.

Implementation Issues

- Educating the workforce
- Communicating results

- Plan maintenance

Causes of Failure/Requirements for Success

To design a plan to ensure the future of our facility by providing the opportunity for employees to share in the financial gains resulting from continuous improvements made through their involvement and superior performance.

The example that follows was developed to guide the efforts of a joint union-management design team:

Our mission is to jointly develop and administer a shared financial rewards program that will foster continuous improvement and job security through better teamwork, more innovation, and reduction of waste.

A third example explicitly addresses the alignment objective:

To provide a framework and guidelines for better aligning [the company's] rewards systems with its evolving team culture and to have a positive impact on the company's long-term success.[1]

To better prepare for the task, design teams often visit other sites with variable pay programs. There is much to be learned from the experiences of others, particularly with respect to the problems and pitfalls encountered. There is often an inclination to limit site visits to companies in the same industry; this parochial viewpoint may, however, deprive the team of insights to be gained from a variety of situations.

The Design Work Plan

The final step to prepare the design team for the challenge of designing a variable pay system is to provide them with a step-by-step work plan.

Designing a variable pay system is, under the best of circumstances, a challenging and difficult proposition. There are many decisions that must be made, and there are often many options for each decision. Many of these decisions cannot be made independently of other decisions, as there are interrelationships among the design components. Further complicating the design process is the likelihood that few, if any, of the design team members will have had any prior experience in designing a variable pay plan.

In view of these circumstances, it is important that the design team be provided with a clear, step-by-step work plan. Without this road map to provide direction and keep the team members on course, it is likely that they will founder and become hopelessly entangled in the complexity of the process. What follows is a basic work plan that could be adapted, or even used as is, for virtually any design team in any industry. It is the evolutionary product of many years of work with a large number of design teams. The order of the steps is a logical one, in that decisions that are dependent on other decisions appear in the right order. An overview of the work plan is provided at this point. In subsequent chapters, we will review each step in greater detail.

1. Review management's business plan, priorities, expectations, and design parameters (see Chapter 4). These all represent important inputs to the design process.
2. Identify performance variables that may be appropriate for inclusion in the variable pay formula. The resulting list may include such variables as productivity, utilization of materials, quality, customer service, safety, delivery performance, and customer satisfaction, to name a few (see Chapter 4).
3. Determine the basic formula approach. Given the key variables identified in the previous step, and considering management's strategy and priorities, what type of variable pay formula should be adopted (see Chapters 4, 5, and 6)?
4. Identify existing measures for each of the variables selected in step 2 (see Chapter 7). For a given variable, such as quality, there may be a number of possible measures: number of defects, customer returns, customer complaints, warranty costs, and so on.
5. Obtain historical data for each of the selected measures, and display these data on line charts (see Chapter 7). An analysis of the dynamics of each of the measures, as revealed by the pattern of historical performance, will be extremely useful at this point and in several future design steps.
6. Use the charts to evaluate the selected measures for suitability for use in the variable pay formula. As a result of this analysis, finalize the selection of measures (see Chapter 7).
7. Develop the equations for valuing gains or goal achievement (see Chapter 8). This step is necessary in order to determine the appropriate bonus level to be paid to participating employees for improvements in the various measures (gain sharing) or for the achievement of goals (goal sharing).
8. Determine initial baselines or goals (see Chapter 9). The baseline is the level of the formula that must be achieved or exceeded in order for there to be a payout.
9. Establish the methodology for resetting baselines or goals in future periods (see Chapter 9). To ensure the continuing credibility of the plan, it is important to clearly define how the baseline will be adjusted in the future.

10. Simulate or model the variable pay system (see Chapter 9). Modeling the system will provide valuable information relative to the dynamics and viability of the system.
11. Establish the sharing ratio, if appropriate (see Chapter 10). What percentage of the gains will be paid out to employees?
12. Establish the frequency of bonus payments (see Chapter 11). The payout period may range anywhere from weekly to annually.
13. Develop a provision to protect against overpayment of bonuses owing to volatility, seasonality, or random variation in the formula measures (see Chapter 11). Formula volatility and variation can cause serious problems and even threaten the viability of the system.
14. Establish the method of distribution of bonuses to employees (see Chapter 11). There are three methods of distributing bonuses to participating employees. There also is a major legal constraint affecting this decision.
15. Define procedures for capital investment adjustments (see Chapter 12). Gains associated with major capital investments are typically not fully shared in order to avoid distorting capital investment decisions.
16. Establish a cap on bonus payments, if appropriate (see Chapter 12).
17. Establish a minimum payout provision, if appropriate (see Chapter 12). Very small bonus payments do not contribute to a positive employee view of the variable pay system.
18. Define eligibility rules for individuals (see Chapter 12). How are new hires, terminations, and leaves of absence to be treated?
19. Document the system (see Chapter 12).

The design team should also address issues relative to the implementation process, such as effective communication of the variable pay system to the employees and establishment of vehicles to ensure that improvement ideas are handled in an expeditious manner (see Chapter 13). This work plan could, of course, be used to guide any design team, whether or not nonmanagement employees are included.

The design team would be well advised to stay on track and deal with one step at a time. It is very easy to get into debates about design issues that appear later in the work plan. This invariably results in a significant expenditure of time and energy, without any concrete results. The whole purpose of the work plan is to provide a systematic framework so that the plan can be developed in an orderly, efficient, and effective fashion. Straying from the plan will simply prolong the design process and increase team frustration. If the plan presented above does not meet the design team's needs, it should develop one that does.

Communications and Support

There are two other practices that the design team should adopt, and both involve communications with various stakeholders. The first is to develop a mechanism for communicating the design team's progress to the rest of the organization. This idea often runs counter to the design team's (and management's) initial instincts. For instance, concerns will be raised about communicating information that has not yet been approved and thus creating expectations that may not be met. The design team may even decide to communicate nothing at all until the plan has been finalized.

This course of action would be a mistake. Variable pay is a compensation system, and the affected employees will be talking about it whether or not information is made available. If factual information is not provided, they will likely assume that this plan will benefit the company at their expense (lack of information, as suggested in the discussion of readiness, leads to low trust), and rumors of a negative nature will quickly spread throughout the organization. As is the case with most business information, the risks associated with communicating nothing probably exceed those of communicating everything. And open communications, after all, go hand in hand with the participative culture that variable pay is designed to support.

The design team's initial communications should focus on basic awareness: What is variable pay, what purposes does variable pay serve, and what kind of culture is variable pay designed to support? As the team progresses through the design process, it can feed the organization substantive information about plan features as they are developed. The team can also use its communication vehicles to define options under consideration and obtain employee input on these options.

Some design teams have gone so far as to create a newsletter for the sole purpose of disseminating information about their variable pay plans. The first issue of such a newsletter by a chemical plant design team contained these features:

- The design team's objective statement
- A letter from the plant manager describing how variable pay fits with the company's business strategy

- The criteria that will be used by the design team to select the variables to be measured
- A detailed project schedule
- Questions raised by employees, along with the answers provided by the design team
- A description of a visit made by design team members to another site with an established variable pay plan
- A brief history of gain sharing
- An announcement of a contest to create a logo for the variable pay process

In addition to building employee trust in and commitment to the plan, open communications during the design process serves another important purpose: It increases employees' understanding of the details of the plan and enhances the final educational process just prior to the launch of the plan.

The second practice that will serve the team well is engaging senior management in a periodic review of its progress. While design guidelines, as discussed above, will have been provided in advance, these guidelines serve only to narrow the boundaries within which the design team will work. They will not ensure senior management's buy-in to any possible plan that could be designed within those boundaries. It would, in fact, be extraordinarily coincidental for the design team to produce a system that precisely met management's expectations.

If the design team completes the design of the plan before presenting it to those who must approve its implementation, the risk of being sent back to the drawing board to rework the plan is high. This turn of events, after the team has spent many months of intense effort and has developed a high degree of ownership for the plan, would be disheartening, to say the least. The team should do all that it can to avoid this outcome.

The only way to lessen the risk of rejection is to obtain feedback from senior management during the design process. The team should seek an audience with key executives about midway (and more often if feasible) through the design process to present the decisions made to date and to seek feedback. Any concerns management may have can then be dealt with and resolved before the plan design is finalized by the team. It is much easier and less painful to change direction in the middle of the design process than after the task has been completed.

If the design team follows these practices, rigorously communicating with the rest of the organization and with senior management as well, the product of the team's efforts will probably sail through the approval process and enjoy the confidence of the rest of the organization.

The team is now ready to begin the actual design process; the remaining chapters will explore the various design steps and the implementation process in detail.

References

1. Darlene O'Neill and David A. Lough, "Team Incentives and TQM: Building Organizational Excellence at National Semiconductor," *ACA Journal*, Spring 1994.

4

Selecting the Basic Formula Framework

The design work plan outlined at the end of the previous chapter will guide the activities of the team charged with designing the variable pay system. The first few steps in this work plan, after a review of management business plans and objectives, relate to the development of the formula. The assumption at this point is that management has determined which employees will be included in the variable pay plan. If this is not the case, the team should address the issue before proceeding to the formula steps.

The *formula* is the core of the variable pay system, for it establishes the type of organizational performance improvement that will generate a reward for the participating employees. The formula also represents the greatest opportunity to tailor the variable pay system to the needs of the business and to align compensation with business objectives. At the same time, the formula is the most complex and difficult element in the variable pay system to design. It is here that the team will spend the greatest amount of time and face some of its greatest challenges.

The design team's very first step—before tackling the formula—is to prepare itself for the task by gaining an understanding of the business issues that will drive decision making regarding the formula.

Step 1. Review Management's Business Plan, Priorities, Expectations, and Design Parameters

Before a team of employees can be expected to create a variable pay system that is aligned with business objectives, the team members must understand what those business objectives are. That this step is even necessary to mention is an indictment of the past practices of most companies with respect to their employees.

Under traditional management philosophies, it was not deemed necessary, or even prudent, to share with employees information about business priorities, strategies, and objectives. Management was the source of all wisdom, and the workplace was designed to minimize the employee's input and impact on the business. What purpose would be served, therefore, by educating the workforce on business issues?

But now businesses are engaging employees in developing a reward system that may have a major impact on the performance of their organizations. And businesses are developing this reward system to support a high-involvement, high-commitment workplace. Those employees charged with designing this system need to understand the mission of the business, the strategic business plan, management's priorities, and the performance variables that are key to achieving business objectives. And while we are at it, this would also be a good time to present management's design parameters as well (assuming that the team has been properly prepared through an educational process on variable pay system design issues).

This step can usually be accomplished through a presentation to the design team by a member of senior management. Appropriate documents, such as the business plan, might also be provided to the design team for review.

Step 2. Identify Performance Variables That May Be Appropriate for Inclusion in the Variable Pay Program

The objective of this step, the first of several that relate to the formula, is to develop a laundry list of performance variables that will serve as raw material for subsequent steps in the formula development process. This list can best be generated by the team via a structured brainstorming process.

It is important to draw a distinction here between variables and measures. The term *variables* is used in this context to mean broad, rather generic, performance areas, such as productivity, quality, and customer satisfaction. *Measures*, on the other hand, are specific indicators through which the variables can be quantified.

There are usually several possible measures for each variable. The variable quality, for example, might be quantified through such measures as rework, customer returns, number of defects, and customer complaints. Measures for the variable safety, as another example, might include recordable accidents, lost-time accidents, and workers compensation costs.

The focus at this stage should be variables, rather than measures, in order to maintain concentration on the broad business issues and limit the number of options that the design team must deal with. Brainstorming measures will likely produce a very large number of items that will be difficult to narrow down to a small number. One design team, for example, brainstormed 130 measures and became hopelessly entangled in the process of selecting the most important ones. Even the list of variables will likely be too long (typically anywhere from fifteen to twenty-five) to deal with at this point, and there will be a need to reduce the number to a manageable few, perhaps six to eight. This is best accomplished through a voting and ranking process.

Each team member might be asked, for example, to select the six variables that he or she believes are the best candidates for inclusion in the variable pay program. To do this effectively, selection criteria are needed. Criteria for selecting among the variables might include:

- *Importance to the business.* It would be a serious mistake to include variables that will increase the company's compensation costs without providing a concomitant business benefit to the company.
- *Controllable by employees.* If variable pay is to be effective in changing employee behaviors, the measures used to determine payouts must be, at least to some degree, under the control of the employees.
- *Impacted broadly.* A variable that is important to the business and controllable, but impacted by only three or four people, would be less desirable than one that is potentially impacted by a large number of people.

One criterion that the team very often wishes to include here is that items be "measurable" or "quantifiable." This is generally not advisable at this point, however. The design team may not be fully aware of all the measures that may exist for a given variable, and it would be unfortunate to eliminate a highly important, highly controllable variable before the team has had the opportunity to explore the measurement options.

When the voting process is complete, the variables can be listed in descending order of votes received, and the top six to ten items can then be selected for further study. An actual example of a rank-ordered list, together with the number of votes received for each variable, is shown in Table 4-1. The team in this case chose to cut off the list at five votes, where there was a natural break point.

The purpose of the voting and ranking process is not to eliminate variables from further consideration but to allow detailed analytical work to commence on those variables that appear most promising. The lower-

Table 4-1.   Example of a rank-ordered list.

Brainstormed Variable	Number of Votes Received
1. Productivity	10
2. Raw materials utilization	10
3. Downtime	8
4. Safety	7
5. Customer returns	7
6. On-time delivery	6
7. Customer satisfaction	5
8. Attendance	5
— — — — — — — — — — — — — — —	
9. Utilization of supplies	3
10. Support staff effectiveness	1
11. Scheduling accuracy	1
12. Estimated cost vs. actual cost	1
13. Rework	
14. Utilization of energy	
15. Raw materials quality	
16. Number of ideas	
17. Cross-training	

ranked variables should be held in reserve for possible reevaluation in the future, if appropriate.

Step 3. Determine the Basic Formula Approach

As suggested above, the formula represents the essence of any variable pay system, for it defines the nature of the performance improvement that will bring financial rewards to participating employees. The formula—more than any other feature of the system—focuses organizational improvement efforts and shapes employee behaviors. The decision made at this step, accordingly, may be of great consequence in determining the effectiveness and viability of the variable pay plan.

In Chapter 1, we identified three categories of variable pay formulas: cash profit sharing, gain sharing, and goal sharing. Each of these categories is clearly definable, and each has its advantages and disadvantages. We will now review each of these categories in detail, followed in the next chapter by a review of some variations on these three basic themes.

Cash Profit Sharing

The simplest, most straightforward formula, *profit sharing*, ties pay to a measure of profits or profitability. And from a contingent compensation point of view, profit sharing makes eminent sense, for profitability is the ultimate determinant of an organization's ability to pay higher compensation. With any other formula, there is a risk that bonuses will be paid when the company's profitability is inadequate or, worse yet, negative. If contingent compensation were the only purpose of variable pay, our discussion of formulas could probably end here.

Profit sharing has a long history, with its first use in the early 1800s in Europe. Profit sharing made its debut in the United States at Procter & Gamble in the 1880s and began to grow in popularity in the 1920s. Until recently, most profit-sharing plans in this country deferred payouts until after an individual's retirement, and were therefore viewed as a retirement benefit. Our definition of variable pay, however, requires that profit-sharing payments be made on a current, rather than deferred, basis. The elimination of deferred profit sharing from further consideration here should not be taken as a criticism of this scheme; it is simply a recognition that the primary objective of deferred-payout plans is to provide retirement income rather than to support organizational change.

Cash payout profit-sharing plans, like other forms of variable pay, began to proliferate when international competition forced American industry to rethink its management and compensation philosophies. A good example of a simple, companywide plan that appeared in a major corporation in the early 1980s provided for a payout pool based on a percentage of after-tax profits, as follows:[1]

Profits exceeding 2.3 percent of sales:	10 percent
Profits exceeding 4.6 percent of sales:	12.5 percent
Profits exceeding 6.9 percent of sales:	15 percent

From a design and administration point of view, this plan is extremely simple; that, as suggested earlier, represents one of the advantages of profit sharing.

As the above example demonstrates, profit-sharing plans can be based on a return measure as well as on absolute dollar profits. Profit-

Table 4-2. Profit-sharing payout schedule.

ROI (%)	Bonus (% of Payroll)	ROI (%)	Bonus (% of Payroll)
20%	10%	26%	16%
21	11	27	17
22	12	28	18
23	13	29	19
24	14	30	20
25	15		

sharing plans, in fact, are often based on measures of return on investment. A good example is a plan that was launched by a subsidiary of an aerospace company in 1985. Designed to support a major organizational change initiative, the plan in its initial year paid out to employees 40 percent of pre-tax profits in excess of the company's target return on investment, as contained in its business plan. Payouts were made on a quarterly basis. In subsequent years, the ROI target was based on the previous twelve quarters' performance, which, unlike the previous example, rewards continuous improvement. This feature, called a *rolling average baseline*, will be discussed further in Chapter 9.

Rather than distribute a percentage of profits, an alternative approach is to establish a fixed payout schedule. An example used by one company is shown in Table 4-2. In this case, the payout amount, expressed as a percentage of the individual's total pay, is specified for various return levels.

A variation on the profit-sharing theme is a plan based on *economic value added* (EVA).[2] EVA is defined as after-tax operating profit less the company's total cost of capital. It quantifies the return that shareholders are earning relative to alternative investment options of comparable risk. Since there appears to be a good correlation between EVA and stock prices, the EVA concept is gaining popularity as the basis for variable pay at the executive level. EVA can, of course, be the basis for variable pay at lower levels as well, and in a few cases, EVA plans have been developed for plant employees. However, it is probably a more appropriate performance measurement vehicle for senior management.

It should be noted that the previous design step—identification of performance variables—is superfluous if profit sharing is selected as the basic formula category for the variable pay system. There is only one variable—profits or profitability—that is relevant here. Presumably profit sharing would have been established as a management parameter at the outset, and the unnecessary step of identifying variables can be skipped.

While cash profit sharing has some obvious attractions, particularly to business owners and senior management, it suffers from a major shortcoming: It probably has little effect on employee behaviors. The profitability of an enterprise is so remote from the average employee's actions on the job that the *line of sight*—the ability of employees to relate their on-the-job efforts to improvements in the variable pay formula—is practically nonexistent. This weakness is exacerbated by the fact that profits are heavily impacted by a variety of forces—such as pricing, material costs, restructurings, marketing expenditures, and accounting adjustments—that are totally out of the control of most employees. Therefore, while profit-sharing plans are excellent vehicles for meeting the contingent compensation objective of variable pay, they are practically useless in supporting the objective of organizational change (except, perhaps, in a very small company).

The ability of profit sharing to reinforce behaviors can be improved somewhat through variations that tie pay to measures of operating profit. This alternative eliminates the effect of interest costs, asset sales, and extraordinary accounting adjustments, which have nothing to do with operating performance and are totally out of the control of most employees. One company, for example, awards all employees a 4 percent bonus if the company achieves its planned operating earnings. The bonus can be as high as 8 percent if operating earnings exceed plan.[3]

The operating-profit alternative is found at the level of an operating unit, such as a plant or a division. The line of sight should be considerably better in this situation as compared to a plan that ties pay to the fully accounted profits of an entire corporation. Profit sharing in any of its forms may be more effective as a behavioral change vehicle in a very small company, where individuals do in fact have some influence on the company's profitability.

Another variation on the profit-sharing theme, which is undoubtedly more effective than pure profit sharing, is what we will call *financially funded goal sharing*. In this approach, the payout potential is determined by a measure of profitability, just as in profit sharing. Unlike profit sharing, however, the payout is not unconditional but is tied to the achievement of additional goals that are more meaningful to and controllable by the participating employees. Employees must "earn" their profit-sharing bonuses by achieving various performance goals. This alternative will be discussed in more detail in Chapter 5.

In summary, cash profit sharing, if looked at strictly from a financial point of view, would appear to be the best vehicle for variable pay. The company bears no risk of paying bonuses, and thus increasing compensation, when financial results do not justify doing so. It is also relatively simple to design and administer. If contingent compensation is the only objective for the variable pay system, cash profit sharing could be the logical choice.

Failing to capitalize on the ability of variable pay to reinforce improvement behaviors and support organizational change, however, represents a lost opportunity of potentially major proportions. For those companies that seek to create a high-involvement, team-oriented organization, a formula other than profit sharing almost certainly makes more sense. If management is concerned about the risk of bonus payments in times of low profitability, mechanisms are available to provide some measure of protection. These mechanisms, which include a profit gate and a variable share, will be discussed in later chapters.

Gain Sharing

Gain sharing is defined for our purposes as any variable pay system that shares with employees the financial gains associated with improvements in measures of team or organizational performance. By utilizing measures of performance, as opposed to measures of profitability, gain-sharing plans are generally more meaningful and relevant to participating employees than are profit-sharing plans. For this reason, they are also more effective at reinforcing behaviors that are important to the success of the business.

The key elements of a gain-sharing program include one or more measures of group performance, a baseline against which improvement can be quantified, an algorithm for each measure that enables improvements to be translated into dollar values, and a sharing ratio for dividing the quantified dollar gains between the company and the participating employees. Clearly, the design of a gain-sharing system is much more complicated than the design of a profit-sharing program.

With gain sharing, there is a wonderful opportunity to tailor the system to the needs and priorities of the business. If reducing costs is the key to business success (as it might be, for example, in a commodities business), the gain-sharing formula can focus exclusively on the management of costs. If, on the other hand, quality is management's top priority, a gain-sharing formula with an emphasis on quality can be constructed. If timeliness and responsiveness to the customer are critical to success, these variables too can be incorporated into a gain-sharing formula. And the same holds true for safety, downtime, inventory management, environmental compliance, attendance, and other variables that may be important to the success of a given business. There are no constraints, other than those imposed by common sense and the needs of the business, on the types of variables that may be included in a gain-sharing program.

Most authorities date the birth of gain sharing to 1935, when the Scanlon Plan was launched at the Empire Steel and Tinplate Company in Mansfield, Ohio. Use of the Scanlon Plan, which shares improvements in the ratio of labor costs to sales (or sales value of production, in a manufacturing facility) was the brainchild of a union leader named Joseph Scanlon. Use of the Scanlon Plan grew slowly through the years and probably reached its peak in the 1970s. Very few examples of the traditional Scanlon Plan formula exist today, largely because labor costs have steadily diminished as a percentage of sales in many industries and because there is no provision in the traditional Scanlon formula for measuring and rewarding improvements in other performance variables, such as quality. Variations on the original Scanlon formula are still prevalent, however, as we shall see below in the discussion of cost formulas.

Because there exists an enormous array of possible gain-sharing formulas, it is helpful to split this category into two subdivisions: those that focus primarily or exclusively on measures of cost, and those that contain multiple measures, often including some that only indirectly affect costs.

Cost Formulas

A *cost formula*, as the name implies, is designed to reward the control of, or reduction in, costs. Cost reduction is important, of course, in virtually any business enterprise, and there are few, if any, variable pay formulas that do not reward cost reduction in some fashion. The cost formula category, however, is distinguished from other approaches in that direct measures of cost are its exclusive or primary focus. Cost formulas will be most attractive where cost reduction is the overriding business priority. This condition might prevail, for example, in commodity businesses or those companies facing severe pricing pressures or financial difficulties.

Selecting Specific Cost Elements

For design teams developing a cost formula, there are two major decisions that must be made early in the process that will essentially define the character of the formula. The first is: *What costs should be included in the formula?* From a business point of view, it would be desirable to include all the costs of the operating entity. The result would then be a system that bears some similarities to profit sharing, in that bonus payouts would reflect the bottom-line performance of the business. Like profit sharing, however, this type of system would be heavily impacted by forces that are out of the control of most employees. There is little that the average employee can do, for example, about depreciation, amortization, interest costs, or marketing expenditures.

An alternative is to include only those costs that are controllable, at least to some degree, by the participating employees. These might include labor, materials, supplies, and energy. If the primary purpose of the variable pay plan is to support employee involvement and organizational change, as opposed to simply creating a system of contingent compensation, this controllable cost alternative probably would be more appropriate, since it excludes, by definition, those costs over which employees have no influence.

Another common alternative, especially in manufacturing organizations, is to measure conversion costs, or those costs that are incurred in the conversion of raw materials to finished products. As a practical matter, this would generally include all manufacturing costs (labor, supplies, energy, etc.) except for raw materials. Companies employing this approach may also incorporate into the plan a separate indicator for raw material utilization, such as scrap or yield, since this variable is generally controllable to a significant degree.

Even where the costs are limited to those that are controllable, it should be noted that there is still a considerable risk of impact from uncontrollable forces, particularly those that relate to the purchase price of the various cost elements. An increase in the price of raw materials or energy, for example, would negatively affect employee bonuses and perhaps offset any improvement that may have been made in the utilization of these elements. Here, again, this is positive from a contingent compensation point of view, as these costs increases clearly impact the bottom line, but negative from an employee-involvement perspective. If management does not want employees to bear any purchase-price risk, it would be better to adopt the second type of gain-sharing formula—the multiple measures approach (see below)—where individual cost elements can be measured strictly on a utilization basis (further elaboration on this point will be found under The Family of Measures later in this chapter). There may also be an impact from changes in selling price, depending on the output indicator used.

Selecting an Output Indicator

This leads to a discussion of the second defining decision to be made relative to a cost formula: *To what output indicator should costs be related?* Rarely are costs measured on an absolute basis in a variable pay program.

Table 4-3. Distribution center cost formula.

Sales	$24,000,000
× Baseline costs (5.2%)	$ 1,248,000
− Actual costs	$ 1,212,000
Bonus Pool	$ 36,000
− Company share (50%)	18,000
= Employee share	$ 18,000

Virtually every organization has substantial costs that vary totally or partly with the volume of products produced or services delivered. There are probably few costs employees can impact, in fact, that are totally fixed in nature. It would generally not make sense, therefore, to tie pay to a reduction in costs on an absolute basis. Costs would increase, in absolute terms, with an increase in output, and employees would fail to be rewarded at the very time when the organization is enjoying improved financial results from that increase in volume. Conversely, bonuses would almost certainly be paid in times of declining volume (as some costs decline in an absolute sense) when the business is in distress. These outcomes would obviously be contrary to the variable pay objectives. To avoid these problems, most cost-oriented variable pay plans measure the relationship of costs to some indicator of output. The common output indicators found in variable pay plans are:

- *Sales or revenues.* A simple example of a cost-to-sales formula developed by a design team for a distribution center is shown in Table 4-3. A baseline ratio of costs to sales is established, based on the prior year's cost performance, and that ratio is multiplied by the current quarter's sales to obtain baseline costs in dollars. Actual incurred costs are then subtracted from these baseline costs to quantify the gain. In this case, all of the distribution center's costs are included in the formula, which is probably about as simple as a cost formula can be.
- *Sales value of production.* A manufacturing facility will often use sales value of production, rather than sales, as the output indicator. This is due to the fact that costs in manufacturing generally track more closely with production than with sales (or shipments). If production exceeded sales

in a given period, the costs incurred by the facility (e.g., materials, labor, supplies) might appear to be quite high relative to sales. When compared to production levels, however, these costs might be quite reasonable. The use of sales as the output indicator could therefore produce distorted results. Sales value of production is generally calculated as follows:

$$Sales\ value\ of\ production = sales \pm change\ in\ inventory.$$

Since an increase in finished goods inventories implies that production exceeded sales, the amount of the inventory increase is added to sales to produce sales value of production. A decrease in such inventories, in contrast, suggests that production was less than sales and is therefore subtracted from sales. Sales value of production can also be calculated by multiplying the units of production by the current selling price.

One retail organization developed a formula for each of its stores that related labor costs to the store's gross margin (sales less the cost of the merchandise sold) rather than to sales. This made business sense because gross margin provides a better indicator of financial results than does sales in the retailing industry.

The major attraction (or disadvantage, depending on your point of view) of a cost-to-sales (or sales value of production) formula is that the selling price of the product or service is factored into the equation. This feature is particularly attractive where management wants employee bonuses to track closely with the profitability of the business. If the formula also includes most of the costs incurred by the business, most of the elements of the income statement are represented and bonus levels will closely reflect the organization's bottom line. If all of the organization's costs are included, there will in fact be something akin to a profit-sharing plan and the comments above relative to profit sharing would apply.

The disadvantage of using sales (or sales value of production) as the output indicator is that pricing is generally market-determined and out of the control of most, if not all, employees. This would be an obvious concern where the primary purpose of variable pay is to promote employee involvement, rewarding employees for their contributions to the success of the business. In this case, other output indicators might be more appropriate.

▪ *Standard cost of production.* A components plant for one of the auto companies eliminated the effect of selling price by relating costs to standard direct labor dollars earned, calculated by multiplying the units produced of each product by its corresponding direct labor standard in dollars:[4]

Table 4-4. Auto plant cost formula.

Direct labor dollars earned	$12,740,000
× Allowable expense factor	178.72%
= Allowable expenses	$22,768,900
− Actual expenses	20,488,900
= Bonus pool	$ 2,280,000

*Standard direct labor dollars earned = units produced ×
direct labor standard in $*

This output measure is then multiplied by an allowable cost percentage, which represents the average cost performance of the previous two years. You will find a simplified version of the formula in Table 4-4 above.

The typical cost formula, as the previous examples show, aggregates the various costs in reporting results. In order to achieve more focus and a better understanding of the plan by employees, some companies limit the number of costs included and break the formula down into separate measures. An example is provided by an aerospace plant, which employs three cost measures:

1. Payroll dollars per unit of output
2. Overhead costs per unit of output
3. Material dollars consumed versus material dollars planned

Measuring each cost separately enables the formula itself to communicate the specific costs included and thus enhances the employees' understanding of the plan.

Units of product produced or services delivered. Adopting units of output as the output indicator also eliminates the effect of selling price on the bonus calculation, and cost-per-unit formulas of various kinds are relatively common as a result. An example is found in a steel mill, where performance in each of the three major production areas is measured through a simple ratio:

$$\frac{Conversion\ costs}{Pounds\ of\ product\ produced}$$

Cost-per-unit formulas do, however, present a significant challenge to the participating employees if performance is measured against a prior period: Their improvement efforts must overcome any inflationary increases in costs before there is any possibility of earning bonuses. This is not nearly as great an issue where costs are related to revenues, as revenues will presumably inflate as well and at least partly offset the effects of inflation on costs.

The inflation effect can be, and often is, eliminated in cost-per-unit formulas by deflating the costs or by adjusting the baseline or target to account for expected inflationary increases. This approach is particularly appropriate when management wants to reward employees for improvements in the utilization of various inputs, a factor which is largely under their control.

Cost-to-Budget Formulas

There is one common alternative approach to the cost formula that does not relate costs to an output variable. That is to reward improvements in costs versus budget. This formula is often favored by management, under the rationale that the business has really not performed to expectations if it has not at least operated within budgeted cost assumptions. If this approach is adopted, the basis for measurement should be a variable budget, in which budgeted costs vary with volume, or the problems associated with absolute cost plans, as discussed above, will be encountered here as well.

The obvious problem with costs-versus-budget plans is the subjective nature of the budget. Budgets in most organizations are not objective documents but are the product of a negotiation process between an organizational unit and the next higher level of management. The resulting budgets may therefore lack credibility with the employees (if not management as well). In addition, budgets often contain considerable "stretch," which increases substantially the employees' task and the risk of having no payout in spite of considerable improvement efforts.

While cost formulas clearly signal to employees that cost reduction is to be the principal focus of their improvement efforts, it should be noted that other critical performance variables can be incorporated into the system while maintaining the primary emphasis on costs. This may be desirable, for example, where a concern exists that the emphasis on costs may lead to a corresponding inattention to quality or customer service. The inclusion of other variables in a cost formula is often accomplished through features variously known as *modifiers, multipliers,* and *gates.* These features will be explored further in Chapter 5.

The Family of Measures

The second category of gain-sharing formulas, encompassing those that go beyond pure cost measures and include a variety of performance indicators, will be identified by the term *family of measures.* A family of measures formula is nothing more than one that contains multiple measures or indicators. The family of measures is an attractive alternative to the cost formula for several reasons:

1. It allows for the explicit inclusion of performance variables that are not cost issues or have only an indirect relationship to costs, such as quality, delivery performance, safety, and customer satisfaction.

2. It allows for cost-oriented variables to be measured in a way that minimizes the impact of uncontrollable variables such as purchase price. If raw materials, for example, were to be included as one of several items in a cost formula, it would be impacted by changes in the price paid for the raw materials. In a family of measures, on the other hand, measures such as "pounds of material per unit produced" or "percentage of material scrapped" could be used to quantify the utilization of material, which is controllable by employees.

3. It highlights and creates a focus on the key improvement opportunities. With a plan that measures cost in the aggregate, employees may not readily discern the key improvement opportunities or priorities. The key improvement opportunities in a plan that measures labor productivity, material usage, waste of supplies, and safety, in contrast, are defined by the formula itself and thus would be readily apparent to the participating employees.

An example of a simple family of measures for a paper mill is shown in Table 4-5. All of the measures in this system are compared to budgeted levels and have an impact on costs. Unlike a cost formula, however, two of the measures—production and waste tonnage—are not, in themselves, cost measures. *Production* is measured on an absolute basis, rather than in an output-divided-by-input format, because the production process is machine-driven, with the manning levels relatively fixed. Any increase in output, therefore, provides a significant financial benefit to the company. External quality, or quality from the customer's point of view, is factored into the equation through a penalty mechanism: *Four times* the number of tons with substantiated defects are subtracted from production. *Manufac-*

Table 4-5. Family of measures for a paper mill.

Variable	Measure
• Production	Tons produced, less 4 × complaint tons
• Manufacturing costs	Manufacturing cost per ton
• Quality	Waste tonnage

Table 4-6. Family of measures for a building products company.

Variable	Measure
• Changeover time	Minutes per changeover
• Run speed	Lineal feet produced per minute
• Plant downtime	Downtime hours
• Material utilization	Scrap by commodity
• Safety	Number of lost-time accidents
• Hazardous waste	Pounds of waste per changeover
• Customer satisfaction	Scrap at customer plants

turing costs are compared to a flexible budget (one that varies with the level of production) to reward employees for reducing waste of energy, manufacturing supplies, maintenance materials, and a variety of other cost elements. Internal quality, or the quality of the production process, is tracked in this plan by measuring the amount of production that must be scrapped. While these three measures are all clearly cost-related, this formula probably produces a greater clarity of understanding on the part of employees than would a cost formula.

An example of a family of measures containing a wide variety of variables is shown in Table 4-6.[5] This plan, which was the initial attempt at gain sharing by a building products manufacturer, was highly successful in terms of the level of improvement obtained.

The productive process for this organization involves manufacturing product on continuously running machinery, and several of the measures are clearly cost-oriented. Reducing *changeover time* and *downtime* and increasing *run speed* in a machine-driven environment will reduce production costs. These variables, which are collectively referred to by the organization as press efficiency, are highly controllable by employees. *Material utilization* also represents an obvious and controllable cost-reduction opportunity.

The remaining measures go beyond cost reduction and focus employee efforts on other priorities or strategic business issues. *Safety* is included in the formula because it represents a value to the organization; cost reduction is secondary for this variable. This notion is reinforced by the fact that this particular measure stands alone in the formula; in other words, a gain in safety cannot be offset by losses in other measures. *Hazardous waste* does have significant cost implications because of disposal requirements, but it also reflects the importance of meeting environmental regulations. Finally, *customer satisfaction* represents a broader and critical strategic thrust for the business. A failure to maintain or increase customer satisfaction may have little immediate cost impact but has major long-term implications for the success of the business.

While the family of measures approach is treated here as a separate and distinct category from the cost formula, there is certainly some potential overlap. A family of measures can, and often does, include one or more cost measures, as the example in Table 4-5 clearly shows.

With a family of measures, then, we are separately quantifying the gains in a variety of variables and adding them together to produce a bonus pool. It should be noted that the vast majority of plans of this type take losses, as well as gains, into account. Losses on any measures, in other words, are subtracted from the pool to produce a *net* gain. If this were not done, substantial losses on one or two of the measures could result in bonuses being paid (for the measures showing a gain) in the face of a decline in overall performance. This outcome would clearly not meet the needs of the business.

While the family of measures formula does provide greater flexibility and the opportunity to include noncost variables in the formula, these benefits do not come without a price. The design time is likely to be greater, as the team may have to sort through and evaluate a large number of potential measures. An organization might have, for example, six different indicators of quality and four ways to quantify safety. The alternative ways to structure a cost formula, by contrast, are likely to be more limited. In addition, the inclusion of noncost items adds some additional complexities relative to the valuation of gains. What is the dollar value of an improvement in customer satisfaction or a reduction in delivery time? The value of a reduction in costs, on the other hand, is self-evident. How these valuation complexities are dealt with will be discussed in Chapter 8.

Table 4-7. Goal-sharing plan for a food processing plant (selected measures).

Variable	Goal	Bonus (per Month)
• Productivity	38,500 lbs./hr.	$20
• Cost performance	$0.009/lb. below standard	40
• Product damage	15 per 10,000 cases	10
• Customer complaints	14 per million lbs.	15
• Shipping errors	5 per wk.	10
• Safety	0 lost-time accidents	10
• Attendance	94%	10

Source: John G. Belcher, Jr., "Gainsharing and Variable Pay: The State of the Art," *Compensation & Benefits Review,* May-June 1994.

Goal Sharing

The third category of variable pay formula differs from gain sharing in one important respect. Rather than create a pool of money based on quantified improvements from a baseline level of performance, goal sharing pays to participating employees a predetermined amount that is tied to the achievement of goals. An example of a goal-sharing formula is shown in Table 4-7.

An organizational goal, rather than a baseline, has been established for each variable in this plan. Associated with each goal is a bonus amount. If the goal is achieved, all employees receive the associated bonus. If the goal is not achieved, there is no payout for that particular variable. While cost issues are well represented in this plan, the formula, like earlier gain-sharing examples, goes beyond traditional variable pay measures to create a focus on quality, customer satisfaction, and safety.

The primary attraction of goal sharing, relative to gain sharing, is its simplicity. Consider what is not present (at least explicitly) in a goal-sharing program:

- The quantification of the difference between actual results and a baseline
- An algorithm to quantify the value of the improvement

- A pool of money that represents the sum of the valued improvements for all of the formula measures
- An employee share percentage
- A mechanism to determine how the employee share of the gains will be divided among the participating employees

In essence, the message sent by the goal-sharing plan is, "If you achieve this goal, you will receive this amount of money." All the calculations are done in advance and built into the system. The process of communicating goal sharing is thus much easier than it would be with a gainsharing program, because virtually all that needs to be known about the system is evident in the formula itself. Participating employees know exactly what they will receive if they achieve the goal for any given measure.

Another advantage, at least from a management point of view, is that no bonuses are paid unless a meaningful improvement is made. In effect, the company retains 100 percent of the gains associated with levels of improvement that fall short of the goal.

Goal sharing also offers an opportunity to directly integrate compensation into the company's strategic or business plan. Goals that already exist in the business plan can, through goal sharing, become the basis for variable pay.

On the downside, a goal-based variable pay system may lack credibility with employees if those employees feel that the goals are set at unrealistically high levels. It may appear to employees that the plan is nothing more than an attempt to get them to work harder with little risk to the company of paying substantial bonuses. This problem can be effectively addressed, of course, by involving employees in the establishment of the goals. One large corporation that has a goal-sharing plan in each of fifty-seven operating units employs a cross-sectional employee committee in each unit to establish the goals. This plan, which has the support of the company's union, paid an average of 6.5 percent in a recent year.[6]

Another possible concern with goal sharing is that this type of system may limit the improvement potential, as there is no motivation to continue improving once the goal is achieved. A related concern is that employees may work hard but fall just short of the goal, which can be demoralizing. This also may increase the risk of failure, as a variable pay system that pays little or nothing in its first year may never get off the ground. This all-or-nothing aspect of goal sharing, in fact, may be its biggest drawback.

These problems can be ameliorated through a system that has multiple goal levels for each measure. An easily achievable goal may carry a modest payout, while a more challenging goal for the same measure produces a larger bonus. A good example of this approach is shown in Table

Table 4-8. Goal sharing with multiple goals.

	Standard Plus	*Goal*	*Goal Plus*
Yields			
Product A	82%	84%	86%
Employee bonus	$50	$100	$150
Product B	74%	76%	77%
Employee bonus	$50	$100	$150
Product C	89%	91%	93%
Employee bonus	$50	$100	$150
On-time delivery	95%	97%	99%
Employee bonus	$50	$100	$150
Cycle time (days)	20	18	16
Employee bonus	$50	$100	$150
Employee development (hours)		40 $50	

4-8. This organization was in the early stages of a self-directed team process and felt a need to provide a pay system to support this change initiative. Because of concerns about the immaturity of the teams, management chose to defer the implementation of a permanent gain-sharing program in favor of the simplicity of a goal-sharing system with an annual payout.

For each variable, there are three goal levels. The term *standard plus* was used to describe a level of performance that was short of the plant's goal for the year, but represented an improvement over past performance. A larger amount was paid out if the plant's goal was achieved, and a still larger bonus was available for performance beyond the goal.

Another example of a goal-sharing plan with multiple goal levels is provided by a major hotel. This plan is also interesting in that it is aligned with the management's concept of a *stakeholders' triangle*. Management believes that it has responsibility to serve three stakeholders: the owner, the customer, and the employee. This concept is displayed graphically as a triangle, with one stakeholder occupying each of the triangle's three points. The hotel's goal-sharing plan, presented in Table 4-9, contains three measures, each representing the organization's performance in serving one of these stakeholders.

Table 4-9. Goal-sharing plan for a hotel.

	Goals			
	Level 1	*Level 2*	*Level 3*	*Level 4*
▪ Employee turnover (employee)	32%	30%	27%	25%
▪ Customer comment card score (customer)	6.3	6.4	6.5	6.6
▪ Hotel profit (owner)	$580,000	$625,000	$670,000	$720,000

Table 4-10. Bonus weightings for a hotel.

	Hourly (%)	*Middle* Management (%)	*Senior* Management (%)
▪ Employee turnover (employee)	25%	50%	25%
▪ Customer comment card score (customer)	50	25	25
▪ Hotel profit (owner)	25	25	50

In view of the fact that the employees' ability to impact each of these measures varies considerably with their position in the organization, the plan weights the payout differently for the various employee groups. Payouts for hourly employees, for example, are most heavily weighted toward the customer variable, while middle management's bonuses reflect a heavier weight on the employee measure. The owner variable, as might be expected, carries the heaviest weight for senior management. The weightings for each of these groups is shown in Table 4-10.

One corporation with multiple business units developed guidelines to ensure consistent application of goal sharing across all units. Each operation was to have three levels of goals, defined as follows:

Baseline: Minimum acceptable level of performance, with 80 percent likelihood of achievement

Figure 4-1.   Goal-sharing plan for electric utility.

Goal 1:   Reduce lost-time accidents to no more than 20.

Goal 2:   Reduce motor vehicle accidents to no more than 90.

Goal 3:   Reduce the average time off per employee for illness or injury to 40 hours or less.

Goal 4:   Limit budgeted operating expenses to $865 million or less.

Goal 5:   Generate 12,600 million kilowatt hours or more at a steam electric plant.

Goal 6:   Attain fossil-fuel plant availability of 81 percent or higher.

Goal 7:   Receive no more than 318 complaints as measured by the Public Utility Commission.

Goal 8:   Increase system sales to 29,770 million kilowatt hours or more.

Goal 9:   Increase sales by 435 million kilowatt hours through economic development and employee marketing efforts.

Challenge: Challenging but achievable, with 50 percent likelihood of success

Stretch: A long shot, requiring significant breakthroughs, with a 20 percent likelihood of achievement.

The simplicity of goal sharing makes it a logical choice for a company seeking to tie the pay of all employees to a single set of companywide measures. This approach became particularly popular in the electric utility industry during the late 1980s and early 1990s. One example is shown in Figure 4–1.

The participants in this plan, which was typical of the industry, were all full-time employees below the officer level. The annual payout was a function of the number of goals achieved. A one-half percent bonus was paid if two goals were achieved, with another one-half percent for each additional goal achieved. The maximum bonus was 4 percent. The goal variables were selected with the intent that each employee could relate to and influence at least one goal.

In view of the fact that most utilities using these systems had thousands of employees, it is questionable whether the plans had any meaningful impact on employee behaviors. They did provide contingent compensation, however, and also served to raise employee awareness about company priorities. More recently, several utilities have modified their variable pay systems to include a departmental goal component in order to increase the impact on employee behaviors (an example is presented in Chapter 6).

As with other forms of variable pay, goal sharing offers ample opportunity to creatively meet the needs of the business. One company, for example, employs as one of its variables a "focus" goal. The variable associated with this goal changes each year to support an organizational focus on a particular performance issue that represents a priority for that year. Examples of past focus areas include participation levels on various committees, developing departmental mission statements, and meeting training schedules.[7]

A Combined Formula

This discussion so far has described gain sharing and goal sharing as separate and distinct options. There is absolutely no reason, however, why these two approaches cannot be combined in one variable pay program. There are many plans that pay out a percentage of the gains on some measures while rewarding the achievement of a goal on other measures. A chemical plant, for example, shares cost reductions from a baseline level and, as part of the same plan, pays fixed amounts for the achievement of safety, environmental, and customer-satisfaction goals.

Making the Right Choice

The advantages and disadvantages of the basic formula categories are presented in Table 4-11.

How does an organization make a choice among the various formula categories, as well as alternative approaches within a category? Part of the answer has been discussed earlier: The formula must meet the needs of the business. If driving down costs, or being the low-cost producer, is key to the success of the business, then a broad cost formula would be a logical choice. If, on the other hand, the key to success lies in being the highest quality, most customer-responsive competitor, then a family of measures, either in a gain-sharing or a goal-sharing format, would provide the flexibility to focus on quality and customer-service issues.

Another part of the answer, however, lies in the relative importance of the two major objectives for the variable pay system (see Chapter 1). If contingent compensation is management's sole or primary objective, then a form of profit sharing, as we learned earlier in this chapter, makes emi-

Table 4-11. Advantages and disadvantages of the formula categories.

Formula Category	Advantages	Disadvantages
▪ Profit sharing	1. Simple to design and administer 2. Cannot pay out when business results are poor 3. Ideal for contingent compensation	1. Difficult for employees to understand 2. Little impact on employee behaviors
▪ Gain sharing	1. Creates focus on key business variables 2. Can reward "soft" variables 3. Supports behavior change objective	1. Complex to design 2. May pay out when business results are poor
▪ Goal sharing	1. Creates focus on key business variables 2. Can reward "soft" variables 3. Simple to understand 4. Can tie pay to business plan goals 5. Supports behavior change objective	1. Goals may lack credibility 2. May limit improvement 3. Higher risk of no payout 4. May pay out when business results are poor

nent sense. Pay would be tied to the bottom line of the business and would therefore fluctuate in concert with the returns to the owners of the business. But if behavioral change is a major management objective for the variable pay system, profit sharing will not get the job done (except, possibly, in a very small organization). Management would be well advised to implement gain sharing or goal sharing, with an emphasis on variables over which employees have a high degree of control.

It is important to note here that management is not forced to choose one objective—contingent compensation or behavioral change—to the total exclusion of the other. Gain sharing and goal sharing do, after all,

Figure 4-2. Formula continuum.

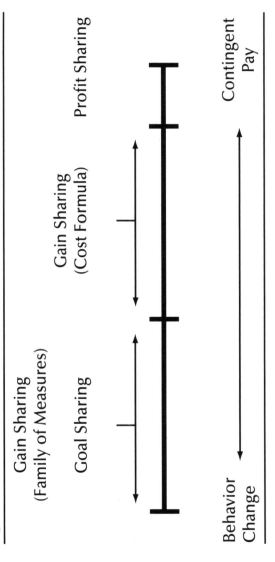

Gain Sharing
(Family of Measures)

Goal Sharing

Gain Sharing
(Cost Formula)

Profit Sharing

Behavior
Change

Contingent
Pay

provide contingent compensation as well as support behavioral change initiatives. They are not, however, as effective a vehicle for contingent compensation as is profit sharing because the basis for pay is not the bottom line of the business.

And there is a great deal of middle ground between pure profit sharing and pure controllable gain sharing/goal sharing. We might think here in terms of a continuum of variable pay plans, with those that best support the contingent compensation objective at one end and those that best support the behavior change objective at the other end. This idea is presented graphically in Figure 4-2.

As the graph suggests, a gain-sharing plan with a cost formula occupies the middle ground between the two objectives. The exact position of such a plan on the continuum depends on the nature of the cost formula. A plan that measures costs as a percent of sales, and includes most or all of the organization's costs, is only slightly to the left of profit sharing. A cost formula that includes only those costs over which employees have a significant degree of control, and which does not factor selling price into the equation, would be closer to the behavior-change end of the continuum. In addition, gain sharing and goal sharing can move more toward the contingent compensation end of the continuum by emphasizing cost-type measures.

There are other formula variations and design options that can move a variable pay plan farther toward one end of the continuum or the other. These include financially funded goal sharing (see Chapter 5) and profit modifiers or gates (see Chapter 10). The point is that management cannot make an intelligent decision about a variable pay framework except within the context of the business needs and the objectives that have been established for the system.

Before proceeding to the next step in the design process, in which individual measures will be identified and evaluated, we will review some variations on the three basic formula categories.

References

1. John G. Belcher, Jr., *Gain Sharing: The New Path to Profits and Productivity* (Houston: Gulf Publishing Company, 1991).
2. Shawn Tully, "The Real Key to Creating Wealth," *Fortune*, September 20, 1993.
3. Paul Barton, "Pay at Risk—Avon Gives Every Employee a Stake in Company Success," *ACA News*, December 1994.
4. Belcher, *Gain Sharing*.

5. John G. Belcher, Jr., "Gainsharing and Variable Pay: The State of the Art," *Compensation and Benefits Review,* May-June 1994.
6. Kathleen M. Davidson, "Goalsharing—Incentive Program Succeeding at Corning Inc.," *ACA News,* December 1994.
7. James P. Guthrie and Edward P. Cunningham, "Pay for Performance for Hourly Workers: The Quaker Oats Alternative," *Compensation & Benefits Review,* March-April 1992.

5

Formula Variations

In Chapter 4, we reviewed the various categories of variable pay formulas: profit sharing, gain sharing, and goal sharing. Before moving on to the next step in the design process, however, we should review some variations on the basic formula categories. These variations have arisen in recent years as organizations have become more creative in designing systems to meet the unique needs of their businesses.

One variation combines a profit-sharing or cost formula with goal sharing in order to capitalize on the best features of each. Another variation involves the use of certain measures as modifiers or multipliers in order to increase the emphasis on certain variables or to deal with a difficult valuation problem. A third shortcuts the payout calculation in order to increase employees' comprehension of the system. The final variation that will be reviewed here makes use of a matrix structure to deal with interrelated variables.

Financially Funded Goal Sharing

In recent years, a hybrid approach to the variable pay formula has become increasingly popular. This alternative employs either a profitability measure or a cost measure to fund a bonus pool, with the actual payout contingent upon achieving certain other organizational goals. We will call this approach *financially funded goal sharing.*

This formula option has become popular because it addresses what is often a major management concern about gain sharing or goal sharing: that bonuses might be paid in times of poor profitability or financial results. This scenario is certainly conceivable if the variable pay formula includes only measures that are highly controllable by employees. The plan participants might improve the gain-sharing measures (or achieve the goal-sharing goals) at a time when market forces are causing a significant decline in profitability. These forces could include an increase in raw

Table 5-1. Financially funded goal-sharing funding mechanism.

Operating Profit as % of Plan	Potential Bonus	Operating Profit as % of Plan	Potential Bonus
>115%	8.0%	95–100%	5.5%
110–115	7.5	90–95	4.0
105–110	7.0	85–90	2.0
100–105	6.5	<85	0

material costs or a heightened competitive challenge that must be met by a reduction in selling prices.

The obvious solution, of course, would be to tie pay to profitability through a profit-sharing plan. This alternative eliminates any risk of high payouts in times of low profitability. As suggested in Chapter 4, however, profit sharing suffers from a major weakness in that it probably does little to change employee behaviors. The financially funded goal-sharing formula addresses this problem in that it enables the company to create a focus on controllable variables while simultaneously ensuring that bonus payments are funded only by increased profitability or reduced costs.

In its most basic form, the pool of money that is available for distribution to employees is a function of profitability, as it would be under profit sharing. If the available monies were distributed to participating employees without further condition, it would in fact be a profit-sharing plan in its traditional form. In this variation, however, the payout is not unconditional but is at least partly tied to the achievement of other goals that are more meaningful to, and more controllable by, the participating employees.

An example is provided by a division of an auto industry supplier.[1] In this plan, potential payouts are a function of the division's operating profits, as shown in Table 5-1. At the level of operating profits equal to that envisioned in the profit plan, a potential payout equal to 6.5 percent of payroll is established. The size of the potential payout increases to a maximum of 8 percent when operating profits are greater than 115 percent of plan, and declines to zero at an operating profit level below 85 percent of plan.

Only half of the potential bonus is paid without further condition, however. The distribution of the remaining half is contingent upon achieving six organizational goals that are more relevant and meaningful to employees. These goals, as well as the percentage of the payout allocated to

Table 5-2. Financially funded goal-sharing goals.

	Percent of Bonus Paid		*Percent of Bonus Paid*
▪ Unconditional	50%	▪ Safety	10%
▪ Productivity	10	▪ Customer rejects	5
▪ Scrap	10	▪ Attendance	5
▪ Rework	10		

each, are shown in Table 5-2. If, as an example, only the productivity and safety goals were achieved, 70 percent of the potential bonus (the 50 percent that is unconditional plus 10 percent for each of the two goals) would be distributed to the plan participants.

This plan capitalizes on the best feature of profit sharing—that bonus payments are always tied to the bottom line of the business—while at the same time establishing line of sight by requiring that improvements be made in variables that are highly controllable by employees. In effect, the employees must "earn" the potential payout accruing from a given level of operating profits by achieving goals in those variables over which they have some degree of control.

A variation on the financially funded theme involves the use of a cost formula, rather than a profitability measure, as the funding mechanism. A distribution operation for a major consumer products company provides a good example of this variation. This plan, in place at several of the company's distribution centers, creates a gain-sharing pool based on improvements in the ratio of each facility's costs to its sales, or value of product shipped. All of the costs incurred in the operation of the distribution center are included, whether they are controllable by employees or not. When costs fall below the baseline ratio, 50 percent of the cost savings are potentially available for distribution to employees, as shown in a hypothetical example in Table 5-3.

This formula was adopted because of a management requirement that any bonuses paid be fully funded by quantifiable cost savings. Another management requirement, however, presented a bit of a dilemma for the design team. Management's top priority at this time was customer service, and each of the distribution centers was being evaluated on the basis of its performance on a customer-service measure. How could a variable pay system be funded by cost reduction, yet reinforce customer service at the same time?

Table 5-3. Distribution center cost formula.

Sales	$24,000,000
× Baseline costs (5.2%)	$ 1,248,000
− Actual costs	$ 1,212,000
= Bonus Pool	$ 36,000
− Company share (50%)	18,000
= Employee share	$ 18,000

One additional complication had to be confronted by the design team. While the cost formula that funded bonuses could be utilized by all distribution centers (there were over 100), there was a desire to allow individual centers the opportunity to tailor the variable pay system to performance variables that were important to each location. One center, for example, may have a need to reduce product damage, while another location might be focusing on the productivity of its delivery truck drivers.

The solution was a financially funded goal-sharing plan: Bonus payments would be funded through cost reduction, but the distribution of these bonuses would be tied to improvements in customer service and any other variables that might be important to a given distribution center. The final allocation of the pool among these various requirements was as follows:

Unconditional:	30 percent
Customer service:	30 percent
Other goals:	40 percent

Thirty percent of the pool is distributed without further condition. An additional 30 percent is paid out if the customer service goal is achieved. Payout of the remaining 40 percent of the pool is contingent upon achieving one to three additional goals established at each location by a management-employee team. The team selects these goals based on the business issues that are important to that particular location. This creative feature accomplishes two things: It provides for employee involvement in the design of the program at the local level, and it enables the system to be customized to the business needs of each location.

Figure 5-1. Distribution center preapproved goal list.

- Warehouse units handled per hour

- Delivery units per hour

- Combined units per hour

- Over/short deliveries as a percentage of sales

- OSHA reportable accidents

- Absenteeism percentage

- Warehouse and truck damage as a percentage of sales

- Finished product difference as a percentage of sales

- Driver performance (e.g., in meeting delivery schedules)

The design team took one further step with respect to the goal-selection process. Given that this plan could ultimately be implemented at over 100 locations, the process of obtaining management approval for each unit's goals prior to the beginning of each year could become very cumbersome and time-consuming. To eliminate this potential bureaucratic complication, a list of ten "preapproved" variables was established, as shown in Figure 5-1. These variables were deemed to be important business issues in every distribution center, and the selection of any variable from the list by any center would be acceptable without further approval. Should any unit desire to set goals on variables not on this list, approval to do so would be required.

Financially funded goal sharing is also an excellent vehicle to focus employees on organizational process objectives as well as performance goals. A medium-size, publicly owned service organization established such a system to support its organizational change initiatives.

This particular company was viewed by Wall Street as a growth company, and the expectations of the investment community for profit growth were high. If these expectations were not met, the company's share price would be vulnerable to a decline. In order to align employee compensation with the interests of the shareholders, the funding mechanism for this company's variable pay system is *earnings per share;* a sliding percentage of the net profits earned in excess of the company's earnings per share goal each semiannual period is set aside to fund bonuses.

The company, which provides information management services, is divided into twenty-five business units. Some of these entities are operating units, with profit-and-loss statements, while others are support groups. In order to increase the employees' line of sight and improve their ability to relate to their business units, the distribution of the bonus pool is tied to the achievement of goals by each business unit. The amount of the potential bonus that any employee receives, therefore, is determined by the level of goal achievement by his or her business unit.

In the initial year of the program, these goals were divided into three categories, reflecting company priorities. These categories, along with their associated weights, were:

Financial objectives:	60 percent
Customer and quality performance:	25 percent
Employee performance:	15 percent

The financial objectives, accounting for 60 percent of the potential payout, consisted of three subgoals for each business unit:

1. Achieve the contribution target (revenues less direct expenses) contained in the business plan. For support groups, the goal was to achieve the unit's expense target.
2. Achieve the revenue per employee target contained in the business unit's plan. For support groups, total corporate revenues were used to establish the target.
3. Achieve improvement over the prior year contribution percentage (revenue less direct costs divided by revenue). Support groups must reduce their expenses as a percentage of corporate revenues.

With 60 percent of each employee's bonus tied to financial measures for his or her business unit, attention to revenue generation and cost control was assured. The remaining 40 percent bonus potential could then be used to increase employee focus on other variables. Since this company had some high-priority organizational change initiatives under way, the decision was made to tie this remaining 40 percent bonus potential to the achievement of process goals rather than to performance in a traditional sense.

The business unit goals for customer and quality performance, accounting for 25 percent of the potential bonus, included:

- Developing measures for six performance criteria identified by a companywide activity-based management process. The measures must be tracked monthly and visibly posted within each business unit.
- Identifying two key activities that relate to customer satisfaction or

process improvement and conducting a process mapping exercise to identify opportunities to eliminate waste or improve cycle times. These maps also must be visibly posted in the work area.

The final 15 percent bonus potential was similarly tied to the implementation of improvement processes, in this case in the area of employee satisfaction and development. The goals were:

1. Complete an employee survey and identify the area of primary concern.
2. Identify employee performance criteria.
3. Complete 100 percent of specified team training modules.

Thus 40 percent of the potential bonus was tied not to performance improvement per se but rather to the implementation of processes, such as developing performance measures and obtaining team training, that were deemed by management to be critical to the success of the business.

Financially funded goal sharing is particularly well suited to this idea, as the funding mechanism ensures that bonus payments are feasible and realistic from a financial point of view. Management is then free to incorporate nonfinancial objectives into the variable pay system without concern about the risk of paying substantial bonuses during times of deficient financial results.

A question that almost always arises with respect to a financially funded goal-sharing system is: What happens to the bonus money that has been funded but is not distributed because of a failure to achieve all the goals? The normal answer is that the company retains those funds, on the rationale that the employees have not earned their full share of the financial gains by failing to achieve the goals over which they have some control. There is an even stronger argument if some of the goals are quality or customer-satisfaction variables; failing to achieve these goals may have a negative impact on the company in the future owing to lost business. As always, of course, exceptions to this generalization can be found. One company, for example, places the unpaid portion of the financially funded pool in a reserve account, to be paid at the end of the year if the goal or goals in question are achieved on an annual basis.

The major disadvantage of a financially funded goal-sharing program is that there is no reward for achieving the goals if the profitability or cost performance is not there to fund the bonus. For this reason, it is probably most appropriate where financial performance is deemed to be a prerequisite before any payout can be justified. Where this is the case, it does represent an improvement over pure profit sharing or an all-inclusive cost formula in that it adds a focus on more controllable or nonfinancial variables.

Because this approach represents a distinct formula type, we will add it to our continuum developed in Chapter 4 (Figure 4-2). Because financial performance is the funding mechanism, financially funded goal sharing is placed toward the right, or contingent compensation, end of the continuum, as shown in Figure 5-2. Its placement roughly corresponds to that of the cost gain-sharing formula. If the funding mechanism is a measure of profitability, it would fall toward the right end of the range shown, as would a cost formula that includes all of the organization's costs. A plan funded by controllable costs, on the other hand, would fall toward the left end of the range.

Modifiers and Multipliers

In the standard approach to the variable pay formula, the performance measures directly determine the magnitude of the bonus payment. In the gain-sharing format, for example, the improvements in the plan measures are determined, the dollar value of those improvements are quantified (see Chapter 8), and a portion of those gains are paid out. In a goal-sharing program, the bonus amount is predetermined and tied to the achievement of specific goals.

An alternative treatment is to treat a specific measure as a modifier or multiplier. When a measure is used as a *modifier* or *multiplier* (the terms will be used interchangeably), the performance on that measure does not directly determine a dollar amount to be paid, but is used to modify (add to or subtract from) the aggregate value of the gains from all the other measures. An example of a customer-complaints multiplier is shown in Table 5-4.

In this example, eight complaints are in essence the baseline; at that level of performance, the variable pay pool is multiplied by 100 percent, which leaves it unchanged. At lower levels of complaints, the multiplier is greater than 100 percent, which increases the size of the overall pool. At higher levels of complaints, the effect of the multiplier is to reduce the pool size.

Modifiers can be extremely simple. A plant with a cost-as-a-percent-of-sales gain-sharing program employs a safety modifier that increases the payout by 25 percent in any quarter in which there are no lost-time accidents.

One advantage of the modifier is that it enables the designers of the variable pay system to sidestep the issue of valuing improvements where it is difficult or impossible to do so. The company is thus able to reward improvements in customer satisfaction without having to quantify the value of a specific level of improvement. In effect, employees are paid a

Figure 5-2. Formula continuum.

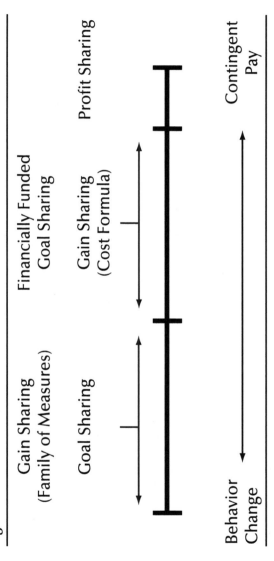

Table 5-4. Customer-complaints multiplier.

Customer Complaints	Multiplier (%)	Customer Complaints	Multiplier (%)
0	120%	10	95%
2	115	12	90
4	110	14	85
6	105	16	80
8	100		

greater portion of the cost savings achieved from other measures on the basis that the company will gain a longer-term, but unquantifiable, benefit from more satisfied customers.

The modifier approach has another potential advantage: It can be used to provide a greater emphasis on and weight to a particular variable that has a higher priority than other measures in the variable pay system. A good example is found in a facility manufacturing air conditioners.[2]

This particular organization implemented a gain-sharing program that included measures of labor productivity, materials utilization, on-time delivery, and safety. Management's top priority, however, was quality, and there was a desire to treat that as a superordinate variable. To achieve that objective, the quality variable was treated as a multiplier, as shown graphically in Figure 5-3.

The quality measure was the score from a regular quality audit conducted by the corporate office. The audit score, on the horizontal axis, was translated into a percentage, shown on the vertical axis, ranging from zero to 110 percent. The gain-sharing pool, representing the aggregate gains from all other measures, was then multiplied by the appropriate percentage to determine the final pool size. If the score was 98, the multiplier is 100 percent, which leaves the pool unchanged. The percentage drops rapidly at progressively lower scores, reaching zero at a score of 78 or lower. Scores above 98 provided for an expansion of the pool, up to a maximum of 10 percent. The modifier in this case serves to provide quality with a greater potential impact on bonuses than would have been possible if it were simply one of several variables contributing to the gain-sharing pool. Poor quality in this organization can cancel out the gains achieved from all of the other measures.

The principal drawback of the modifier is that its effectiveness in rein-

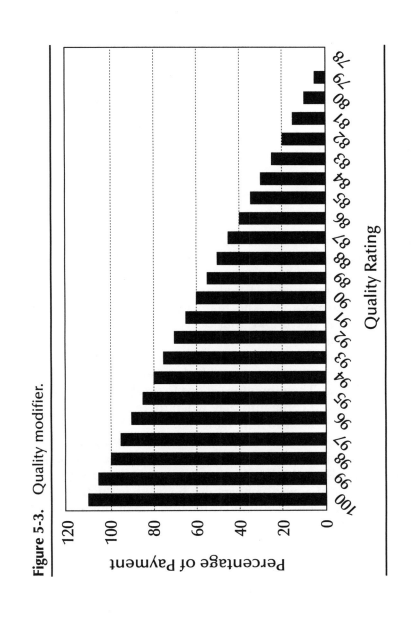

Figure 5-3. Quality modifier.

Table 5-5.   Alternative customer-complaints schedule.

Number of Complaints as Percent of Orders Booked	Payout per Participant
0.8%	$ 0
0.7	50
0.6	100
0.5	150
0.4	200

forcing behavior is dependent upon the magnitude of the improvements in the other variables. If there are little or no gains to be modified, its power is greatly diminished.

One design team solved this problem by developing an alternative approach to the modifier. The team developed a customer-complaints modifier that was not unlike that described earlier and shown in Table 5-4. The team was very concerned, however, that the complaints modifier would have no effect if there were no gains in the other variables. Reductions in customer complaints should, they reasoned, be rewarded under any circumstances. They therefore chose to establish an alternative payout schedule that would come into play when there were no gains to be modified. This schedule is shown in Table 5-5.

This approach enabled employees to earn bonuses for reductions in customer complaints, even when the modifier would not have been otherwise operative. The scheduled payout approach used by this team to increase the power of a modifier can also be used as the basis for the overall payout from a variable pay plan, as we will see in the next section.

Scheduled Payout Plans

The payout calculation in a gain-sharing program generally involves a series of calculations, some of which might be rather complex. First, the gain must be valued in dollars. These dollars are aggregated to form a pool, a percentage of which is set aside as the employee share. The employee share is then allocated to the individual participants in some fashion. Only

Table 5-6. Profit-sharing payout schedule.

ROI	Bonus	ROI	Bonus
20%	10%	26%	16%
21	11	27	17
22	12	28	18
23	13	29	19
24	14	30	20
25	15		

then does an individual learn what his reward is for contributing to the achieved gains.

As we discussed in Chapter 4, goal-sharing plans reduce all this complexity to a simply communicated idea: "If you achieve this goal, you will receive this reward." A great deal of this simplicity can also be achieved with a gain-sharing plan, through the mechanism of a *scheduled payout*.

Scheduled payout plans are similar to goal sharing in that the payments for achieving given levels of performance are predetermined and communicated in advance. Unlike goal sharing, which generally involves a single or very small number of goal levels for each measure, a scheduled payout plan communicates the bonus payments for many small increments of improvement. It is, in essence, a gain-sharing program with the gains grouped into steps, with the associated payouts defined and communicated in advance. An example of a scheduled payout profit-sharing plan was discussed in Chapter 4 and presented in Table 4-2. The plan is reproduced here as Table 5-6.

For each increment of profitability, as measured by return on investment, the payout, as a percent of each individual's pay, is shown in the table. The participating employees can thus ascertain the value of their bonuses at any level of profitability without having to go through several calculations to determine the size of the pool, the employees' share of the pool, and the distribution percentage.

In some cases, the gain-sharing pool (or the employee share of the pool), rather than the individual payout, is the information communicated for each increment of improvement. An example is provided by a materials-waste measure for a packaging plant, as presented in Table 5-7.

As in the earlier example, a number of calculations have been made

Table 5-7. Scheduled payout — materials waste.

Improvement Over Baseline (%)	Employee Share ($)	Improvement Over Baseline (%)	Employee Share ($)
.05–.15%	$ 1,440	.85– .95%	$12,960
.15–.25	2,880	.95–1.05	14,440
.25–.30	4,320	1.05–1.15	15,840
.35–.45	5,760	1.15–1.25	17,280
.45–.55	7,200	1.25–1.35	18,720
.55–.65	8,640	1.35–1.45	20,160
.65–.75	10,080	1.45–1.55	21,600
.75–.85	11,520		

Table 5-8. Unit cost matrix (bonus percent paid).

Cost per Unit	Units Produced (000)						
	36	34	32	30	28	26	24
$16.10	4.5	5.2	5.9	6.7	7.5	8.3	9.0
16.40	3.8	4.4	5.1	5.8	6.5	7.4	8.1
16.70	3.1	3.7	4.3	4.9	5.7	6.5	7.2
17.00		3.0	3.6	4.2	4.9	5.6	6.3
17.30			2.9	3.5	4.2	4.8	5.5
17.60				2.8	3.4	4.0	4.7
17.90					2.7	3.3	3.9
18.20						2.6	3.2
18.50							2.5

in advance for the employees. In this case, the employee share of the gains, rather than the payout to each individual, is communicated for each one-tenth of 1 percent reduction in the waste of materials.

The Matrix

Design teams will invariably encounter complex situations that test their ingenuity and ability to solve problems. One that often leaves them greatly perplexed is where the value of an improvement in one variable is dependent on the level of another variable. A given improvement in variable *x*, in other words, may represent a substantial benefit to the company at one level of variable *y*, but much less of a benefit, or even no benefit at all, at a different level of variable *y*.

A variable pay program in a manufacturing organization provides an illustration. The formula is a basic cost formula, with the measure being total manufacturing cost per unit produced. Measured costs include indirect costs, support costs, depreciation, and other fixed costs as well as variable costs. Because of high fixed costs in this operation, changes in volume have a significant effect on cost per unit. A given cost per unit might therefore represent an exceptional performance at one level of volume, but a poor performance at higher level of volume. While the traditional approaches to cost formulas do not attempt to adjust for volume, management in this case felt that the effect of volume was too great to ignore. The solution was the matrix shown in Table 5-8.

The threshold for bonus payments in this plan is a cost performance of $18.50 per unit. This cost level justifies a payout, however, only if volume is 24,000 units or less. At higher volumes, progressively lower cost-per-unit levels are required in order for bonuses to be paid. At the highest volume shown on the chart (36,000 units), the cost per unit must be $16.70 or less to trigger a payout. The matrix has thus allowed the organization to construct a variable pay plan that reflects the reality of the high degree of interdependence between volume and costs.

The matrix can also be used to tie the entire payout from a variable pay plan to a superordinate goal, such as profitability. A subsidiary of a company in the electronics industry developed a plan that incorporated six quality, customer service, and cost measures (Figure 5-4) into what is known as an *objectives matrix*.[3] Through this vehicle, ten levels of performance are established for each measure, and a number of points are assigned to each of the performance levels. The points awarded for each measure are weighted based on the relative importance of each variable, and an overall score, between 0 and 1,000, results.

Management of this company wanted employee bonuses to reflect

Figure 5-4.   Electronics company measures.

- Reliability
- Line rejects
- Delivery performance
- Plant yield
- Material utilization
- Productivity

Table 5–9.   Electronics company matrix.

Controllable Profit	Performance Index		
	< 400	*400–700*	*> 700*
$$$$	4%	6%	10%
$$$	2	4	7
$$	1	3	5
$	0	1	3

both the score from the objectives matrix and the subsidiary's profitability. The solution was the matrix shown in Table 5-9. Bonuses, ranging from zero to 10 percent, are a function of both the objectives matrix score (shown on the horizontal axis) and the subsidiary's profits (shown on the vertical axis).

A company in the service industry integrated the objectives matrix format into a more elaborate payout matrix (Figure 5-5) based on the increase in the profitability of the business. In this case, ten measures made up the objectives matrix, producing a performance score from 0 to 1,000. Various performance scores, in increments of 100, are shown on the vertical axis of the matrix. The horizontal axis represents various levels of profit improvement over the prior year. Each cell of the matrix contains the range of individual payouts that would be made for a particular combination of performance and profit improvement. The precise amount of the payout is determined through a rather complex formula; the ranges are shown in the matrix for ease of communication. As can be seen, there is no payout if the performance score is 300 or less, or if the year-over-

Figure 5-5. Payout matrix.

Index	0–4%	4–8%	8–12%	12–16%	16–20%	>20%
0–300						
301–400		up to $82	$83–$198			
401–500		up to $103	$104–$239	$240–$408		
501–600		up to $144	$145–$321	$322–$532	$533–$775	
601–700			$145–$350	$351–$589	$590–$681	$864–$1,166
701–800				$351–$618	$619–$919	$922–$1,253
801–900					$619–$939	$942–$1,294
901–1000					$619–$960	$963–$1,335

Percent Profit Increase

Performance Score

Table 5-10. Budget performance matrix.

Number of Goals Achieved	Conversion Cost Variance From Budget				
	<95%	95–99%	100–104%	105–109%	110% +
4	0	2.5%	3.0%	3.5%	4.0%
3	0	2.0	2.5	3.0	3.5
2	0	1.5	2.0	2.5	3.0
1	0	1.0	1.5	2.0	2.5
0	0	0	0	0	0

year increase in profits is less than 4 percent. As performance scores improve, at a given level of profit improvement, the bonus paid increases accordingly. Likewise, higher profits produce higher payouts for a given level of performance.

What is accomplished through these last two matrix examples—larger payouts for a given level of performance as profits increase—can also be effectuated through a variable share mechanism, which will be reviewed in Chapter 10.

An analogous situation involves the use of a matrix to vary the payouts based on budget performance, an example of which is shown in Table 5-10. In this case, organizational goals were established by management on four variables: productivity, quality, schedule performance, and safety. The annual payout was a function of both the number of goals achieved and the variance from budget for conversion costs (the costs incurred in converting raw materials to finished product). A maximum bonus of 4 percent was paid if all four goals were achieved and the conversion cost variance from budget was 110 percent or greater.

The matrix can also be used to reward cost reduction while ensuring that the proper amount of work gets done by the group in question. This approach was adopted by an organization in which maintenance represented a major cost and was a critical aspect of the business.

The design team's initial inclination was to employ a simple measure of maintenance costs versus budget as one of the measures in the organization's variable pay formula. A concern was raised, however, that the maintenance department could reduce its costs by failing to carry out preventive maintenance activities. This could be disastrous, for the company's business was extremely dependent on the reliability of its capital equip-

Table 5-11. Maintenance cost matrix.

Percent Preventive Maintenance Tasks Completed	Costs as Percent of Budget					
	100%	99%	98%	97%	96%	95%
100%	$ 0	$15,000	$35,000	$60,000	$90,000	$140,000
98	(5,000)	5,000	15,000	30,000	60,000	90,000
96	(10,000)	0	5,000	15,000	30,000	60,000
94	(20,000)	(10,000)	0	5,000	15,000	30,000
92	(30,000)	(20,000)	(10,000)	0	5,000	15,000
90	(40,000)	(30,000)	(20,000)	(10,000)	0	5,000
88	(50,000)	(40,000)	(30,000)	(20,000)	(10,000)	0

ment. The team ultimately adopted the matrix shown in Table 5-11 to protect against this outcome.

The horizontal axis of the matrix contains the maintenance department's cost performance versus budget. The numbers on the vertical axis represent the percentage of scheduled preventive maintenance tasks completed. Each of the cells contains the amount added to (or subtracted from) the bonus pool. The payout for a given level of cost performance declines, and may even become negative (which would subtract from the gains on other measures), if the preventative maintenance tasks accomplished fall short of those scheduled.

An innovative use of the matrix format can be found in a plant in the forest products industry. A union-management design team here struggled with a vexing problem. The team agreed that improvements in productivity and on-time delivery, among other things, should be rewarded through the variable pay system. What complicated matters for the design team was the fact that delivery performance was related to the level of capacity at which the plant was operating. When the plant was overbooked (orders exceeded the capacity of the plant), on-time deliveries, as might be expected, were generally lower than when the plant was operating below capacity.

To further complicate matters, delivery performance and productivity were interrelated. When the plant was operating at or near capacity, a major mechanism for improving on-time delivery was increasing the out-

Table 5-12. Employee share of productivity gains.

Percent of Capacity	On-Time (%)		
	<90%	*90–95%*	*95–100%*
105–110%	60%	65%	70%
100–105	55	60	65
95–100	50	55	60
<95	50	50	50

put per hour, or improving productivity. Productivity, therefore, was more than a cost issue; it represented the major means of improving delivery performance, and therefore customer satisfaction, in times of high production.

The final problem faced by the design team was the issue of valuing improvements. While it was relatively easy to place a value on productivity gains, this was not the case for improvements in on-time deliveries, which resulted in greater customer satisfaction (the subject of valuing improvements in customer satisfaction will be explored further in Chapter 8).

The team finally hit upon a creative (albeit complicated) solution for the valuation problem: The employee share of any productivity gains would be determined by the level of on-time deliveries. The rationale was that a given level of productivity is of greater value to the company when it is accompanied by improved delivery performance. This left the problem of the capacity relationship to delivery performance. The solution was a matrix, as shown in Table 5-12. As the plant's production schedule approaches and then exceeds capacity, the greater difficulty of achieving on-time performance, as well as the greater importance of productivity improvement, is reflected through the increasing share of productivity gains paid out to employees.

While modifiers, matrices, and the scheduled payout alternative have been reviewed as part of the discussion on Step 3 (selecting the basic formula structure), the decisions to use these approaches will normally not be made by the design team until later in the plan development process. It is unlikely at this early stage of the design process that the team will have encountered the measurement and valuation complications which these variations are designed to address.

The decision to adopt the financially funded goal-sharing approach, on the other hand, may well be made at this early stage in the design process in order to comply with a management guideline or to meet an obvious business need.

Before we leave the discussion of the various formula categories, we need to explore two additional approaches that are not actually distinct formula categories but represent alternative ways of structuring variable pay around different organizational entities.

References

1. John G. Belcher, Jr., "Group Incentives: Improving Performance Through Shared Goals and Rewards," in Howard Risher and Charles Fay, *The Performance Imperative* (San Francisco: Jossey-Bass, 1995).
2. John G. Belcher, Jr., *Gain Sharing: The New Path to Profits and Productivity* (Houston: Gulf Publishing Company, 1991).
3. An example of an objectives matrix can be found in "Measuring White Collar Work," a paper by the American Productivity and Quality Center, Houston, 1988.

6

Multi-Tiered Plans and Small-Group Systems

Chapters 4 and 5 reviewed the basic categories of variable pay formulas, along with several variations. Most of that discussion took place within the context of a plan that measures and rewards the overall performance of an entire organizational business unit, whether it be a plant, a warehouse, a division, or an entire company. The only possible exception discussed so far was the financially funded goal-sharing approach, in which subgroups within an organization might receive different bonuses based on their specific performance. These plans are still funded, however, by the performance of a discrete organizational entity.

There are two categories of variable pay plans that do not fit the above description. In one category, which we will call *multi-tiered plans*, bonuses are funded by the performance of two or more distinct organizational units. Participating employees therefore receive two (or even three) separate and distinct bonuses.

The other category, *small-group plans*, measures performance exclusively at the subgroup level and pays out on that basis. Within a given organizational unit, therefore, there will be many subunit formulas, with different payouts associated with each.

Multi-Tiered Plans

As suggested in Chapter 1, there are two primary objectives for variable pay: implementing contingent compensation and supporting organizational change. The point was also made that the ideal measurement vehicle for the contingent compensation objective—corporate financial results—is ineffective in supporting the objective of organizational change. The idea behind the two-tiered system is to employ two (or even three)

Table 6-1.   District formulas.

Measure	Valuation Method
Payroll/gross margin	50% of savings
Inventory turns	Dollars of inventory saved × one-half the carrying cost
Receivables days outstanding	$100 per employee for each day improvement
Percentage of on-time delivery	$20 per employee for each .1 percentage point improvement
Hours without a lost-time accident	$1 per employee for each hour

separate and distinct formulas in order to effectively support both objectives.

A two-tiered plan is one in which participating employees receive bonuses from two or more separate and distinct formulas, each of which measures performance at a different organizational level. In its most common form, one bonus is based on corporate profitability while the second is tied to site or operating unit performance. The two-tiered plan differs from financially funded goal sharing in that separate bonuses are funded and paid based on the performance of two organizational entities.

Some Examples

A company in the distribution business provides an example. Employees receive bonuses from two formulas, one based on companywide performance and the other on district, or geographical area, performance. Both formulas are a family of measures. The companywide formula, which is somewhat atypical for this type of plan in that it goes beyond corporate financial results, includes three measures:

Net income per employee:	25 percent of the amount in excess of a target level is added to the pool.
Sales of slow-moving inventory:	5 percent of such sales are added to the pool.

Table 6-2. Electric utility, tier I.

Earnings per Share	Points	Earnings per Share	Points
$2.61	0	$2.80	20
2.65	5	2.85	25
2.70	10	2.90 (target)	30
2.75	15	2.95	35

Safety: 100 percent of the value of improvements are added to the pool.

At the district level, a common set of measures is employed, but the baselines vary, based on each district's past performance. The district measures, along with the valuation methods, are shown in Table 6-1. The variable pay of this company's employees is thus tied to both corporate profitability (along with other variables) and operating unit results.

An interesting example of a *three-tiered plan* can be found in an annual payout plan for an electric utility. The three tiers, along with their respective formulas, are:

- Corporate earnings per share
- Departmental cost control
- Team performance against goals

The performance level for each tier is translated into a predetermined number of points. They are based on tables established each year by the corporation. Examples of the award tables are shown in Tables 6-2, 6-3, and 6-4.

The corporate tier (Table 6-2) is quite straightforward. Earnings per share must exceed a predetermined threshold amount ($2.61 in this example) before any points are awarded, and the number of points increases proportionally from that point. At the target level of earnings ($2.90 in this example), thirty points are awarded. The earnings-per-share threshold also serves as a *gate*, or condition that must be satisfied for the entire plan; no bonuses are paid for any tier if earnings fall below that level.

At the department level (Table 6-3), the number of points earned is a function of the department's cost performance versus its budget. Depart-

Table 6-3. Electric utility, tier II.

Costs vs. Budget (%)	Points	Costs vs. Budget (%)	Points
+ 4.51% or more	0	−1.01 to 5.00%	31–34
+ 2.51 to + 4.50	12–3	−5.01 to 10.00	35–39
+ 0.51 to + 2.50	24–15	−10.01 or more	40
0.00 to 1.00	30		

ments do not have to meet or beat their budgets in order to earn points; the minimum acceptable performance for an award from this tier is a cost level of 4.5 percent over budget. This feature reflects the fact that budgets are very tight in this company, partly because cost savings from any year are incorporated into the following year's budget. Thirty points are earned for a department that achieves its cost budget for the year, with a maximum forty-point award for holding costs under budget by 10 percent or more.

The team award is more complex than the two higher tiers. Team boundaries are defined by each business unit and therefore vary in size. Some business units—where there is high interdependence between groups—choose to define the team as an entire facility, while others have defined teams at the work-group level. Each team has a package of goals, which are developed within the context of the corporation's stated values and emphasis areas. Each of the goals carries a weight reflecting its importance to the business. Various levels of performance on each goal equate to percentages, which are then weighted to produce an overall percentage for the team. This percentage is found on the vertical axis of the matrix shown in Table 6-4. One hundred percent in this context would mean that the team achieved maximum performance on all of its goals. The horizontal axis on the matrix contains the goal achievement percentage for the company's highest-level operating goals, which are contained in the company president's goal package. The design of this matrix ensures that teams earn maximum points only when the corporation is also achieving its operating goals. As with the higher goal tiers, there is a threshold of performance below which no points are earned.

The payout to each individual is determined by multiplying the total points by the target award level, which is established each year by management, divided by 100. If the target award were, for example, $1,050, each point would be worth $10.50.

Table 6-4. Electric utility, tier III.

Team Performance %	Corporate Performance							
	100%	*95%*	*90%*	*85%*	*80%*	*75%*	*70%*	*65%*
100%	40	37	34	31	28	24	20	17
95	37	36	33	30	27	23	19	16
90	34	33	32	29	26	22	18	15
85	31	30	29	28	25	21	17	14
80	28	27	26	25	24	20	16	13
75	24	23	22	21	20	19	15	12
70	20	19	18	17	16	15	14	11
65	17	16	15	14	13	12	11	10

Small-Group Systems

Small-group variable pay plans are those systems that measure and re-ward the performance of groups within an organization rather than the entire organization as one unit. These groups might be departments, pro-duction lines, or teams. The systems are variously referred to in the litera-ture as small-group incentives, team rewards, and a variety of other names.

The advantages of team-based variable pay were described in Chap-ter 2. When performance is measured at the team level, the team members have greater control over the measures that determine their reward than would be the case if the entire organization were being measured. In addi-tion, it is likely that employees will have a greater understanding of the measures and will be better able to relate the pay system to their activities on the job.

These advantages presumably increase the employees' motivation to improve performance and more effectively promote behavior change. There are important tradeoffs for these advantages, however. The teams will naturally focus on their internal performance rather than on their im-pact on other parts of the organization. If there is interdependency among teams, the outcome could be poor interfaces and suboptimization of per-formance. Another concern arises from the fact that bonus payments will vary from group to group. This inevitably leads to perceptions of inequity; those teams that consistently earn lower bonuses will find fault with the system and may ultimately withdraw their support for the variable pay process. Other disadvantages, such as administrative complications and excessive payouts when some groups improve while others do not, were also mentioned in Chapter 2.

Given these considerations, small-group incentives probably make the most sense for relatively large organizations (where employees would feel that their impact on organizationwide performance is extremely small) and/or those with little interdependence among teams. For a small, interdependent organization, team incentives could actually do more harm than good. In any event, any company considering the implementation of a small-group system would be well advised to evaluate the trade-offs associated with this approach before adopting it.

Some Examples

Team-based variable pay systems can employ any of the formula approaches reviewed in Chapters 4 and 5 (although profit sharing would not be meaningful in most cases), and the discussion of pros and cons in those chapters apply here as well. An example of a simple, straightforward team-based plan is provided by a manufacturer of agricultural equipment.[1]

During the mid-1980s, the markets for agricultural equipment were deeply depressed, and this company, like many others in its industry, faced a survival situation. As a response to this threat, management initiated an employee-involvement process and adopted a team gain-sharing plan.

The obvious business need in this case was to reduce costs without sacrificing quality. Since this operation was relatively labor-intensive, the logical focus of the team incentive was labor productivity. Productivity was measured in each department through a simple output-over-input formula:

$$\frac{Pounds\ of\ quality\ products\ manufactured}{Hours\ worked}$$

It was imperative that product quality be maintained while productivity was being improved. To ensure that outcome, customer rejects and returns were deducted from the output of the department responsible.

A family of measures can also be employed in a small-group plan. One major corporation with a long-term commitment to team-based work systems implemented a small-group plan throughout the company in the early 1980s. In the company's manufacturing units, the plan applied to

Table 6-5. Department/unit goals.

Measure	Minimum Opportunity		Target Opportunity		Maximum Opportunity	
	Performance	Percent	Performance	Percent	Performance	Percent
Cost/unit	$2.85	0.34%	$2.78	0.83%	$2.72	1.66%
Percentage Availability	79	0.33	84	0.83	90	1.67
Number of accidents	17	0.33	12	0.84	6	1.67
		1.00%		2.50%		5.00%

individual product or process teams whose members generally numbered in the 50 to 200 range. Each manufacturing team was measured on a common set of variables:

- Manufacturing cost
- Quality
- Delivery performance
- Inventories
- Housekeeping and safety

This plan was terminated after several years because the company was experiencing one of the problems associated with small-group systems: Employees were focusing on their team's performance to the detriment of overall business results. It was replaced by a financially funded goal-sharing system, with the funding mechanism based on business unit profitability.

A different approach is illustrated by a service company that adopted a form of goal sharing at the department or unit level. Bonuses in this company are tied to the achievement of three unit-specific objectives, as established by each department or unit with assistance from the corporate staff. Three performance levels—designated as minimum performance, target performance, and maximum performance—are defined for each objective, as shown in the example in Table 6-5.

Table 6-5 also shows the percentage payout associated with each performance level. The achievement of minimum performance on all three measures would result in a 1 percent bonus payout to the unit members. The achievement of target or maximum performance on all three measures would produce a 2.5 percent or 5 percent bonus, respectively. Pay-outs are made on an annual basis.

This organization also employed a multiplier (see Chapter 5) based on corporate profitability. Minimum, target, and maximum performance levels were established for the corporation's return on equity, and the percentage payout to each department or unit was multiplied by 0.8, 1.0, or 1.2, based on the performance level achieved. If the corporation failed to achieve at least its minimum ROE performance goal, there were no payouts made to any employees.

A surrogate for profit sharing at the team level was adopted by an insurance company.[2] This company replaced its traditional organization structure with multifunctional teams to better serve the customers. Each team produced a "profit" by reducing expenses below the pricing assumptions utilized for the insurance product the team was managing. A portion of this profit, with the amount based on the team's performance in meeting certain quality and customer satisfaction standards, was distributed to the team members.

Measuring Performance of Administrative Groups

Any organization that develops a small group variable pay system faces a vexing problem: how to measure the performance of administrative and support groups. White-collar departments have always represented a challenge from a measurement point of view, apart from the question of variable pay. Part of the problem lies in the fact that most such groups do not produce discrete and homogeneous units of product or service that are susceptible to traditional productivity and quality measurement techniques. Furthermore, maximizing their outputs, as opposed to maximizing the value of the services provided to the organization, would not even make business sense for many support departments. The measurement problem is further exacerbated by the nature of support departments' customers. They are internal customers, and few organizations have systems in place to monitor the satisfaction of these customers or the quality of the services provided.

There are basically two practical formula alternatives for administrative and support departments.

1. *Goal sharing.* In this instance, the goals are derived from the department's business plan or management objectives. While some sort of cost or productivity goal may be appropriate, there should normally be an emphasis on goals relating to the company's strategic objectives or to the value of the services provided to operating groups.

The company whose team-based manufacturing variable pay plan was described above also had a separate plan for the administrative and support groups. This plan was actually a form of financially funded goal sharing (see Chapter 5). At the start of each year, each of the support teams developed a minimum of five strategic or human resources goals relating to the business of the division or group (or the corporation, for corporate staff groups) with which the support team was associated. At the end of each quarter, each team received a score from 0 to 100, based on the degree of goal achievement. This score represented the percentage of profits of the relevant business unit, in excess of that budgeted, that would be shared with these support teams.

The finance department of one corporation also implemented a financially funded goal-sharing system. The funding mechanism was departmental cost reduction; an employee share of savings in controllable costs (labor, travel expense, office supplies, and outside services) versus the previous year's level determined the size of the pool. The distribution of this pool was dependent on the achievement of the department's business goals, of which there were seven. For each goal achieved, one-seventh of the pool was paid out to the department's employees.

2. *Average bonus.* The support departments receive the average bonus achieved by the operating teams they support. For administrative and support groups, this method is simpler and may often be more appropriate, sending a very clear signal that the mission of these departments is to support the operating units, and that the support departments will be rewarded only to the extent that the line organization performs. This may be particularly effective as part of a process to change a traditional and bureaucratic organization, where the staff groups in the past have viewed their role as controlling the operating units rather than supporting them.

An example is the plan for the corporate staff of a manufacturing business. Gain-sharing plans existed in all four of the company's manufacturing units, and it was a simple matter to calculate the average payout, as shown in the following example:

Springfield:	3.6 percent
Valdosta:	7.1 percent
Evansville:	2.9 percent
Cedar Rapids:	4.0 percent
Average	4.4 percent

In this case, the plants were weighted equally. Other alternatives would include weightings based on the number of employees at each plant or the dollar volume of business at each location.

* * * * *

It should be noted that the company whose manufacturing and support team plans were described in this section restructured their variable pay systems in the late 1980s, so that bonuses are now based on the overall performance of the business unit rather than that of the individual team. This modification came about because of one of the problems discussed earlier: The employees related more to their teams' objectives than they did to those of the company or business unit.

Team variable pay systems that stand alone (i.e., that are not part of a multi-tiered plan or financially funded goal-sharing system) are actually not as common as one might expect. This is probably because of the risks and complications associated with this approach, as discussed in Chapter 2 and reviewed again earlier in this chapter.

Having completed Step 3, the design team has settled upon the basic formula approach and is now ready to begin the process of selecting the specific measure or measures that will constitute the variable pay formula.

References

1. John G. Belcher, Jr., "Rewarding Teams," *Continuous Journey* (publication of the American Productivity and Quality Center), December 1993-January 1994.
2. R. A. McDonald, "Getting Bottom Line Performance," *Best's Review,* September 1993.

7

Selecting and Evaluating Measures

At this point, the design team has a list of variables that are the top candidates for inclusion in the variable pay formula, and the team has decided on the basic formula framework. The next step involves the identification, evaluation, and selection of specific measures for each of the candidate variables.

Step 4. Identify Existing Measures for Each of the Variables Selected in Step 2

The task at this step of the design process is to identify various measures that might be employed to quantify performance improvement for each of the variables included in the design team's working list developed in Step 2. This list, you may recall, was confined to broad business variables (such as productivity and quality), as opposed to specific measures that are quantifiable.

The emphasis here should be on *existing* measures, for two reasons. First, the design process will obviously be simplified, and administrative burdens minimized, if the design team does not have to create entirely new measures along with supporting data-collection systems. Second, historical data will normally be available for existing measures. As we shall see later, these historical data will be invaluable in determining the suitability of various measures, in establishing baselines, and in evaluating the need for a smoothing mechanism. These tasks will be considerably more difficult if historical data are lacking.

Design teams sometimes have difficulty identifying existing measures for certain variables and are quick to conclude that few or none exist. Experience has shown, however, that there are generally more mea-

Table 7-1.   Productivity measures.

- Units/direct labor hours
- Units/total labor hours
- Standard direct labor hours earned/actual hours
- Direct labor variance
- Sales/payroll costs
- Labor costs vs. budget

Table 7-2.   Quality measures.

- Number of defects
- Defects/total units produced
- Rework costs
- Cost of quality
- Customer returns

sures available than a cursory assessment may reveal. It may be necessary to conduct some research or call upon in-house experts to uncover all the possibilities. Tables 7-1, 7-2, and 7-3 show the lists of measures identified by one design team for the variables productivity, quality, and safety, respectively.

In many cases, as in the example just cited, the list of measures generated by the team at this step will be too large to allow for an efficient and timely analysis. There will likely be a need, therefore, to reduce the list to a more manageable number. This step is analogous to a similar exercise in Step 2, where the number of variables was reduced before proceeding further. As a general guideline, the team should select no more than two or three measures for each variable for further analysis.

In making the selection, team members should ask themselves such questions as the following:

1. *Which of the measures are the most valid and accurate indicators of the variable in question?* One design team, for example, concluded that cus-

Table 7-3. Safety measures.

- OSHA recordable accidents
- Lost-time accidents
- Lost-time days
- First-aid cases
- Incident rate
- Severity rate
- Workers compensation costs

tomer returns was not as valid a quality measure as some other options because the company allowed its distributors to return merchandise for reasons other than quality problems.

2. *Which of the measures provides the best alignment with company business objectives?* Measures of external quality, such as returns or customer surveys, may be more appropriate than internal quality measures (such as scrap or rework) for a company whose top business priority is improvement in customer satisfaction.

3. *Which of the measures would provide the greatest benefit to the company if improvements were made?* All other things being equal, the design team would probably choose those measures that provide the greatest payout potential.

4. *Which of the measures is least susceptible to distortion from outside influences?* Costs as a percent of sales, for example, is impacted by changes in selling price, whereas a cost-per-unit measure is not.

5. *Which of the measures is impacted by the largest number of participating employees?* A measure that can be impacted by 75 percent of the employees is obviously more desirable, all other things being equal, than one that can be impacted by only 10 percent of the employees.

6. *Which of the measures will be easiest for people to understand and relate to their actions on the job?*

A thorough discussion of these questions, as well as any others that the design team may deem to be appropriate, should result in a shorter list of candidate measures and a readiness to proceed to the next step.

Step 5. Obtain Historical Data for the Selected Measures and Display These Data on Line Charts

Step 5, along with Step 6, is among the most important ones in the design team's work plan, for these steps will provide an analytical tool that will prove to be invaluable in several subsequent steps of the design process.

The objective of Step 5 is to obtain data that then can be utilized in Step 6 to facilitate the making of the final selection of measures that will constitute the variable pay formula. These data will also be extremely useful, as suggested above, in establishing baselines or goals (see Chapter 9), in determining the payout frequency (see Chapter 11), and in selecting a smoothing mechanism (see Chapter 11).

Attempting to design a variable pay plan without thoroughly understanding the history and dynamics of the plan measures is folly. Such an endeavor is analogous to developing a strategic plan without any knowledge of the business or the strengths and weaknesses of the organization. No rational businessperson would develop a strategy without that information, and no design team should develop a variable pay plan without a basic comprehension of the history and dynamics of the plan's measures.

Charts are invaluable in gaining that understanding. They enable the team members to quickly grasp and comprehend past trends, the degree of variation, and any seasonal patterns underlying the measures. Without charts, these features would have to be discerned by analyzing a series of numbers—a formidable and tedious task under the best of circumstances.

The team should endeavor to obtain three years' worth of history, by month (if monthly payouts are an option) and by quarter. This step will normally have to be carried out between team meetings; each of the team members might accept the responsibility of obtaining data on one or more of the measures and conveying these data to the designated chart maker (usually someone who knows how to create charts on a personal computer).

Step 6. Use the Charts to Evaluate and Finalize the Selected Measures

The design team's task now is to analyze the various measurement options and make the final selection of the measures to be incorporated into the variable pay plan. This analysis is conducted by examining the charts produced in the previous step and weighing the conclusions drawn against the questions asked in Step 4.

In analyzing the charts, the team members should look for certain phenomena that would complicate their design decisions and therefore reduce a measure's attractiveness and utility.

Trends

The first thing the design team should look for on the charts is the existence of underlying trends in the data. Figures 7-1 and 7-2 display the charts of two measures that might be under consideration by a design team. The points plotted on the chart represent three years of history, by month. Both charts show considerable month-to-month fluctuations. The noteworthy difference between the two charts, however, is the long-term trend (represented by the straight line on the charts) underlying the short-term fluctuations. The trend shown in Figure 7-1 is basically flat; there has been little fundamental change in the level of the measure over the three-year period. Figure 7-2 represents a very different situation. The measure here has clearly shown a steady improvement over the same period.

Which of these two measures would be more suitable for a variable pay program? The answer is the measure depicted in Figure 7-1, all other things being equal. The process being measured here appears to be stable, with performance basically flat, as shown by the trend line. If, after variable pay is installed, performance begins to trend upward, the design team can reasonably conclude that something has changed. What has changed, presumably, is that the variable pay system, supported by employee involvement, has brought about a greater focus by employees on this particular variable. Management should have no qualms about sharing these gains with employees.

Figure 7-2, on the other hand, presents the design team with a major complication. With an improving trend already clearly established, what would constitute a gain in this situation? If next year's improvement falls right on the trend line, has anything really changed? One could argue that improvement simply reflects the impact of existing forces, whatever they may be, and that the improvement would likely have occurred without variable pay. Management may well feel that it is inappropriate to reward employees for an improvement that would have been obtained anyway.

If you accept this position, the conclusion would be that only gains in excess of those implied by an extension of the trend line should be shared. But how can we be sure that the trend would in fact continue if nothing else changed? Nothing increases forever, and assuming that past forces will continue unchanged in a turbulent business environment may not be realistic. One might also argue that past improvements came about, at least in part, as a result of employee efforts for which they received no financial reward. It would only seem fair that employees now be recognized for continuing these efforts.

(text continues on page 120)

Figure 7-1. Flat trend.

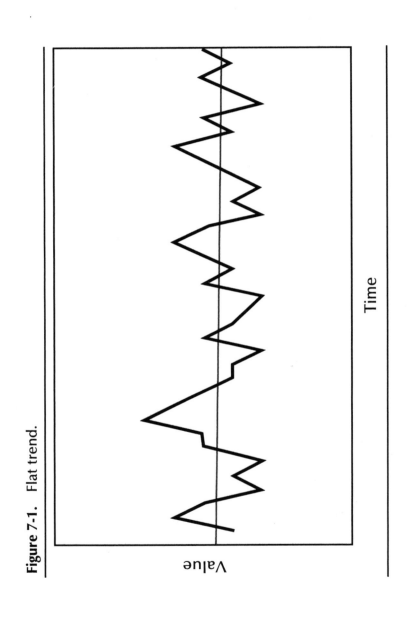

Figure 7-2. Rising trend.

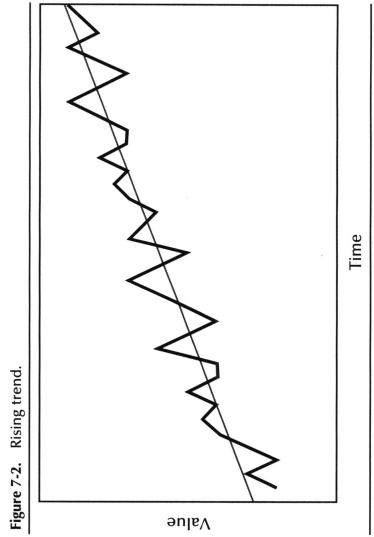

Time

Value

clearly, establishing a fair and acceptable baseline for the measure depicted in figure 7-2 would be a challenge for the design team, particularly when compared to the relatively uncomplicated situation represented in Figure 7-1. While the measure in Figure 7-1 would appear to be an easy choice here, the phrase used earlier, "all other things being equal," must be taken into consideration. If the answers to the questions posed in Step 4 would heavily favor the other measure, it may be a better choice in spite of the complication presented by the trend.

The existence of an underlying trend, then, is not reason in and of itself to eliminate a potential measure from further consideration. It does represent a complication, however, that should be taken into account by the design team when making the final selection of measures.

Volatility

The second condition the design team should investigate through its charts is the volatility of the measures under consideration. Figures 7-3 and 7-4 present the charts for another two measures that might be under consideration by a design team. In this case, the team does have to worry about complications associated with trends: Both measures display a flat trend. A glance at Figures 7-3 and 7-4 immediately reveals, however, a different distinction between the measures: The measure depicted in Figure 7-4 is far more volatile than the measure shown in Figure 7-3.

Volatility introduces some serious complications for our variable pay plan. How does a design team know when there is a true gain on a measure, such as the one depicted in Figure 7-4? If, in a given month, this measure shows an improvement versus the baseline, does it represent a real gain that should be shared, or is it simply part of the normal variation that underlies the measure? There is a clear risk here that the company will pay employees for an apparent gain, only to see that gain subsequently offset by a loss of comparable magnitude. The net effect would be higher compensation costs for the company with no real improvement in performance. Such an outcome does not bode well for the long-term viability of the variable pay plan. The measure in Figure 7-3 would be clearly preferable to that shown in Figure 7-4, all other things being equal.

If the more volatile measure is nonetheless chosen, the negative consequences of the volatility can be lessened through infrequent payouts (such as semiannual or annual) or such vehicles as deficit reserves, rolling payout calculations, and year-to-date payouts (see discussion of these smoothing mechanisms in Chapter 11). Incorporating one of these features in the plan design would indeed be critical if a volatile measure were selected.

Figure 7-3. Low volatility.

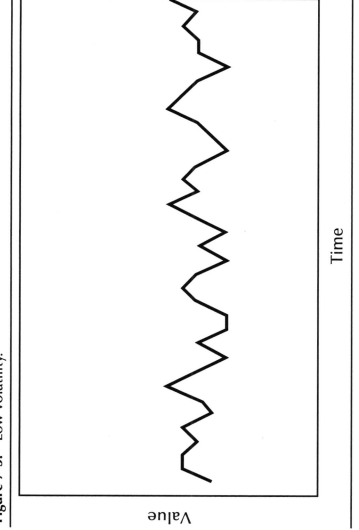

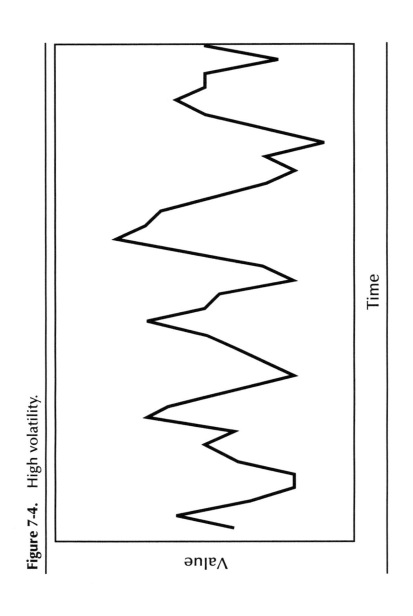

Figure 7-4. High volatility.

Aberrations

The third phenomenon that the charts will reveal is the existence of any aberrations in the data. The feature that stands out in the chart in Figure 7-5 is the one data point that is clearly out of line with all the others. It is imperative that the cause of this aberration be ascertained by the design team.

An aberration such as this one can mean one of two things. The first possibility is that some unusual event or set of circumstances (a special cause, in the jargon of statistical process control) occurred that caused a significant deviation from the normal chart pattern. Were a similar event to occur again in the future, it could have a major impact on the bonus calculation in that period: It could well produce a very large gain, or, if the impact was in the opposite direction, a very large loss. This outcome may not be appropriate, as the gain or loss is of short-term duration and may be due to forces that are totally out of the control of plan participants. The cause of this aberration must therefore be determined, and the use of this measure in the plan may call for some special provisions to protect against that eventuality.

The second possible explanation for an aberration is that the abnormal point is simply an error in the data. If this is the case, the design team should be concerned about the usability of this measure, as it would be unwise to tie pay to a measure whose accuracy cannot be relied upon. If the measure is to be utilized in the variable pay system, the cause of the error must be ascertained and corrected.

Seasonality

One final chart pattern must be reviewed here, and an example is presented in Figure 7-6. Note that performance for this measure is significantly different for three months out of every year. This pattern is suggestive of seasonality, one of the most troublesome of characteristics as far as the design of a variable pay plan is concerned.

The long-term trend in this case is flat, and a design team might well decide to use the historical average for the three-year period as the baseline. But what are the consequences of such a decision? In all likelihood, every year the variable pay plan will show a gain for three months and a loss for the other nine months, even if nothing changes. Or, if the seasonal period is one of poor performance, the team would expect to see nine months of automatic gains and three months of predictable losses. These purported gains and losses are not real, however, but are simply a reflection of the seasonal nature of the data.

The effects of seasonality, if they are significant, must be eliminated

(text continues on page 126)

Figure 7-5. Aberration.

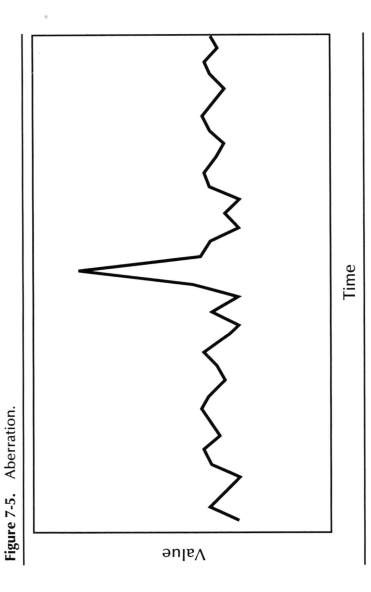

Value

Time

Figure 7-6. Seasonality.

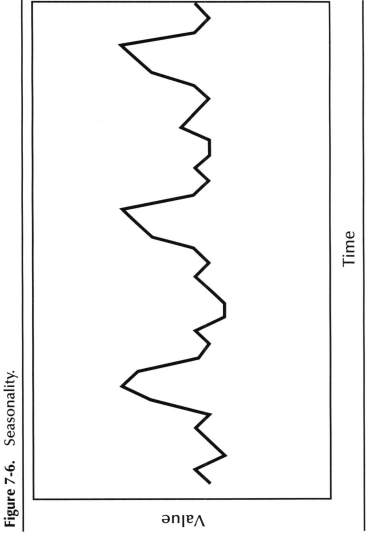

Value

Time

from the variable pay system or serious distortion will result. Bonuses, rather than reflecting performance, will be a function of the time of year. There are not many companies that would like to increase compensation simply because it is spring.

There are basically three ways to deal with a seasonality problem: an annual payout frequency (see Chapter 11), a four-quarter rolling payout (see Chapter 11), or separate baselines for the seasonal period (see Chapter 9).

By way of summary, the design team employs charts of historical data as a tool to evaluate the various measures under consideration and to assist it in finalizing its choice of measures. The existence of trends, high volatility, aberrations, or seasonality is vitally important information for the design team, as these phenomena create serious complications that, if not addressed in the design process, could produce a seriously flawed plan. The existence of complications such as these should not necessarily disqualify a measure from use in the variable pay system, however. The questions asked by the team in Step 4 should also be taken into consideration before reaching any final conclusions regarding a measure's usability. The design team may have to accept, and deal with in later design steps, a certain degree of complication if a measure otherwise appears to be a significantly better choice than other options.

At this point, the design team should have finalized its choice of measures for the variable pay system and be ready to move on to the next step.

8

Assigning Values to Gains or Goals

Now that the design team has selected the measure or measures that will drive the variable pay program, it faces what may be one of its most challenging tasks: developing a method for quantifying the value of improvements (in the case of gain sharing and profit sharing) or the worth of goal achievement (in the case of goal sharing).

If the variable pay plan is to meet the needs of the business and enjoy the support of management, the bonus payments must bear some relationship to the financial benefits realized by the company. This outcome cannot be assured unless the value of the improvements can be quantified with a reasonable degree of accuracy. How, after all, can a design team make a rational decision about the magnitude of the payouts if it cannot ascertain the value of the improvements?

This task is challenging because it requires, at a minimum, some analytical skills and perhaps even some knowledge of accounting. It is at this stage in the design process that the analytical or technical members of the design team earn their keep. The job is further complicated by the fact that the value of the gains for some variables, such as customer satisfaction, are virtually impossible to quantify with any degree of confidence.

The fact that certain variables may present seemingly insurmountable challenges from a valuation standpoint, however, should not prevent the design team from exploring all the options. It would be unfortunate to exclude from the variable pay system a measure that is critical to the success of the business, and is highly controllable by employees, simply because its value does not lend itself to precise quantification. If every pay increase issued under our traditional pay systems had to be justified on a financial basis, pay would surely be fixed for a very long time.

Step 7. Develop the Equations for Assigning Values to Gains or Goal Achievement

The approaches used to evaluate improvements cannot be discussed in a generalized fashion because they vary widely depending on the variables being analyzed. We will, therefore, review separately the methods typically employed for each of the more commonly used variables.

Costs

Improvements in cost measures (as well as profitability measures) are generally the simplest to appraise because the value of the improvement is normally provided as a by-product of the measure itself. Take, for example, the simple cost-to-sales formula shown in Table 8-1.

There is no need to develop a method of valuing the gain, for the answer is already there: The value of the gain in this example is $400,000. This is the amount by which the company's bottom line has improved (all other things, of course, being equal). All a company need do now is multiply this gain by the employee share percentage and distribute the resulting pool to the participating employees.

The same comments would apply to a costs-versus-budget formula: The gain and its value are the same. If the formula is of the cost-per-unit variety, however, such as the one in Table 8-2, there is one additional, but still very simple, step required. The gain per unit must be multiplied by the number of units produced or the number of services delivered in order to ascertain the value of the total gain.

The use of any measure that is denominated in dollars (as cost measures, by definition, are) clearly simplifies the design process by eliminating the need to develop a complicated equation to convert the gain into dollars. Allowing only dollar-based measures does, however, considerably limit the measurement options, and therefore the flexibility of the variable pay system, as discussed in Chapter 4. This is another situation

Table 8-1. Cost formula.

Sales	$12,000,000
× Baseline costs (60%)	$ 7,200,000
− Actual costs	6,800,000
= Gain	$ 400,000

Table 8-2. Cost-per-unit formula.

Actual costs	$7,980,000
÷ Units produced	950,000
= Cost per unit	$ 8.40
Baseline cost per unit	$ 8.70
Gain	$ 0.30
× Units produced	950,000
= Total gain	$ 285,000

Table 8-3. Labor cost formula.

Sales	$12,000,000
× Baseline payroll costs (20%)	2,400,000
− Actual costs	2,250,000
= Gain	$ 150,000

where you may have to accept some complications in order to have a meaningful and effective system.

Productivity

Measures of labor productivity are probably second only to cost measures in their frequency of use in variable pay plans. The textbook definition of productivity is "output divided by input," and this variable can, of course, be structured as a cost measure by replacing "costs" in Table 8-1 with "payroll cost," as shown in Table 8-3. In this case, the comments above relative to a cost measure apply: The value of any improvement is produced as an outcome of the measure itself.

Measuring productivity in this fashion, however, does not provide a true picture of the utilization of labor, as this ratio is impacted by changes in the selling price of the product or service, as well as by improvements in the efficiency of labor. If it is the desire of management to reward true improvements in labor productivity, the measure should be constructed

Table 8-4.   Valuation of productivity gain.

Units produced	75,600
÷ Baseline units/hour	3.6
= Baseline hours	21,000
− Actual hours	18,000
= Gain in hours	3,000
× Average wage rate	$ 12.40
= Value of gain	$37,200

using physical outputs and inputs. This is commonly done through some sort of *units per hour* measure. The output units may be tons of steel, cases of cereal, number of service calls, or whatever else the organization produces or provides as a service.

The valuation of gains in a units-per-hour measure is only slightly more complicated than it is for a cost measure. Let us assume the following facts, which are all we need to know in order to value the gain:

A.	*Units produced*	75,600
B.	*Hours worked*	18,000
C.	*Units per hour (A/B)*	4.2
D.	*Baseline units per hour*	3.6
E.	*Average wage rate*	$12.40

Given these facts, it is clear that we have a gain of 0.6 units per hour (4.2 minus 3.6). The question is, what is the value of that gain? The answer is found in Table 8-4.

Basically, we determine the hours that would have been incurred at the baseline productivity level, and then subtract from that figure the hours that were actually incurred. The resulting gain, in hours, can then be multiplied by the average wage rate to quantify the value of the gain in dollars. As a variation, we can add to the average wage rate, if desired, the cost of benefits.

The denominators in units-per-hour measures traditionally have been limited to the hours worked by hourly paid labor or, even more narrowly, by direct labor (those employees who directly produce the product or deliver the service). Organizations today, however, must be concerned about the productivity of all employees, not just those who happen to fall into certain artificial classifications. The fact that an individual is paid on a salaried, rather than hourly, basis does not make his or her pay any less costly to the company. For variable pay purposes, therefore, it is desirable to include the hours of all employees (assuming that all employees are participants in the plan) in any productivity measure. Doing so, of course, may require that past history be recalculated to include all hours.

While units-per-hour measures have great appeal because of their simplicity, there is usually a complication that diminishes that advantage. That complication is *product mix*. Few organizations today produce a single product or service; they more likely produce a variety of outputs, some of which require more labor hours than others. Should the mix of the units produced become more heavily weighted toward high-labor products or services, the units produced per hour will decline, all other things being equal. The opposite outcome will occur, of course, if the mix shifts toward less labor-intensive outputs. If significant mix changes do occur, and their impact on the productivity measure is material, they should be adjusted for. Mix changes are totally out of the control of employees, and their effect on a units-per-hour measure does not represent a change in productivity.

The usual solution to the mix problem is a *weighting system*. The output of each type of product or service could be multiplied by a factor that represents its relative labor content. Take, as a simple example, a system that produces two products, one of which requires twice as much labor to produce as does the other. Eliminating distortion from mix changes would require that all units of the high-labor content product be multiplied, or weighted, by 2.

Most companies, of course, produce more than two products; it is not unusual for manufacturing facilities to produce hundreds, or even thousands, of different products. The task of developing a weighting system, however, need not be as daunting as it may seem. There may even exist a ready-made weighting system, in the form of production standards. If not, a large number of products can normally be assembled into a smaller number of product lines or groups that are relatively similar in terms of labor content.

An alternative solution to the mix problem is to separately measure the productivity of each product or product grouping . The plan would then contain several productivity measures, each of which would independently contribute money to the bonus pool. The feasibility of this approach may be limited in many companies, however, by an inability to accurately allocate hours to the various product lines.

While the word *productivity* is normally used to refer to the utilization of labor, it can be more broadly applied to the utilization of any input,

Table 8-5.   Valuation of materials productivity gain.

Tons of production	8,125
× Baseline % scrap	3.2%
= Baseline scrap tons	260
− Actual scrap tons	238
= Gain in tons	22
× Average cost per ton	$ 280
= Value of gain	$6,160

such as raw materials, energy, or supplies. The basic valuation method for labor productivity shown in Table 8-4 can be employed for any productivity measure that is expressed in an output-divided-by-input format. Table 8-5 presents, as an example, an analogous valuation approach for the utilization of raw materials.

Some organizations choose to employ their standard cost systems, rather than the output-over-input approach, to measure labor productivity. In a standard cost system, the units of output of each product or service are multiplied by the number of direct labor hours that theoretically should be expended in producing each unit of that product. The result of that calculation, typically called *standard hours earned* or *earned hours,* represents the total number of direct labor hours expected for the particular volume and mix of products or services produced during a given period. The standard hours earned can then be divided by the actual hours incurred to produce an indicator that is often called *efficiency.* This alternative to measuring labor productivity readily produces a gain in hours, as a typical example shows in Table 8-6. These hours need only be multiplied by the average hourly wage rate to produce a gain valued in dollars.

There are two problems, from a variable pay point of view, associated with standard cost systems.

1. *Such a system generally measures only the productivity of direct labor.* The productivity of a major part of the workforce—the indirect or support employees—is therefore excluded from the measure. This is not desirable, as the earlier discussion of units-per-hour measures suggested. The problem can be solved by adding an additional measure of indirect labor productivity or by applying some sort of multiplier to the earned hours to account for indirect labor.

Table 8-6. Gain from standard cost system.

Standard hours earned	46,840
× Baseline efficiency	86.7%
= Baseline hours	40,610
− Actual hours	38,390
= Gain in hours	2,220

2. *The standards generally change from time to time.* This severely complicates the management of baselines (see Chapter 9). Assume, as an example, that the variable pay plan provides for baselines to be reset each year to a level equal to the average performance of the prior two years. If the variable pay measure is performance against standard, and the standards have been tightened during the prior two years, the level of productivity that produced a 90 percent efficiency result two years ago may generate only an 85 percent efficiency level against current standards. The prior two years' performance data for efficiency are no longer valid as historical indicators against which to measure improvement. This problem can be solved only through some complicated arithmetic or by freezing standards for the purpose of variable pay computations.

Before we leave the subject of productivity, it should be noted that there is one other, very different, method that is sometimes used to value productivity improvements. Rather than valuing productivity improvement from an input point of view by quantifying the savings in wage and salary costs, a design team could adopt an output perspective: Higher productivity produces more units of product or service for the same amount of labor input. These additional units will, assuming they can be sold, add to the company's bottom line by the amount of gross margin realized per unit. This incremental gross margin could be the basis for valuing the productivity improvement. This is not a widely used valuation method, however, in view of the added complexity involved.

Quality

Few companies today can ignore the issue of quality, as the widespread emphasis on total quality management and all its variants would attest. And if it is indeed a corporate priority, management can hardly ignore quality in the design of a variable pay system. Failing to reward quality improvement would certainly damage the credibility of management's exhortations to place quality above all else.

Some would argue that cost formulas provide reinforcement for quality, on the assumption that quality improvements directly reduce costs. While this assumption, which was popularized by Phil Crosby,[1] is undeniably true with respect to many aspects of quality, the problem is that cost formulas, by definition, explicitly measure costs and not quality. As a result, it would be risky to assume that all employees understand the relationship between quality and costs, and that constant exposure to a cost measure will keep quality in the forefront of their improvement activities.

The costs-reinforce-quality argument begins to lose credibility, furthermore, when we draw a distinction between internal quality (the quality of the process that produced the product or service) and external quality (the quality of the product or service as delivered to the customer). It is certainly conceivable that an organization could report excellent levels of internal quality (little or no scrap and rework, for example), with its attendant low costs, by shipping defective product to the customer.

Because of its indirect relationship to costs, quality is one of those variables that supports the argument for a family of measures framework (see Chapter 4) for a variable pay system. Quality can then be made an explicit, rather than implied, variable. If the design team is empowered to go beyond profits or costs as the basis for the variable pay formula, quality will likely be at the top of their list of potential variables.

When it comes to valuing gains in quality measures, generalizations are more difficult than with cost or productivity measures, as there are a greater variety of possible measures. It may be helpful to think in terms of two categories of quality measures, as described above: internal quality measures and external quality measures.

1. *Internal quality measures.* The focus of internal quality measures is the quality of the organization's processes, rather than the quality of the final product or service as delivered to the customer. As such, internal quality measures are generally valued by quantifying the costs associated with failing to produce the product or service right the first time. Common examples of internal quality measures used in variable pay systems include the following:

- Scrap
- Rework
- Cost of quality
- Defective units

If the quality measure tracks absolute dollars, as it might with any of the first three measures above, valuing the gain is straightforward. As

Table 8-7. Scrap cost formula.

Sales	$89,000,000
× Baseline scrap costs (2.1%)	1,869,000
− Actual scrap costs	1,690,000
= Gain	$ 179,000

with any cost measure, the quantification of the gain is also the value of the gain. The value of $100,000 reduction in scrap or rework costs is simply $100,000.

As often as not, however, these measures are related to an indicator of volume on the basis that a higher level of production would be expected to produce a higher absolute level of scrap or other quality-related costs. The variable pay metric might be, for example, "scrap as a percentage of sales." In this case, the valuation equation, such as the example shown in Table 8-7, looks much like that of a typical cost-to-sales formula, as presented in Table 8-1.

2. *External quality measures.* External quality measures are indicators of quality from the customer's point of view. They gauge the degree to which the organization's products or services are meeting the external customer's requirements. While the benefit of improvements in internal quality is lower costs, a major benefit of better external quality is more satisfied customers (see discussion of customer satisfaction below).

Common measures of external quality include warranty costs and customer returns.

Placing a valuation on *warranty costs* is not a problem; like other cost measures, the gain in warranty costs is denominated in dollars and is therefore self-valued. It should be noted, however, that the true impact of warranty costs, as it is with any external quality measure, is probably much greater than the immediate cost effect. Not only does the company incur the cost of fixing or replacing the product but it may also lose the customer's confidence and future business.

Valuing *customer returns* presents a bit more of a challenge. The value of a return depends on whether the customer purchases a replacement from the organization or takes his business to a competitor. If the customer purchases a replacement, the loss to the company is the cost incurred in producing the returned product, less any recovery attained by recycling or reselling the product. If, on the other hand, the customer takes his business to a competitor, the company has lost a sale and the value of a return is therefore equal to the lost revenue associated with that sale. Even that may severely understate the ultimate value of the return; as in the case of warranty costs, the dissatisfied customer may take all future business to the competitor, in which case the true loss to the company may be many times the value of that return.

As a practical matter, it is rarely possible to ascertain the effect on future business of a customer return. Most variable pay programs, therefore, use either the production cost or the lost revenue to value returns.

Customer Satisfaction

As global competition intensified during the 1990s, the focus of many companies' improvement efforts switched from internal efficiency to the satisfaction of the external customer. Having the lowest costs in the industry will not guarantee a company's viability if its customers are not pleased with its products or services. If it is indeed a business priority, customer satisfaction should be rewarded through the variable pay system, as would any other performance variable that is key to the organization's success.

Some would equate customer satisfaction with quality, and there is certainly some overlap (as you will see below, a measure of returns is discussed under both categories). Customer satisfaction, however, goes beyond the quality of the product. The perfect product or service will not satisfy the customer if it is not delivered on time, when the customer needs it. Responsiveness to problems, as well as prompt and satisfactory resolution of problems when they do arise, will also contribute to the customer's overall satisfaction.

Some companies, however, are reluctant to incorporate a measure of customer satisfaction into their pay programs because it is a "soft" variable: An improvement in customer satisfaction does not normally have an immediate impact on the bottom line. The benefits of more satisfied customers will more likely become manifest in the future, in the form of greater customer loyalty, more repeat business, and greater market share. The value of these future benefits are, of course, impossible to quantify with any degree of confidence.

Nonetheless, many organizations are concluding that the need to reinforce customer satisfaction as a critical performance variable outweighs the problems associated with valuing its improvement. As a result, it is not difficult to find customer-satisfaction measures in variable pay programs today. The four most common measures of customer satisfaction are returns, customer complaints, delivery performance, and customer survey results.

1. *Returns* is the one measure in the customer-satisfaction category

Table 8-8. Goal-sharing plan for a food processing plant (selected measures).

Variable	Goal	Bonus (per Month)
▪ Productivity	38,500 lbs./hr.	20
▪ Cost performance	$0.009/lb. below standard	40
▪ Product damage	15 per 10,000 cases	10
▪ Customer complaints	14 per million pounds	15
▪ Shipping errors	5 per wk.	10
▪ Safety	0 lost-time accidents	10
▪ Attendance	94%	10

that is susceptible to valuation on a current-cost basis. It is also a measure of external quality, and the methodology for valuing returns was discussed in the earlier section on quality measures.

2. *Customer complaints* has become a popular variable pay measure in recent years, as companies in highly competitive industries have developed ever tighter standards of quality and customer satisfaction. Minimizing returns is no longer good enough in many industries; complaints of any kind must be eliminated. Valuing customer complaints, however, presents a greater challenge to the design team than does returns. At least with a return, there is a tangible item that has a quantifiable cost associated with it. The resolution of a complaint, on the other hand, may involve little or no direct cost. But companies do not incorporate customer complaints in their variable pay plans because they are costly; they are there because a complaint is evidence of an unhappy customer, and an unhappy customer can mean the loss of that customer's future business. And in some industries, such as those that supply the automobile manufacturers, the loss of a single customer can threaten the very viability of the business.

Obviously, it is impossible to place an accurate dollar value on a possible loss of future business. The design team, therefore, has to seek other alternatives for valuing improvements in the number of customer complaints. One option is simply to assign an arbitrary value. The team might choose, for example, to add $2,000 to the bonus pool for each unit reduction in the number of complaints. The goal-sharing formula outlined in Table 4-7, and reproduced here as Table 8-8, provides an example of a company that applied an arbitrary value ($15 per employee per month in this case) to the achievement of a customer-complaints goal.

Arbitrary valuations, of course, cannot be justified to the accountants; they represent a business judgment. The fact that the accountants cannot find the amount in question on the income statement, however, should not serve as a reason to eliminate from consideration those measures that represent critical business issues to the company. Management, after all, makes spending and investment decisions every day based on uncertain returns or highly subjective estimates of cost savings.

Another alternative for valuing improvements in a measure such as customer complaints is to treat the measure as a modifier or multiplier. Examples of modifiers and multipliers were presented in Chapter 5. This alternative is popular because it does not require that a specific value be placed on improvements in customer satisfaction.

3. *Delivery performance.* Like customer complaints, delivery performance has become a widely used variable in gain-sharing and goal-sharing programs. The customer expects a product or service to be delivered on time, when it is needed. For a manufacturing organization operating on a just-in-time system, timely delivery may in fact be vital to its very ability to operate.

As with complaints, the gains from improved delivery performance are primarily future-oriented and therefore difficult to value. In one of the few attempts to place a cost value on delivery performance, one firm concluded that the effect of failing to meet delivery schedules was increased inventories. When an order fails to ship on time, incremental inventory carrying costs (either work-in-process or finished goods) are incurred until the date of delivery. The value of these incremental carrying costs could be analytically estimated for any given percentage of late deliveries.

More typically, however, the same choices that are available for a customer-complaints measure—arbitrary values or modifiers—are also used to determine the payout associated with delivery performance. One plant, for example, assigned arbitrary values to various levels of schedule accomplishment, as shown in Table 8-9.

4. *Customer-survey results.* The results of customer surveys will occasionally be used as a customer-satisfaction measure in variable pay programs. This type of measure is not nearly as common as customer complaints or delivery performance, partly because many companies lack comprehensive and well-established survey vehicles, and partly because the gains from improved survey results are even more intangible and difficult to quantify than those from the other customer-satisfaction options.

The same valuation options discussed earlier apply here. A service

Table 8-9. Schedule-accomplishment values.

On Time (%)	Value
90%	$ 5,000
92	10,000
94	15,000
96	20,000
98	25,000
100	30,000

Table 8-10. Municipality variable share.

Percent Satisfaction	Employee Share
<60%	0%
60–70	2
70–85	3
>85	4

company, for example, developed a modifier based on the results of a regular telephone survey, while a distribution center employed a creative option called a variable share.[2] With this option, which will be discussed in more detail in Chapter 10, the employee share of the gains in a gain-sharing or profit-sharing program is a function of some other variable—in this case a customer-satisfaction survey.

A variable share based on customer satisfaction has even been employed in a public sector plan.[3] A municipality implemented the public-sector equivalent of profit sharing (the excess of city revenues over expenditures) with the objective of improving productivity in order to meet a projected budget shortfall. Since increasing the public's satisfaction with city services was also deemed to be an important objective, the employee share of the profit-sharing pool was based on the results of a community survey, as shown in Table 8-10. The program apparently succeeded; a projected budget deficit of $500,000 turned into a $2.4 million surplus, and community satisfaction reached 90 percent.

Safety

In many organizations today, safety is a stated priority, often taking precedence over all others. References to a safe workplace are often found in corporate mission and values statements. It should be no surprise, therefore, that safety measures are commonly found in variable pay programs.

There are a variety of ways to measure safety performance, of which the most common are OSHA recordable accidents, lost-time accidents, OSHA incident rate, OSHA severity rate, first-aid cases, and workers compensation costs.

The last item is the only option listed that directly quantifies cost savings, and as a result, it is favored by some organizations. Workers compensation, however, suffers from some serious drawbacks. First, there is a considerable lag between any improvement in safety performance and its manifestation in lower workers compensation costs. Reinforcement for improvement is therefore not timely. Second, workers compensation costs are also impacted by forces other than a given company's safety experience, such as changes in rates. An improvement is safety performance might therefore be offset by these uncontrollable factors.

Because of these weaknesses, the other options listed above are probably more widely utilized in variable pay systems. As with other measures that are not already denominated in dollars, improvements in these indicators must be converted to a dollar value before bonuses can be paid.

- *OSHA recordable accidents.* One common approach to valuing gains in safety is applicable when the measure encompasses all, or at least all of the serious, accidents. An example would be OSHA recordable accidents. This statistic is readily available because it is required to be tracked and reported to the Occupational Safety and Health Administration (OSHA). Any accident that requires medical treatment beyond first-aid (or meets some other tests) qualifies as a recordable accident. The valuation method involves adding up those costs incurred over the past one to three years that can be directly attributed to accidents, such as workers compensation costs and medical payments. These costs can then be divided by the number of accidents during the period to obtain a per-accident cost estimate. This figure can then be used to value reductions in the number of accidents.

Design teams that adopt this approach, however, often run into a problem. When the potential gains are calculated and the company share subtracted, the remaining amount often provides for a relatively small payout for the plan participants. One team discovered, for example, that the probable payout from safety would amount to $12 per person per quarter. This raises obvious concerns about the motivational power of the safety measure.

Actually, the directly measurable costs understate the true cost of poor safety because accidents generate a variety of indirect costs as well. A machine may have to be halted for an extended period, for example, resulting in lost output. The injured party may have to be replaced by a temporary or less skilled worker, causing a decline in productivity and/or quality. Supervisory time may be diverted from more productive pursuits to deal with the accident and process paperwork. There may be property damage as well. While few companies even try to track these indirect costs, they are no less real.

If the indirect costs need to be recognized in order to create a meaningful bonus potential for safety, there are two options available. One is to multiply the direct costs by some factor to account for the indirect costs. Research into the cost of accidents suggests that the indirect costs may amount to as much as four times the direct costs. Multipliers of 2, 3, or 4 times the direct costs are, therefore, commonly found when valuing safety in variable pay programs.

The other option is to provide for a 100 percent employee share on the safety measure. In effect, the employees receive as a reward all of the direct costs, while the company keeps the indirect cost savings. In some cases, both an indirect cost multiplier and a 100 percent share are utilized. These companies are willing to give back to employees all possible gains from safety because safety is viewed as a company value rather a cost-savings opportunity.

- *Lost-time accidents.* If the safety measure selected by the design team is a subset of total accidents, such as lost-time accidents, the valuation technique described in the preceding paragraphs is not applicable unless the direct costs can be separated between lost-time and non-lost-time accidents. There is an alternative available, however, for the valuation of lost-time accidents. The National Safety Council (NSC) periodically publishes a study of the average cost of a lost-time accident in American industry. This cost, which includes both direct and indirect costs, was reported to be $27,000 in a recent report.[4] The NSC figure is often used as a valuation tool for lost-time accidents in variable pay programs. It should be noted, however, that there is considerable variation from industry to industry in the true cost of these accidents.

- *OSHA incident rate and OSHA severity rate.* If the safety measure chosen is the incident rate or severity rate (two measures that are also required to be reported to the Occupational Health and Safety Administration), the cost per accident must be converted to a cost per rate point. While this is a straightforward arithmetic exercise, care must be taken to account for the measurement period being used (a given incident rate implies more accidents, and therefore a higher cost per rate point, in a quarter than it does in a month).

Because it is a top priority in many manufacturing facilities, safety is sometimes used as a gate, or a condition that must be achieved if any bonuses at all are to be paid from the variable pay system. As an example, a provision in the variable pay plan for a plant in the paper industry states that no bonuses will be paid in any period in which a lost-time accident occurs. A gate accords the safety variable a very high priority (it can eliminate the gains from all other variables) without being forced to place a value on it.

Attendance

The attendance variable is unique in that it presents the design team with two very distinct and very different options. On the one hand, it can be treated like any other variable pay measure—that is, a baseline or goal is established for the group, and any bonus payments earned are paid to all members of the group (an example can be found in the goal-sharing program shown in Table 8-8).

However, if this option is chosen, the team faces another difficult valuation issue, for the cost of poor attendance is not easy to determine. One possibility is to assume that the jobs of the absent individuals will have to be covered by other workers on an overtime basis, with the attendant premium compensation costs. But there is also the possibility of indirect costs, the primary ones being reduced productivity and quality owing to a less experienced person filling in for the absentee. One might argue, on the other hand, that these added costs would be reflected, and thus accounted for, in any productivity or quality measures that are part of the variable pay formula. After all is said and done, the valuation of improvements in attendance is arbitrary as often as not.

What makes attendance unique is the alternative option that is available to the design team: It can be treated as an individual penalty rather than as a group measure. In this treatment, a standard or acceptable level of absences is set, and any individual who violates that standard loses part or all of the bonus. An excellent example, from a plan at the plant level in an automotive company, is provided in Table 8-11. Here, any individual that misses just one day (eight hours) receives only 75 percent of the bonus to which he or she would otherwise be entitled. After two days' absence, the bonus is down to 50 percent, and the entire bonus is forfeited with three days' absence. And these requirements cover a semiannual payout period!

Table 8-11. Attendance penalty.

Hours Missed	Bonus Paid
<8	100%
8–15	75
16–23	50
>23	0

The advantage of the individual penalty, of course, is that it harms those who have poor attendance and would therefore be expected to bring about some change in the behavior of those offenders. Absences are now very expensive, perhaps costing the absent individual hundreds or even thousands of dollars. For that reason, the individual penalty alternative is far more common in variable pay programs than is the group measurement.

The group measure does have one advantage, however, that is lacking in the individual penalty: It brings about some degree of peer pressure on the miscreants who, by their absences, are impacting the bonus opportunity of all participants in the variable pay program.

One enterprising design team attempted to get the best of both worlds by employing a group absenteeism measure, but paying any bonuses earned on this variable only to those employees with perfect attendance for the period. If the number of employees with perfect attendance is relatively small, the payout to these individuals could be quite substantial, and the perfect-attendance roll would undoubtedly increase dramatically as a result.

One issue almost always arises, and usually leads to some lively debate, when attendance is considered as an individual penalty: Which absences should be counted? One faction may want to count all absences of any kind, on the basis that an individual cannot contribute to the performance of the organization if he or she is not on the job. Others will argue for including only those absences that are unexcused, unpaid, or otherwise deemed to be inappropriate. If company policy or a union contract allows or sanctions certain absences, would it not be unfair to penalize, through the variable pay system, the people involved in these absences? There is, of course, no right or wrong answer to this question, and the design team must resolve it through the application of consensus decision-making skills.

Other Variables

The foregoing review of the more common variable pay measures is, of course, far from complete. As variable pay has become more widespread, the measurement boundaries have expanded considerably. Today, there is virtually no business measure that cannot be found somewhere as part of a variable pay system. Some of the less common, or more specialized, measures, along with the usual approach to valuing improvements, include the following:

    ▪ *Downtime.* Maintaining continuous operation of the machinery is a critical variable in continuous-process industries such as chemicals and paper manufacturing. As such, downtime measures are quite prevalent in these industries. Valuing downtime is a bit more complicated than many other measures because the effect of downtime is lost production (and therefore less absorption of overhead) rather than increased costs. Some companies with machine-driven production processes use machine hours, rather than labor hours, to absorb overhead costs for accounting purposes.

    If this is the case, there may be an established absorbed-cost-per-machine-hour number that can be used for valuation purposes. Other companies calculate the amount of production lost as a result of the downtime and then estimate the bottom-line effect of that lost production. This might be done by multiplying the lost production by an average profit contribution (sales less direct costs) per unit.

    ▪ *Inventories.* Inventories are very costly to carry and therefore represent a significant improvement opportunity for some organizations. In addition, the use of just-in-time manufacturing systems has increased the emphasis on reducing inventory levels. This variable would probably be more common than it is in variable pay programs were it not for concerns about employees' ability to influence and control inventory levels.

    Where it is employed, a measure of inventory turnover, rather than the absolute inventory level, is generally selected by the design team to allow for higher inventories to support higher sales levels. The usual approach to valuing improvements in inventory turnover is to translate the turnover improvement into a dollar value of inventory and then multiply that figure by an assumed inventory carrying cost, such as 25 percent of the value of the inventory.

    ▪ *Sanitation.* This variable is of paramount importance in the food and beverage industries, as poor sanitation can cause extremely costly product contamination problems and may even lead regulatory agencies to shut down operations. Because sanitation is an absolute requirement in these businesses, it is often incorporated into the variable pay system as a *gate.*

Table 8-12. Sanitation modifier.

Audit Score	Modifier (%)	Audit Score	Modifier (%)
87	125%	81	95%
86	120	80	90
85	115	79	85
84	110	78	80
83	105	77	75
82	100		

As suggested earlier, a gate is a condition that must be satisfied in order for there to be a payout from the variable pay plan. One example is found in the distribution operation of a major consumer products company, whose formula was discussed in Chapter 5. This plan provides that no payout will be made in any quarter in which a rating below "excellent" is received from a regulatory inspection. This treatment sends a message that poor sanitation is not an acceptable tradeoff for cost reduction.

Where sanitation is used to provide a bonus opportunity (as it sometimes is in a goal-sharing program), the payout must by necessity be arbitrary. The bonus amount tends to be relatively small in these cases, partly because of the impossibility of valuing the achievement of sanitation goals and partly because meeting sanitation standards is expected as part of the job. In one example found in a food plant, a 0.5 percent bonus is paid for achieving an "excellent" rating on corporate sanitation audits.[5]

An alternative treatment for sanitation is as a modifier (see Chapter 5). A modifier developed by one gain-sharing design team is shown in Table 8-12. The formula in this case is a family of measures, including such variables as waste of raw materials and safety. The sanitation indicator is a score, as provided by a regular internal audit. The gain-sharing pool in this case is subject to a modification of + or − 25 percent based on the results of the sanitation audit.

• *Environmental incidents.* For companies in such industries as chemicals and oil refining, the avoidance of environmental incidents represents a major management priority. Not surprisingly, measures based on the number of these incidents can be found in variable pay programs in these industries. Valuing improvements in this measure is greatly complicated by the fact that the cost of an environmental incident can range from minor to catastrophic. Furthermore, the immediate and direct costs of an environmental incident do not take into account the possibility of regulatory sanctions and the impact on community relations and the public image of the company.

Some plans set the value of an environmental incident as the average direct costs incurred in past incidents. Others apply a multiplier to the average cost to account for the other, less tangible, risks. Still others simply apply arbitrary values to each incident. This type of variable could also be used as a modifier or gate.

- *Employee involvement.* A few companies have incorporated measures of employee involvement into their variable pay systems. The rationale for doing so is that the involvement process is critical to the organization's success, and people should therefore be reinforced simply for taking the initiative to be more involved. Presumably, the greater level of involvement will enhance the improvement process and produce a higher level of performance for the organization. The value placed on the increased involvement, as one might expect, is virtually always an arbitrary amount.

Probably the most commonly used measure of employee involvement is the number of suggestions submitted to a formal suggestion program. One service organization, for example, contributed $100 to the gain-sharing pool for each suggestion submitted by participating employees to an existing suggestion program. To encourage teamwork in developing ideas, there was an added proviso that the suggestion be submitted by a team in order to qualify for the gain-sharing contribution. Note that this measure is normally based on suggestions submitted, rather than suggestions implemented or the dollar value of approved suggestions. Remember, the intent here is to reward the degree of employee involvement rather than the actual improvement.

Another company included as a gain-sharing measure the number of team meetings held because of a management concern that employees were not spending enough time getting together to solve problems. Where managers are not comfortable with the idea of increasing pay for involvement per se, the use of employee-involvement goals would likely be more acceptable when they are among the qualifying goals for a financially funded goal-sharing formula (see Chapter 5).

Clearly, the valuation of gains or goal achievement is an important step in the design process. The consequence of doing it poorly is a flawed system that either fails to provide a proper return to the business or is inequitable for the participating employees. Depending on the measures selected, it can also be one of the most complicated steps in the process. The design team should ensure that it has, or can call upon, the needed analytical skills to accomplish the task effectively.

At this point, the design team has finalized the variable pay measures and has established the various methodologies for valuing gains or goal achievement. It has, therefore, completed the variable pay formula and is ready to proceed to the remaining design components.

References

1. Philip B. Crosby, *Quality Is Free* (New York: McGraw-Hill, 1979).
2. John G. Belcher, Jr., *Gain Sharing: The New Path to Profits and Productivity* (Houston: Gulf Publishing Company, 1991).
3. "City Boosts Productivity as Alternative to Tax Hikes, Service Cuts," *National Productivity Report*, October 15, 1985.
4. "Accident Facts" (Itasca, Ill.: National Safety Council, 1995).
5. James P. Guthrie and Edward P. Cunningham, "Pay for Performance Hourly Workers: The Quaker Oats Alternative," *Compensation & Benefits Review*, March-April 1982.

9

Establishing Baselines and Modeling the System

Now that the variable pay formula has been created, the next logical step in the design process is to establish the baselines or, in the case of goal sharing, the goals. The baseline for a gain-sharing or profit-sharing measure is the level of performance that must be exceeded in order for there to be a gain. Without a baseline, it would be impossible to ascertain the magnitude (or even the existence) of a gain. For a goal-sharing plan, the baseline is the goal that, if achieved, triggers the predetermined payout for that measure.

Step 8. Determine Initial Baselines or Goals

This step is a critical one for the design team, for if it is not done properly, it could well cause the variable pay plan to fail. What is required here is a delicate balance. If the baselines are easily achievable, bonuses may prove to be excessive relative to the benefit obtained by the company, and the plan will lose the support of management. If, on the other hand, there is too much stretch in the baselines, the plan will lack credibility with employees and there will be a significant risk that payouts will be insignificant or nonexistent. Either way, the viability of the plan would be in jeopardy.

Adding to the complexity of this decision is the fact that for most measures, there are a very large, if not infinite, number of possible choices for the baseline number. Obvious examples include the prior year, the prior two years, the best prior year, the current year's budget, a competitor's performance level, the world-class performance level, and any goals that might be established through the business planning process.

It can be helpful here to think in terms of two categories of baselines.

The first of these is historical baselines. A *historical baseline* is one whose value is equal to some past level of performance. The past period used to establish the baseline could be the previous quarter, the previous year, or the average of several past quarters or years. It could also be the best performance achieved in any prior year.

The second category is target baselines. In this case, *the target baseline* is one whose value is established at some level of performance better than that achieved in the recent historical period. Goal sharing, by definition, falls in this category, as bonuses are tied to the achievement of goals that would normally represent some level of improvement over past performance. Profit-sharing and gain-sharing plans, however, can also have target baselines. In this case, the threshold level of performance at which the company begins to share gains would be higher than it would be if a historical baseline were employed. In effect, the company retains 100 percent of the first increment of gains over past performance and then shares the additional gains achieved beyond the target baseline.

Historical Baselines

The principal advantage of historical baselines is that they are objective and would generally be perceived by the plan participants as being fair. Past performance is a reality; the subjectivity associated with establishing goals or targets is not an issue. To most employees, the notion of sharing gains from past or current performance levels would seem equitable and fair. Historical baselines also minimize the risk of the plan's failing to pay out during the first few periods. This can be an important advantage, as a variable pay plan is fragile in its infancy and a lack of bonuses for an extended period may cause a new plan to lose credibility with the participants before it gets off the ground.

A previously achieved level of performance may be an appropriate target where there has been a decline in performance in recent years. This prior level is obviously achievable, assuming there has been no fundamental change in the business to explain the decline, and it may be difficult to convince management that bonuses should be paid for performance that is below that achieved in the past.

Historical baselines could be a serious mistake, on the other hand, under certain conditions:

- *A major capital investment, physical expansion, or process change has taken place in the historical period under consideration.* The historical data in these circumstances would not be an accurate reflection of the current operating environment.
- *A major change in the business, such as the addition of a new product line*

or the entry into new markets, has taken place in the recent past. In this case, past performance may be invalidated for baseline purposes.

- *A significant improvement in performance has taken place in recent periods.* Developing a baseline by averaging results over this time frame may seriously understate current performance and produce large bonuses that are not funded by new improvement.
- *Past performance is unacceptable.* It may not make business sense to reward employees for improvements from a level of performance that is depressed, noncompetitive, or unacceptable for other reasons.

Target Baselines

Some would argue for target baselines, on the basis that additional compensation is justified only if significant improvement occurs or key business goals are achieved. Modest improvements in performance may in some companies be viewed by corporate management as expected, at best, and substandard at worst.

The basis for establishing target baselines varies. Some of the more common include the budget, strategic or business plan goals, and competitive benchmarks.

- *Budget.* The budget is probably the most prevalent basis for establishing target baselines. Often viewed by management as the minimum acceptable level of performance, the budget would seem to be a logical starting point for measuring and rewarding gains. It may be difficult to convince management that increased compensation is justified if the budget, by which management's own performance is being measured, has not been achieved.

There are two problems with using the budget to establish a baseline for a variable pay plan. First, the budget is not an objective benchmark and therefore may lack credibility with employees. In most organizations, the budget is the outcome of a negotiation process between one level of management and the next higher level. The negotiation often ends when management at some level dictates its desires to the next level down, and it cascades on down from there. Nonmanagement employees generally have little, if any, input to this process. It should not be a surprise, therefore, when employees question the validity of a baseline that is derived from the budget.

The second problem arises from the fact that budgets in many companies have a significant amount of "stretch" built into them. As such, there is a high probability that the budgeted levels of performance will not be achieved. And while it may not be desirable to launch a variable pay plan that requires little effort on the part of the employees, it is also not advantageous to implement a plan that carries a high risk of never paying out. For this reason, the starting point for paying bonuses in some plans is set at a performance level that is somewhat worse than budget (see the electric utility example in Chapter 6). Budgets are most useful for establishing baselines, therefore, where the probability of their achievement is reasonably high and where employees below the management level have some input to the process of budget development.

- *Strategic or business-plan goals.* Business goals that have been established as part of the strategic or business planning process are often used in setting target baselines. This option may be a particularly popular choice among management, as it serves to explicitly align variable pay with the business strategy and goals. The same cautions suggested above with respect to budgets, however, apply here as well.

- *Competitive benchmarks.* These would seem to be an excellent basis for establishing baselines, as the meeting of a competitive challenge would be a very desirable outcome of the change process. Their use is fairly uncommon, however, probably because of a lack of reliable comparative data in most industries. In addition, a competitive benchmark in some cases may represent too great a reach for the organization.

Target baselines, and goal sharing in particular, may make eminent sense if the organization's performance is being impacted by forces of a temporary nature. A design team at a beverage plant was faced with just such a problem. The team was in the process of designing a gain-sharing plan with historical baselines when the closure of another of the company's plants was announced. A substantial portion of the closed plant's volume was to be transferred to the design team's plant during the first quarter of the gain-sharing plan's operation. With an anticipated 60 percent increase in volume, the historical data collected by the design team was obviously useless. The team's solution was to have an interim goal-sharing plan for the first quarter, with bonuses tied to goals associated with an absorption of the additional volume with minimal product and material losses and a reasonable on-time delivery performance. The plan would then revert to one based on the original measures, with baselines that reflected the higher volume achieved in the previous quarter.

Target baselines or goal sharing also are obvious choices in startup operations. Many new startups today are designed to be team-oriented, high-involvement systems from the first day, and as a result, there is often a desire by management to implement congruent reward systems such as variable pay from the outset. Target baselines make sense in these situations for two reasons.

Table 9-1. Historical vs. target baselines.

Historical	Target
1. Objective — based on actual data.	1. May be applicable where capital investments or other changes have occurred.
2. Will likely be perceived as fair.	2. Can reflect continuation of improvement trend.
3. Maximizes probability of payout.	3. Appropriate where past performance is unacceptable.
4. Appropriate where past performance is high.	4. Can be tied to organizational goals.
	5. Required where history is nonexistent.

First, there is typically an established set of startup goals (achieving a certain level of production by a specific date, attaining a certain level of quality within a specific time period, and so on) and the key business need generally is to achieve these goals. Second, no history exists for a startup operation, by definition, and target baselines therefore represent the only real option. Even though targets or goals invariably represent the initial baseline feature, there is often a plan to convert to historical baselines once the startup period is completed and the facility is in a reasonably stable operating condition.

The Choice of a Baseline

Table 9-1 summarizes the arguments and advantages of historical and target baselines.

As with any other design decision, the choice between a historical and a target baseline should ultimately be based on the circumstances, the business needs, and the impact on the plan's credibility.

The charts developed in Step 5 (see Chapter 7) will be invaluable when making the baseline decisions. The design team should refer back to these charts for guidance in selecting the value for each measure's baseline. By way of illustration, the charts shown in Figures 7-1 and 7-2 are reproduced here as Figures 9-1 and 9-2.

The point was made in Chapter 7 that the baseline decision is a rela-

(text continues on page 156)

Figure 9-1. Flat trend.

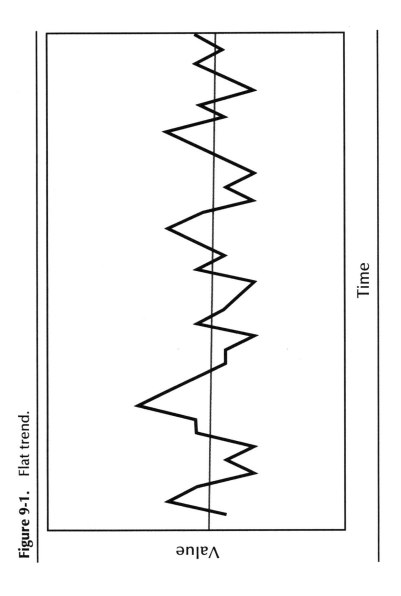

Value

Time

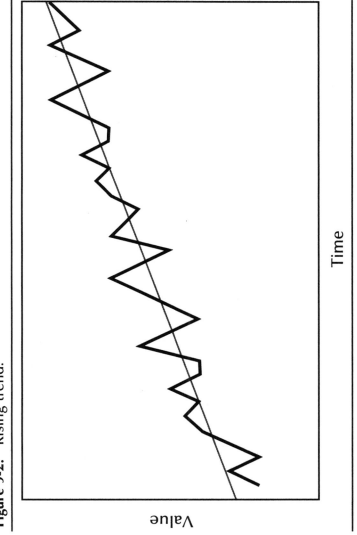

Figure 9-2. Rising trend.

tively simple one for a measure displaying a flat historical trend, such as the one in Figure 9-1. Assuming that a historical baseline (rather than a target) has been deemed by the design team to be desirable, the obvious choice in this case is the average performance level for almost any period covered by this chart. Whether the team chooses to average one, two, or three years, the result will be virtually the same. It is unlikely that anyone would consider such a baseline to be unfair, as it represents a level of performance that is stable and has been maintained for a considerable period of time. If, after the installation of the variable pay system, performance on this measure improves, it would be hard to argue that employees do not deserve to be rewarded.

The measure represented in Figure 9-2 is a different matter. Depending on the historical period chosen, widely different baselines would result. Table 9-2 contains the thirty-six data points underlying the chart in Figure 9-2. The various baselines that would result from averaging different time periods are as follows:

3 months:	147
6 months:	143
12 months:	141
24 months:	131
36 months:	120

These data clearly illustrate the danger of adopting and applying predetermined baseline rules without evaluating the history underlying the measures. If the design team in this case had decided that the baselines for each measure should be equal to the last three years' performance, the baseline for the measure in Figure 9-2 would have been established at a level (120) far below the current level of performance (155 in the most recent month). Had performance remained flat after the launch of the gain-sharing program, management would have received an unpleasant surprise: large bonuses for no improvement at all. In fact, bonuses would be paid in this case even if performance declined substantially from its current level. This is undoubtedly not what management had in mind! More than one variable pay program, in fact, has lost management support for this very reason.

What is the proper level of the baseline in this situation? There is good reason to ask whether a historical baseline is even appropriate for this measure. There clearly are existing forces that are driving continuous improvement here. A case could be made that a real gain has not been made unless performance under variable pay exceeds that which would have been expected without any change in the pay system. This line of

Table 9-2. Data points for 36-month chart in Figure 9-2.

Month	Value	Month	Value
1	80	19	130
2	90	20	125
3	80	21	120
4	90	22	130
5	100	23	135
6	105	24	130
7	100	25	140
8	110	26	130
9	100	27	130
10	100	28	140
11	120	29	150
12	110	30	140
13	100	31	130
14	110	32	140
15	120	33	150
16	130	34	140
17	120	35	145
18	110	36	155

argument might lead the team to extrapolate the trend line to determine the baseline for the upcoming periods.

As suggested in Chapter 7, on the other hand, there might be other points of view. Can the existing rate of improvement really be maintained without the help and commitment of the workforce? And did not employees contribute to past improvements? It should be apparent now why the assertion was made in Chapter 7 that a measure with a flat history would provide fewer complications for the design team, other things being equal, than would one that has a pronounced trend.

If history is to be the basis for establishing the baseline for this measure, only a short time period—such as the last three to six months—would be appropriate. Even then, some of the bonus subsequently paid to employees might reflect improvements that occurred prior to the implementation of the variable pay plan.

It should be noted that management sometimes does wish to reward employees for past improvements, either because they have been unable to compensate people appropriately through their traditional pay systems or because they want to ensure that some bonuses are paid immediately to get the plan off to a fast start. If this were the case, a historical baseline would accomplish this objective nicely in this situation.

To the extent that the measure displays a seasonal pattern, the baseline decision becomes even more complicated. The chart depicting such a measure in Chapter 7 is reproduced here as Figure 9-3, with the addition of a line representing the thirty-six-month average.

We don't have a significant trend here, so one might conclude that the thirty-six-month average would be a good choice for the baseline. The problem with doing so, however, should be obvious. In one quarter of every year, performance will almost certainly exceed the baseline, and performance will just as certainly fall short during the other three quarters. These outcomes would not be due to any effort or failure on the part of employees, but would simply be a reflection of the seasonal nature of the business.

When faced with a pronounced seasonal pattern such as this one, the design team basically has three choices:

1. *Pay out on an annual basis.* This option may not be advantageous because the benefits of frequent reinforcement for improvement are lost (see Chapter 11).
2. *Use a rolling four-quarter or rolling twelve-month payout method.* By basing the payout on the average performance over the past year, rather than on the current month or quarter alone, the seasonal distortions (as well as any others) are smoothed out and eliminated from the system (see Chapter 11).
3. *Adopt dual baselines.* Use one baseline for one quarter and a different one for the other three quarters.

The first and second solutions, which are independent of the baseline, are discussed in more detail in the chapters indicated. The third option is the only solution that directly affects the baseline decision. The design team could establish one baseline for the quarter in which the pronounced seasonal effect occurs, based on the performance achieved in that same quarter during the previous one, two, or three years. The team would then formulate a separate and distinct baseline for use in the other three quarters, based on the relevant historical data for these quarters. The variable

Figure 9-3. Seasonality.

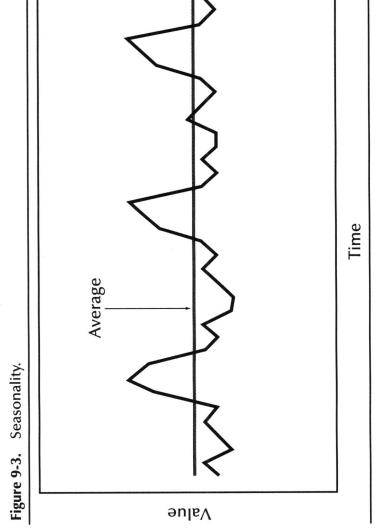

pay plan would then have a realistic basis, free of distortions from sea-sonal influences, for quantifying improvement in any period during the year.

It should be noted that the design team does not have to select one basis—history or target—to the exclusion of the other baselines. Nor does it have to adopt the same historical period for all measures. One design team, for example, found that the previous year's performance produced a suitable baseline for all measures except one; safety performance, as measured by the number of recordable accidents, had deteriorated over the past two years. The team members agreed that it would be inappropri-ate to reward employees for safety results until performance had at least returned to the level of two years ago. Hence, a different basis was se-lected for establishing the baseline for the safety measure alone.

Some Other Considerations

Complications can arise when the level of a particular measure is heavily impacted by another variable that is external to the organization. A plant design team encountered this vexing problem when it discovered that la-bor productivity, an important measure for the company's gain-sharing program, was significantly affected by the average order size, which var-ied greatly from period to period. Relatively small order sizes required frequent changeovers and smaller production lots, and were usually ac-companied by lower productivity as a result. How could an appropriate baseline for productivity be established when the average order size was not known in advance?

The team's creative solution to this problem was to adjust the produc-tivity baseline each period, based on the order size. The adjustment turned out to be quite simple: The baseline was established by multi-plying the previous year's productivity level by the following ratio.

$$\frac{Current\ average\ order\ size}{Previous\ year's\ average\ order\ size}$$

If the current period's order size was larger than that of last year's, this ratio would be greater than 1, and would therefore increase the pro-ductivity baseline. The amount of the increase would be proportional to the difference in order size. The reverse would be true if the current order size was smaller than last year's. Examples of the calculation are shown in Table 9-3.

Establishing baselines is clearly not a science, but requires some anal-ysis and the exercise of judgment and common sense. There are generally

Table 9-3. Baseline adjustment for order size.

Average Order Size			Original Baseline	Adjusted Baseline
Current	*Previous*	*Cur./Prev.*		
40	42	0.95	125	118
42	42	1.00	125	125
47	42	1.12	125	140

many possible baseline options for a given measure, and rarely does one alternative stand out as an obvious choice. Ultimately, however, the baseline decision must make business sense. The rigid application of a predetermined formula, such as averaging the last twelve months, without the application of some common sense, can produce an untenable result.

Step 9. Establish the Provision or Formula for Resetting Baselines in Future Periods

Before the design team can dispose of the baseline issue, it must answer one more question: How will the baselines change in the future? Failing to clearly address this issue can cause serious problems down the road.

One company learned this lesson the hard way. An excellent gainsharing plan was developed by a design team, and it paid off nicely during its first year. Both management and the participating employees were pleased with the result. Management then announced a new, and tighter, set of baselines for the plan's second year. This course of action seemed perfectly reasonable to management, for the difficult competitive environment in the industry demanded continuous improvement. Unfortunately, the workforce did not share this perspective, and the baseline changes were interpreted by many employees as an attempt by management to manipulate the system and reduce their bonuses. Trust was damaged, credibility was lost, and the effectiveness of the plan was seriously impaired.

In reality, changing baselines or goals is the norm in variable pay plans today. The problem arises when this provision is not clearly articulated in the design of the plan and not communicated to the participating employees.

Flexible Baselines

Fixed baselines were not uncommon some years ago. The early genera-
tions of gain-sharing programs, such as the Scanlon Plan, often established baselines that did not adjust on a routine basis. The arrival of
international competition, however, changed all that. Continuous improvement became a survival issue for those organizations facing the
rigors of a global economy, and anything else did not justify a reward.

Concerns may be expressed that a changing baseline will not be perceived by employees as fair. After all, the reasoning goes, the company
continues to benefit from the previous years' gains; why should not employees continue to share in these ongoing gains? In a highly competitive
environment, however, the company's share of any gains has probably
been transferred to the customer in the form of lower selling prices. Where
competition is intense, the company has little latitude to raise prices to
recover increases in labor, material, and other costs. It may even be forced
to implement an absolute reduction in prices to maintain its volume of
business and market share. The company's share of any year's improvements in this scenario does not enhance the bottom line year after year,
but serves merely to offset any increases in the price paid for labor, materials, and so on, in that year. In effect, the customer has ended up with the
company's share of the gains and there is nothing left to share in future
years.

If, in subsequent years, the company continues to reward past years'
performance improvements, that added compensation is funded out of
the profits of the company. This cycle, if carried to its ultimate conclusion,
could result in bankruptcy of the company. Variable pay is supposed to
enhance the viability of the business, not destroy it!

Most variable pay plans today, then, have a provision that allows for
a regular and routine adjustment of the baselines or goals. It is generally
desirable that the nature of the adjustment be predefined and objective.
This is not always possible with goal-sharing plans, particularly those that
are based on the annual business plan, which obviously cannot be known
years in advance. For gain-sharing or profit-sharing plans that use historical baselines, however, a simple, objective adjustment is quite feasible
and realistic.

The most common adjustment methods reset the baseline to a level
equal to the performance of the previous year, previous two years, previous three years, previous eight quarters (or twenty-four months or four
semiannual periods), and previous twelve quarters (or thirty-six months
or six semiannual periods).

From a management point of view, the first option seems to best meet
the needs of the business. Bonuses would reflect only the current year's

performance, and only new improvements would be shared in each subsequent year. To the participating employees, on the other hand, this may seem to be a very demanding system, and there could well be concerns that a pace of significant improvement would be difficult to maintain for more than a few years. To improve the perception of fairness and equity, and to extend the life of the plan before it requires a major overhaul, a rolling average baseline, such as one of the other options listed above, may be advantageous.

With the two-year and three-year rolling averages, the baseline is reset on an annual basis, and employees in effect share gains for two or three years, respectively. Should continuous improvement cease, however, the baseline eventually catches up with the actual performance level and bonuses are eliminated.

The eight-quarter and twelve-quarter rolling average adjustments differ from the two-year and three-year options in that the baseline change occurs on a more frequent basis (quarterly, in this case). The effect is that any quarter's performance will immediately be reflected, in part, in the next quarter's baseline. Over any given period, therefore, a quarterly adjustment will produce smaller bonuses, assuming the same level of performance improvement, than will an annual adjustment.

Another implication of quarterly adjustments is that changes to the baseline are more gradual and thus produce less variability in payouts. With an annual adjustment, bonuses in the first quarter of a new year may drop precipitously as the history from two or three years back is suddenly replaced by the past year's performance, which may be considerably higher. With a quarterly adjustment, in contrast, only one-eighth or one-twelfth of the baseline data is being replaced with each baseline adjustment.

With goal sharing, the question of baseline change is really not an issue. By definition, goal-sharing plans reward participants for achieving goals. It is unlikely that employees would expect organizational performance goals to remain at the same level indefinitely (with the possible exception of a variable in which performance is presently at a very high or near-perfect level). The only issue is how the goals are reestablished each new year. Nonetheless, it behooves the design team to clearly spell out the fact that the goals *will* change every year to ensure that there are no misunderstandings.

It is important to note that the baseline change decision should be completely independent of the decision to establish the initial baseline. A common mistake made by design teams is to assume that the period of the initial baseline should correspond to the rolling average period that will be used on an ongoing basis to reset the baseline. This may be inappropriate, as using a three-year average for the initial baseline often results in large payouts that are reflective of improvements that took place before the variable pay system was installed (see the discussion under Step 8 earlier in this chapter).

Some Potential Future Developments to Consider

A question that inevitably arises relative to a baseline adjustment provision is: *What happens when performance declines?* If there is no provision to the contrary, the baseline in this circumstance would have to be loosened in the period following the decline to reflect the impact of the lower performance. An average of the past two years is, after all, an average of the past two years.

However, many plans contain a provision to the contrary. They state that the baseline can never decline to a lower performance level (barring, of course, a major change in the business). The argument for this provision is that a deterioration in the baseline following a period of poor performance would ultimately enable employees to earn higher bonuses in future periods than would have been possible had performance levels been maintained. This outcome may not be deemed by management to be justified.

Another question that comes up is: *What happens to the variable pay program when no more improvement is possible?* This concern will likely be raised by the design team and is certainly a legitimate one. While performance on some variables, such as productivity, could theoretically improve almost indefinitely, there are obvious limits on others. An organization cannot improve on zero defects, for example; nor can it have fewer than no accidents. While these absolutes may never be reached, it is certainly conceivable that such high performance levels could be attained that there would be little opportunity of and minuscule financial gain from a further improvement. At that point, an automatically adjusting baseline becomes an impediment, for it will eventually coincide with this high performance level, and motivation to maintain this performance will be lost.

An oil refinery faced just this dilemma with its gain-sharing program. Included in its formula was a measure that compared the refinery's output of gasoline and other products to the volume of crude oil that was input to the process. The intent, of course, was to operate the refinery so as to minimize the loss of raw material. By the second year of the plan, employee efforts had improved this measure to the maximum level that was technically possible. Since the gain-sharing plan contained an eight-quarter rolling average baseline, any bonus opportunity from this measure would be eliminated in two years.

How could the focus on this important variable be maintained? The union-management design team elected to freeze the baseline for this one measure, so that bonuses would continue to be earned by maintaining this industry-leading level of performance. Payouts of this type are termed *maintenance bonuses;* employees are rewarded for maintaining, rather than improving on, a very high level of performance. (There are other options for dealing with this situation; these will be discussed more fully in Chapter 13.)

This anecdote underscores the importance of having an effective mechanism for modifying the variable pay plan. In a turbulent and rapidly changing business environment, the ability to modify a variable pay plan is critical to its long-term viability. The process for accomplishing these changes will be discussed in detail in Chapter 13.

When Fixed Baselines May Be the Better Choice

Profit sharing represents a partial exception to the generalization that baselines are adjusted in variable pay plans on a routine basis. Those plans that share profits from the first dollar obviously do not incorporate a baseline-change provision. This is also true of some plans that share profits in excess of a specified return on assets or return on investment. Other plans of this type, on the other hand, adjust the return baseline to reflect changing management or shareholder expectations.

There are also certain circumstances when a fixed baseline may be justified in a gain-sharing plan. Where base levels of pay are low relative to the market, or where no increases in base pay are contemplated for an indefinite period, there may need to be a substantial bonus potential in order to provide employees the opportunity to earn a market or above-market level of total compensation. Without such an opportunity, the organization may have difficulty retaining good employees. With baselines fixed, the potential for high bonuses can be established and maintained.

If the variable pay system is replacing another form of compensation, a stronger argument can be made for fixed baselines. One corporation that eliminated traditional production incentives replaced these incentives with team-based variable pay systems with fixed baselines. This was done to ensure that workers formerly earning incentives could maintain their previous compensation levels without adding the former incentive amounts to base wages (and thus increasing fixed compensation). In those cases where the employees' previous incentive compensation is added to the base, on the other hand, a fixed baseline would probably be inappropriate.

The ultimate criterion for the baseline decision, as with any other component of a variable pay system, is that it make business sense. And barring circumstances such as those just described, a fixed baseline probably will not pass this test in a highly competitive industry.

Step 10. Simulate or Model the Variable Pay System

With the formula and baselines established, the variable pay design team is now ready to conduct some simulations of the system. The purpose of this step is to test the system in order to understand its dynamics and to ensure that it produces reasonable results under a variety of scenarios.

The modeling of the variable pay system is important for several reasons:

1. *The range of possible payouts must be ascertained and evaluated for reasonableness from both a company and a participating employee point of view.* Experience suggests that a variable pay system should offer potential payout opportunities in the range of 3 percent of pay or more if it is to motivate improvement and change behaviors. If the simulations suggest that that level of bonuses is unlikely, the design must be reconsidered. It makes little sense to implement a pay plan that will not likely stimulate behavioral change.

At the other end of the spectrum lies a different problem. If it appears that the system may pay very large bonuses, the design must be carefully reviewed to ensure that the baselines are reasonable and that there are no errors in the formula calculations. If the formula holds up under this scrutiny, the design team should then consider whether such large payouts will be acceptable from a management point of view. If not, the bonus potential can be moderated by tightening the baselines, reducing the employee share of the gains, or other methods.

2. *The relative payout potential of the various measures needs to be determined when a family of measures formula is used.* If the payout potential from one measure far exceeds that of the other measures, the team can expect that employee attentions will be inordinately focused on that particular variable. This may be entirely appropriate, since that measure represents the area where the greatest financial benefit can be obtained for the company.

On the other hand, the lack of attention to the other variables may be a concern if their importance goes beyond short-term financial benefits. This concern may apply, for example, to such variables as safety and customer satisfaction. This point is illustrated in Table 9-4, which contains a simulation conducted by one organization's design team. The team estimated the amount of improvement that could reasonably be expected for the five measures in the variable pay plan. The team then applied the valuation techniques developed in Step 7 to determine the value of those improvements. The employee share of these gains was divided by the participating payroll to determine the percentage payout.

Table 9-4. Variable pay plan simulation.

	Gain (%)	Value
Productivity	3%	$ 284,000
Quality	5	22,000
Materials utilization	4	65,000
Delivery performance	8	28,000
Safety	12	13,000
Total		$ 412,000
× Employee share @ 40%		$ 64,800
÷ Participating payroll (520 empl)		3,180,000
= Percent payout		5.2%

While the resulting percentage was deemed to be adequate to influence behaviors, the design team noted a problem of a different kind: Almost 70 percent of the payout would come from productivity improvement. With only a small fraction of the bonus potential arising from quality improvement, would not the employees place an inordinate emphasis on productivity, perhaps even sacrificing quality in order to maximize productivity? The situation with safety was even worse; the anticipated improvement would produce a quarterly payout averaging only $10 per person. This plan might well produce behaviors that are not in the best interests of the business or the employees.

Facing a situation like the one presented in Table 9-4, the design team may wish to artificially inflate the payouts of other key variables (or reduce the payout of the high-potential variable) in order to obtain a better balance among the various measures. Methods to increase the potential payout on certain measures include a higher employee share or the application of arbitrary multipliers on those measures.

3. *The model is a way to obtain data that can be reported to management when seeking approval to implement the variable pay process.* Management will almost certainly want to know what can be expected in terms of bonus payments, particularly if this is the organization's first attempt at implementing variable pay. The simulation will enable the design team to provide concrete answers to that question, while simultaneously impressing management with the thoroughness of the team's work.

For a goal-sharing system, this modeling step is simple and straight-forward; the design team need only consider the predetermined payouts earned when the goals are achieved. It is a more complex undertaking for a gain-sharing system. The design team must make assumptions relative to the amount of improvement that might be realized for the various measures, apply the calculations developed to value those improvements (see Chapter 8), accumulate the gains into a pool, and make a tentative decision regarding the employee share of those gains (the final decision on the sharing ratio will be made after the simulations are completed).

Spreadsheet software on a personal computer will be an invaluable tool for the design team, as it will allow the system to be modeled under a variety of different scenarios with ease. At a minimum, the design team should examine these three scenarios:

1. A minimal amount of improvement occurs.
2. The expected amount of improvement occurs (based on the design team's best guess).
3. The maximum foreseeable improvement occurs.

The modeling can, of course, go well beyond these scenarios and include an evaluation of the effects of increases in some variables along with a decline in others, a change in volume, a change in mix, and so on. The more scenarios the design team models, the greater will be the team's, as well as management's, comfort with the system.

Assuming that the system holds up under the simulations, the design team will have reached a milestone: The heart of the system—the formula and baselines—has been completed. The most difficult part of the design process is behind it, and the team is now ready to move on to the remaining design steps.

10

Sharing the Gains

As suggested at the conclusion to Chapter 9, the design team at this point has completed the most complex and demanding part of the design process. Under the best of circumstances, creating a variable pay formula and the associated baselines involves a great deal of analytical effort and solving some difficult measurement and valuation problems.

The team's remaining tasks revolve around design features that are peripheral to the formula. This characterization should not be taken to mean that these decisions are trivial or necessarily simple to make; in many cases, they will have a significant impact on the employees' perception of the fairness of the plan and therefore on the plan's effectiveness in changing behaviors. But with a few possible exceptions, they should not present as great a challenge as those faced in developing the formula.

The immediate next step for the design team is to determine how the gains will be shared between the company and the participating employees.

Step 11. Establish the Sharing Ratio

The sharing ratio, like everything else in a variable pay system, must be determined in advance. As one might imagine, the choice made by the design team on this feature can have a major effect on the magnitude of the payouts and on the perception of the plan's fairness.

It should be noted here that one form of variable pay—goal sharing—does not contain an explicit sharing arrangement. Since predetermined payouts are associated directly with the achievement of goals, there is no pool of savings created and therefore no need to have a sharing ratio. The same holds true for those gain-sharing plans with scheduled payouts (see Chapter 5). The absence of this feature is one reason why both of these approaches are simpler to communicate and to understand.

The choice of a goal-sharing or scheduled payout plan does not allow the design team to skip this step, however. The key word in the previous paragraph is *explicit*. While the sharing ratio in these approaches is not discernible to the plan participants, it is nonetheless there. How else could the design team set the payouts for the achievement of goals in a goal-sharing program? To rationally do so, the team must at least estimate the value realized by the company upon achieving each goal and allocate a portion of that value to fund the bonus payment. The sharing ratio is therefore implicit, rather than explicit, in these variable pay programs.

The Employee Share

The employee share in most gain-sharing programs falls somewhere in the range of 25 to 50 percent of the gains. If the employee sharing ratios from a large number of programs were plotted on a graph, however, there would not be an even distribution across that range. What there would be is a skewed curve with a definite clustering at the 50 percent point.

The popularity of 50/50 shares in variable pay programs is due to one simple fact: It sounds fair. Few employees would argue that they are not receiving a fair share of the gains when those gains are equally divided between the company and the participating employees. And often there is little more thought than that given to this issue by the design team. Unfortunately, it is not that simple an issue.

While a perception of fairness is undeniably important to the success of a variable pay program, this design feature should not be disposed of so casually. There are a variety of circumstances, in fact, which might justify a lower employee share than 50 percent:

- A comprehensive formula
- An undemanding baseline
- A capital-intensive business
- A growth business
- High base pay relative to the market

The first point above refers to the nature of the variable pay formula. A comprehensive formula is one that comprehends, or includes, most or all of the key variables affecting the business. Profit sharing is the ultimate example of a comprehensive formula, in that it reflects the impact of all possible variables on the business's performance. And it is here that there are generally the lowest employee shares (further discussion of profit sharing follows). An example of a comprehensive gain-sharing formula would be a cost formula that includes most or all of the organization's costs. A

Table 10-1. Distribution center cost formula.

Sales	$24,000,000
× Baseline costs (5.2%)	$ 1,248,000
− Actual costs	1,212,000
= Bonus pool	$ 36,000
− Company share (50%)	18,000
= Employee share	$ 18,000

formula that is not comprehensive, in contrast, would be one that includes only one performance variable, such as labor productivity.

Comprehensive formulas tend to have lower employee shares for several reasons:

- *The company must retain more of the gains in order to fund key corporate needs.* A company in a competitive business environment must continuously improve performance in order to fund reinvestments in the business, offset increases in costs without passing these increases through to the customer, and reward the owners of the business for supplying capital. If the company is committed to share with employees the improvements in only a limited number of variables, it presumably can apply to these corporate needs 100 percent of any gains that may be achieved in other variables. Should the company share a high percentage of the gains in a comprehensive formula, on the other hand, it might find itself with inadequate funds for these other imperatives.

- *The potential bonus payments are larger.* The greater the number of costs or variables that are included in the variable pay formula, the larger the potential payout becomes. A given target level of bonuses could therefore be achieved with a lower employee share than would be possible with a narrow formula.

- *There is a greater likelihood of gains from uncontrollable sources.* A broad cost formula, such as the one presented in Table 4-3 and reproduced here as Table 10-1, has the potential of producing substantial bonuses from favorable pricing decisions, increases in demand, changes in product mix, or other factors that are out of the control of the employees. Some would argue that the potential for such "windfall" bonuses justifies a lower employee share than would be appropriate for a plan that rewards only improvements that are controllable by employees.

The second point in the above list of circumstances that would justify a lower employee share suggests that baseline decisions should also be considered when addressing the share component. The guideline here is that the employee share should bear some relationship to the amount of effort that will be required to earn bonuses. Consideration should be given to both the initial baseline (Step 8) and the provision for changing the baseline (Step 9).

Where the initial baseline is equated to some past level of performance, as opposed to a target that represents considerable improvement over past performance, a lower employee share can be justified on the basis that gains will require relatively less effort to achieve. By the same token, a program with a fixed baseline could be expected to have a lower employee share than one in which the baseline tightens on a routine and recurring basis. Where a fixed baseline exists, a 50 percent employee share may in fact be fiscally imprudent in a competitive environment (if the fixed baseline itself is not).

A third circumstance in which an employee share below 50 percent may be appropriate is in a capital-intensive business. In such a situation, the company may need to retain a larger proportion of the improvements in order to fund ongoing reinvestment in the business. A labor-intensive business, on the other hand, may have considerably less need to retain funds for reinvestment.

A rapidly growing company represents another situation in which a lower employee share could be justified. Growth companies generally do not pay substantial dividends to their shareholders because of the need to retain capital to fund the company's growth. For the same reason, it may be inappropriate to pay large bonuses to employees as well.

Finally, those organizations that maintain base pay at high levels relative to the market could be expected to have an employee share that falls toward the low end of the normal range. With pay already high, the amount of additional compensation that the business can realistically tolerate in a competitive environment may be limited.

The above guidelines are not hard-and-fast rules, and exceptions are not hard to find. They are merely factors that should be taken into account when considering the employee share component of the variable pay system. Some companies, in fact, opt for a 50/50 share even where circumstances could justify a lower employee share in order to improve the perceived fairness of the program among the participating employees.

Profit-Sharing Plans

As suggested earlier, profit-sharing plans represent an exception to the generalization that the employee share falls within the 25 to 50 percent range. The exception specifically applies to those plans that share profits from the first dollar. Many of the points made earlier relative to circumstances that justify a lower employee share apply here in the extreme. Profit sharing is the broadest of formulas, and profits generally represent the main source of funds for reinvestment in the business and for rewarding the owners of the business. Profits are also impacted by a wide ranges of factors that are out of the employees' control, ranging from market conditions to arcane accounting adjustments. And the baseline could hardly be less demanding than in a plan where the sharing begins with the first dollar of profits. As a result, the employee share in first-dollar profit-sharing plans generally does not exceed 15 percent. We even saw, in Chapter 8, an example of a public-sector organization that pays out a maximum of 4 percent of its income.

Profit-sharing plans that share only profits in excess of a target level, on the other hand, do often have employee sharing ratios that fall more in line with the normal range for other types of variable pay programs. It is not unheard of, for example, to share 50 percent of profits in excess of a budgeted level of profitability.

Multiple Sharing Ratios

While variable pay plans have traditionally employed a single sharing ratio, this is certainly not a requirement. This constraint could, in fact, present a problem where a family of measures formula is adopted. What is a fair and reasonable share for one measure may not be appropriate for another measure.

A wire manufacturing plant with a family of measures formula was not willing to be constrained by the traditional approach.[1] Its formula consisted of three measures: value added, quality complaints, and safety. Management felt that no single sharing ratio was appropriate in this case. Value added, at one extreme, is impacted by a wide variety of forces, many of which are out of the control of employees. The selling price of the company's products and the cost of its raw materials, for example, directly impact value added, but they are largely determined by the marketplace. In addition, improvements in value added are the main source of capital for reinvestment in the business and for rewarding the owners of the business. It would probably be inappropriate, therefore, to pay employees a sizable percentage of improvements in value added.

Table 10-2. Variable share on profitability.

Return on Investment (%)	Employee Share (%)
>20%	50%
15–20	40
10–15	30
<10	20

At the other extreme was safety. Safety is almost entirely controllable by employees, and management viewed safety improvement as a company value rather than as a source of capital. The nature of this formula called for a nontraditional sharing arrangement. The plan was therefore implemented with the following employee shares:

Value added:	30 percent
Quality complaints:	50 percent
Safety:	100 percent

A 100 percent employee share of safety improvements is actually more common than one might expect. As was suggested in the discussion on valuing gains (see Chapter 8), the direct costs of accidents may prove to be too small to generate an intense employee focus on safety, and a 100 percent employee share helps fatten the payout. And the company still gains from savings in indirect costs, assuming those costs have not been included in the valuation scheme.

The Variable Share

As with other design elements, there are creative options with respect to the share component. Foremost among these is the *variable share*. With this innovative option, the variable pay pool is determined in the normal fashion, such as by aggregating the gains from a family of measures. The sharing arrangement is not a fixed percentage, however, but is a function of some other variable, such as quality or profitability.

Profitability as a Basis for Variable Share

A variable share based on profitability might look something like that shown in Table 10-2. In this example, the employee share of the variable

Table 10-3. Payout limited by profitability.

Return on Assets (%)	Maximum Payout (%)	Return on Assets (%)	Maximum Payout (%)
6.8%	4.5%	4.8%	2.5%
6.4	4.1	4.4	2.1
6.0	3.7	4.0	1.7
5.6	3.3	<4.0	1.4
5.2	2.9		

pay gains can be 50 percent, but only if profitability is high enough to allow for substantial payouts. At progressively lower levels of profitability, the employee share declines.

In some plans, the employee share may even be zero if profitability is very low or negative. The profitability in question can be that of the company, business unit, or site. It can be operating profits, fully accounted profits, or a return measure of some kind (such as return on investment).

The purpose of this form of variable share is to moderate the payouts when profitability is inadequate and thus reduce the company's financial exposure at a time when substantial cash payouts might be financially imprudent. In a twist on the variable share idea, one plant used a profitability measure, return on assets, to limit the payout from its gain-sharing program, as shown in Table 10-3.

A related feature of the variable share is the *profit gate*. In earlier chapters, we defined a gate as a condition that must be met if there is to be any payout from the variable pay program. In its most basic and common form, a profit gate would simply require that the organization be profitable in order for bonuses to be paid. As with the variable share, the profit gate can apply to the bottom line of any organizational unit.

The obvious rationale for the profit gate is that the business cannot afford to pay bonuses if it is unprofitable. The counterargument, of course, is that the organization's losses would have been even greater had performance not improved on the plan's variables.

Some plans require that a minimum level of profitability be achieved to enable payouts. These gates are generally established at a return level that is considered to be minimally acceptable by the shareholders or owners of the business. One plan, for example, pays bonuses only if a 6 percent return on assets is achieved during the bonus period.

The disadvantage of the profit gate and the variable share based on

Table 10-4. Variable share on quality.

PPM Customer Rejects (Parts per Million)	Employee Share of Bonus Pool (%)
<3,000	0%
1,851–3,000	25
1,501–1,850	50
451–1,500	55
0–451	60

profitability is that the participants in the plan may become disgruntled and distrustful of management when bonuses are reduced or eliminated by this provision. It therefore represents another example of a design feature that makes sense from a business point of view but may have negative consequences for the credibility of the variable pay plan. As such, it probably is most appropriate where employees have a good understanding of business issues or where it would cause a financial strain for the organization if it were compelled to pay out substantial bonuses in times of low profitability. A variable share of this type would also be more credible if the profitability of the business unit or site, rather than of the entire corporation, is used.

Quality as a Basis for Variable Share

A variable share can be structured around other key variables, such as quality. An excellent example is provided by a supplier to the auto industry.[2] In this case, the gain-sharing pool is an aggregation of the savings in labor and material costs versus standard. The employee share of those gains, rather than being a fixed percentage, is based on customer rejects, expressed in parts per million, as shown in Table 10-4.

If rejects exceed 3,000 parts per million (0.3 percent), the employee share of the cost savings in this plan is zero and there is therefore no payout. As the number of rejects declines, the employee share of the cost savings increases, to a maximum of 60 percent.

Through the use of a variable share, this company has accomplished two things. First, it has incorporated an important customer-satisfaction measure into its gain-sharing program without being forced to place an explicit value on improvements in that variable. In that sense, it is similar to the modifier concept discussed in Chapter 5. More important, however,

Table 10-5. Quality-index components.

Component	Weight (%)
Returned product	35%
On-time delivery	20
Product inspections	30
Customer complaints	15

Table 10-6. Variable share on quality index.

Quality Index	Employee Share (%)
951–1000	50%
851–950	48
751–850	46
651–750	44
551–650	42
451–550	40
351–450	38
251–350	36
151–250	34
51–150	32
0–50	30

it has accorded a very high priority to customer satisfaction; poor performance on this variable can override and eliminate any cost savings that may have been achieved. Through the variable share vehicle, the company has created a self-funding variable pay plan while ensuring a high focus on customer satisfaction. The message to employees is clear: We will share cost savings with you, but not if they are obtained at the expense of customer satisfaction.

One manufacturing facility employed a quality index to determine the employee share of gains in labor productivity (as measured by pounds per hour) and scrap. The index was based on the weighted performance of four quality measures, as shown in Table 10-5. The range of the employee share was from 30 to 50 percent, as shown in Table 10-6.

Table 10-7.   Graduated variable share.

Cost Ratio (%)	Employee Share (%)	Cost Ratio (%)	Employee Share (%)
>95%	0.0%	88–89%	21.0%
94–95	4.0	87–88	23.0
93–94	7.5	86–87	25.0
92–93	11.0	85–86	26.5
91–92	14.0	84–85	27.5
90–91	16.0	83–84	28.5
89–90	19.0		

We discussed in Chapter 5 two organizations that adopted a variable share based on the results of a customer-satisfaction survey.

Other Bases and Uses for Variable Share

A variable share can also be employed for a different purpose than that of the previous examples. It can be used to provide for a graduated payout as the magnitude of the improvement increases. Higher performance, in other words, results in an ever larger employee share.

An example of this type of variable share can be found in Table 10-7. This company's variable pay formula measures total operating costs as a percent of sales. Since all of the company's operating costs are included in the formula, the company is effectively sharing operating profits. If operating costs exceed 95 percent of sales (or, looked at another way, operating profits are less than 5 percent of sales), there is no payout. As the cost ratio declines, the employee share increases, reaching a maximum of 30 percent (remember, from the earlier discussion, that broad formulas and fixed baselines justify a lower employee share). As the company points out to its employees, there is a double benefit for reducing costs: A larger percentage of a larger bonus pool is paid out.

As the examples illustrate, the addition of the variable share option to the design team's bag of tricks enhances considerably the sharing ratio's utility. This component can now go beyond the mundane purpose of splitting the pie and can also be used to better influence behaviors in desired directions and tailor the plan to meet specific company needs and priorities.

The placement of the employee share decision in the step-by-step design plan is no accident. It follows the baseline steps because, as discussed above, baseline decisions should be taken into account when considering the employee share. It also follows the system simulation step because preconceptions about the employee share may need to be modified based on the magnitude of the potential payouts.

The ultimate criterion for the employee share decision is the same as that for all other design decisions: It must make business sense. There is nothing inherently right or fair about a 50/50 division of the gains, and the best interests of the variable pay plan will be served if the design team is not too quick to jump to conclusions on this design issue.

References

1. John G. Belcher, Jr., "Gainsharing and Variable Pay: The State of the Art," *Compensation & Benefits Review*, May-June 1994.
2. Ibid.

11

Paying Bonuses

With the finalization of the employee share decision, the variable pay plan design has reached the stage where the amount of money to be paid to the participating employees can be determined. The design team can now turn its attention to the distribution of this money.

To accomplish this distribution, the team must define the frequency of bonus payments and the method of distribution to individual employees. It must also decide whether a need exists to smooth or level out short-term gains and losses to ensure that the corporation does not pay out more than is justified on the basis of the sustained improvement.

Step 12. Establish the Frequency of Bonus Payments

Unlike most other decisions faced by the design team, the basic options available for the frequency component are limited in number and easily defined. These options are:

- Weekly
- Monthly
- Quarterly
- Semiannually
- Annually

While the options are clear, the best choice may not be so apparent. The advocates of relatively frequent payouts, such as weekly or monthly, have one powerful argument, while those who favor less frequent payouts can marshal several arguments to support their cause.

Frequent vs. Infrequent Payouts

The major argument for frequent bonus payments is the need to *reinforce desired behaviors*. A major purpose of our variable pay system is, after all, to

Table 11-1. Monthly gains ($000).

January	$20	August	$(30)
February	(20)	September	30
March	20	October	(20)
April	(30)	November	20
May	30	December	(20)
June	(30)		
July	30	Total	$ 0

encourage employee involvement and teamwork in pursuit of continuous improvement. It obviously is in the best interests of the company to modify employee behaviors toward this end as expeditiously as possible. It only stands to reason, then, that employees should be reinforced promptly through the variable pay system when these behaviors occur. If the reinforcement is far distant in time from the occurrence of the behaviors, companies should not be surprised if the pace of change is relatively slow.

If behavior reinforcement were the only consideration, we would expect to find the vast majority of variable pay plans paying bonuses at least monthly. But this is not the case. There must, therefore, be some advantages to less frequent payouts.

One such advantage is the potential for *larger payouts.* A system with an annual payout, for example, has the potential to produce a much larger bonus check than does one with a monthly payout provision. Which situation would produce greater reinforcement—a $50 check every month or a $600 check at the end of the year? It may be advantageous to trade off frequent reinforcement for the high impact of a large bonus payment.

Another benefit of infrequent payouts is the *smoothing effect.* Consider a hypothetical gain-sharing program in which the dollar gains recorded for a variable pay program over a twelve-month period are presented in Table 11-1.

The total gains over the course of the year, for the purposes of the bonus calculation, will vary considerably, depending on the payout frequency chosen:

Monthly:	$150,000
Quarterly:	$50,000
Semiannually:	$10,000
Annually:	$0

In our example, monthly losses exactly offset monthly gains, and there is no improvement for the year. With a monthly payout provision, however, bonuses would have been paid in the six months when a gain occurred. The company would have incurred increased compensation costs with no concomitant benefit. Such an outcome is surely not what management had in mind and does not bode well for the company's continued support for the variable pay plan.

With less frequent payout periods, there is some offsetting of gains and losses, and total bonus payments over the course of the year are reduced accordingly. But only an annual payout in this case will save the company from paying some bonuses in a year when no net improvement occurred.

The hypothetical situation portrayed in Table 11-1 is exaggerated for effect; a company that experiences alternating gains and losses on its performance variables every month has problems that variable pay won't solve. However, where payouts are relatively frequent, such as monthly, even an occasional deficit in a gain-sharing or profit-sharing program can result in excess bonus payments. There are other solutions to this problem without resorting to annual payouts and therefore losing the benefits of frequent reinforcement. These smoothing mechanisms will be discussed in detail later in this chapter as Step 13.

The third advantage of less frequent payouts is *lower administrative costs*. The distribution of bonuses does involve some costs, such as those associated with cutting and distributing checks, and updating payroll and accounting records. Clearly, less frequent payouts will reduce these particular costs. The system should be designed to minimize these costs, however, and this argument should be secondary to the other criteria.

A research project sponsored by the American Compensation Association found that the prevalence of the various frequency alternatives for "operational plans" (defined by the researchers as those based on formulas other than bottom-line measures) were as follows:[1]

Annually: 34 percent
Semiannually: 4 percent
Quarterly: 26 percent
Monthly: 19 percent
*More frequently
    than monthly:* 17 percent

The fact that annual payouts represented the most widely used alternative undoubtedly relates to management's desire that bonus payments reflect the full year's performance. It may also be a reflection of management's experiences with executive bonus systems, which generally pay out on an annual basis. The tradeoff, however, is infrequent reinforcement of desired behaviors, as discussed above. This is probably not a good trade-off when the primary purpose of the variable pay plan is to support cultural change.

The study found that annual payments were even more prevalent (67 percent) for plans that are based on bottom-line measures—basically the equivalent of profit sharing as we have defined it. This is not surprising when one considers that behavioral change is often less of an objective with profit-sharing plans. The point must be stressed again, however, that any company that does not have behavioral change as an objective is missing a major opportunity to use its pay system to support development of a high-involvement, high-performance culture.

A few plans accrue bonuses on a monthly basis but pay out quarterly (or accrue quarterly and pay out annually). A bonus earned in any month, in other words, is unconditionally earned and cannot be offset by a loss incurred in another month. This approach enjoys some of the benefits of a quarterly payout (larger amounts, lower administrative costs), while having a greater reinforcement effect than would a pure quarterly payout. It does however, sacrifice the smoothing effect of a quarterly payout.

Unequal Payout Periods and Variable Frequencies

There is no rule, of course, that requires that all payout periods be of equal length (every three months, every six months, etc.). One components plant in an automotive company has a very successful gain-sharing program that pays bonuses twice a year. What is unusual is that the payout periods run from January through July and from August through December. This seven-month/five-month arrangement came about because of the complications presented by the annual model changeovers in the auto industry.

More than one organization has adopted a monthly frequency, with the payout periods coinciding with a four-week, four-week, five-week accounting cycle rather than with the calendar months. Coinciding payout periods with the accounting cycle saves a considerable amount of administrative work in these cases.

Another variation from the standard frequency options is *variable frequency*. With this alternative, the payout period is not fixed. Rather, a gain-sharing pool accumulates until it contains a predetermined amount of money. The pool might continue to build, for example, until it contains $50,000, at which point it is paid out.

A variable frequency serves two purposes. First, it ensures that bonus payments are always substantial and therefore strongly reinforce the behaviors that brought about the improvement. Second, it provides some protection against the payment of bonuses for short-term gains (at least those that are less than the payout threshold level) that are not sustained.

Frequency of Communication of Results

Before concluding our discussion of frequency, one related issue must be touched upon: the frequency of communication of results. Regardless of the payout period, plan performance should be communicated to the participating employees at least monthly. Feedback is a powerful tool; it reinforces positive improvement behaviors, and it enables employees to problem-solve around issues that are impeding improvement in the plan measures. Without feedback, employees have no way of knowing whether their efforts are producing the desired results. (This subject will be explored further in Chapter 13.) The less frequent the payout period, the more important this interim communication becomes. Failing to provide monthly updates would be a major mistake in a semiannual or annual payout plan.

Step 13. Develop a Provision to Protect Against Overpayment of Bonuses

The feature addressed by the design team at this juncture in the design process is an optional one; a variable pay plan *can* function without a smoothing mechanism. This step, however, must not be ignored, for it may have great bearing on the viability of the system. If the team chooses *not* to have a smoothing mechanism, the reason should be that there is no need for one, not that the team failed to consider this step.

A *smoothing mechanism* is most needed when payouts are relatively frequent and where there is a substantial risk that some periods may produce a loss, rather than a gain. In these situations, it is critical that the design team develop a provision to protect against overpayment owing to business volatility, seasonality, or random variation in the formula measures.

As an illustration, assume that a design team developing a gain-sharing program has opted for a quarterly payout. Hypothetical results, assuming a 50 percent employee share, are shown in Table 11-2. Over the course of the year, the company in this scenario would pay bonuses of $40,000 on a gain of $60,000. Without a smoothing feature, the company's share of the full-year gains would amount to 33 percent rather than the intended 50 percent.

Now look at the example in Table 11-3, where the fourth quarter gain

Table 11-2. Quarterly payout, I ($000).

	Gains	Employee Share
Quarter 1	$20	$10
Quarter 2	(20)	—
Quarter 3	30	15
Quarter 4	30	15
Total	$60	$40

Table 11-3. Quarterly payout, II ($000).

	Gains	Employee Share
Quarter 1	$20	$10
Quarter 2	(20)	—
Quarter 3	30	15
Quarter 4	(30)	—
Total	$ 0	$25

is turned into a loss. In this scenario, the company paid $25,000 in bonuses. Unfortunately for the company, there was no gain to fund those bonuses for the year. As suggested earlier in the discussion on payout frequency, paying bonuses when no net improvement has occurred is not meeting the needs of the business and will not gladden the hearts of management or shareholders.

One solution to this problem, as we learned previously, is to lengthen the payout period. By doing so, gains realized in one quarter would be at least partly offset by losses incurred in other quarters. Extending the payout frequency to an annual basis, in fact, would eliminate the problem. It is impossible to pay out a greater than intended share of annual gains if the bonus is based on annual results.

There are other solutions, however, that would at least partly protect

Table 11-4. Quarterly payout with deficit reserve ($000).

	Gains	Employee Share	Reserve	Amount Paid
Quarter 1	$20	$10	$ 3.0	$ 7.0
Quarter 2	(20)	—	(10.0)	—
Quarter 3	30	15	4.5	10.5
Quarter 4	30	15	4.5	10.5
Total	$60	$40	$ 2.0	$28.0

the company against overpayment of bonuses while allowing for the greater reinforcement that comes with more frequent payouts.

Deficit Reserve

The most widely used mechanism is the deficit reserve. Under this alternative, a percentage of the employee share is withheld and credited to a special account established for this purpose on the books of the company. When a deficit occurs, the employee share of this deficit is charged against this reserve account. At the end of the plan year, the balance in the reserve account is zeroed out. If there is a positive balance, it is paid out to the participating employees; if the balance is negative, it is written off and absorbed by the company.

The scenario in Table 11-2 is shown again in Table 11-4, but with the addition of a 30 percent holdback for a deficit reserve. The amount paid out to employees over the course of the year has now been reduced to $28,000. We have solved the company's excess payments problem without resorting to annual payouts. Note that the $2,000 remaining in the reserve at year-end must be paid out to the participating employees in order to bring their share of the full year's gain up to 50 percent.

The deficit reserve does not, however, provide absolute protection against overpayment of bonuses by the company. Looking back at the scenario in Table 11-3, it is apparent that no reserve amount, short of 100 percent, will enable the company to avoid paying some bonuses in a year in which it realized no net improvement. And a 100 percent reserve would be pointless, as it would be no different than an annual payout.

A variation on the traditional approach to the deficit reserve is to deduct the reserve amount from the total gain rather than from the em-

Table 11-5. Quarterly payout with deficit reserve deducted from total gain ($000).

	Gains	Reserve	Net Gain	Employee Share
Quarter 1	$20	$ 6	$14	$ 7.0
Quarter 2	(20)	(20)	—	—
Quarter 3	30	9	21	10.5
Quarter 4	30	9	21	10.5
Total	$60	$ 4	$56	$28.0

ployee share of the gain. This alternative, which is demonstrated in Table 11-5, may improve employee receptivity to a deficit reserve, as there often exists a perception that it is unfair to hold back part of the employee share only. If this variation is employed, two changes to the arithmetic must be made: 100 percent of the deficit must be charged to the reserve account, and only the employee share of any positive balance at year-end should be distributed to the participating employees. The final result obtained is then exactly the same as that of the more traditional approach.

The percentage withheld for the deficit reserve varies widely, with most plans falling within the range of 10 to 50 percent. The appropriate percentage should be a function of the risk to the company; the greater the risk of losses, the higher the percentage should be. The design team can gauge this risk by referring back to the charts developed at Step 5 (see Chapter 7). A high degree of volatility in the plan's measures would argue for a relatively high reserve percentage. Before adopting a high percentage, however, the design team should consider two potentially negative effects:

1. A high reserve percentage may reduce the amount available for payouts to a level that is inadequate for effective reinforcement of desired behaviors. Whether or not this is a problem can be ascertained by reviewing the simulations conducted at Step 9 (see Chapter 9).
2. A high withholding may not be well received by the participating employees, particularly where they lack knowledge about the dynamics of the formula that justify the high percentage.

The year-end treatment of the deficit reserve must also be defined by the design team. As was suggested earlier, most plans provide for the balance in the reserve account to be zeroed out at year-end. If the balance is positive, it is necessary to pay out this amount to the employees in order to bring their total payments up to the full employee share as defined in the plan. If the balance is negative, the company absorbs the amount in question in order to start the new year fresh.

There is an alternative to this traditional year-end treatment. In some plans, the reserve balance is maintained and carried over into the new year. Termed a *continuous accrual reserve*, this option practically eliminates the risk that the company will incur a deficit in the variable pay plan and be unable to recover that deficit from future gains in the same year.

If this approach is adopted, however, one additional complication must be addressed. If deficits are small relative to gains or infrequent in their occurrence, the magnitude of the reserve balance may grow quite large, and employees will rightfully want to receive their fair share of gains that may have occurred long ago. This problem is handled by establishing a *trigger mechanism:* When the reserve balance reaches a certain predefined level, it is at least partly paid out.

The deficit reserve is by far the most common approach to the volatility problem. The design team, however, should not conclude from this fact that the deficit reserve is the best solution to the problem. There are several additional, lesser-known, alternatives that may prove to be both more effective and easier to sell to the participating employees.

Rolling Average Payout

One of these alternatives is the *rolling average payout*. In this approach, two or more periods are averaged in order to determine the gain to be shared. Assuming a quarterly payout and a two-quarter rolling average, the pool for the first quarter would be calculated by averaging the gains achieved in the first quarter and the fourth quarter of the previous year. The second quarter pool would be based on the average gain from the first and second quarters, and so on. This rolling average technique ensures that a loss in any quarter will be offset against the subsequent quarter's gain (if there is one). Looking back at the scenario in Table 11-2, the employee share in the third quarter would be reduced from $15,000 to $5,000 (50 percent of the average gain from the second and third quarters) with a two-quarter rolling payout.

The number of periods over which gains may be averaged is not limited to two. A four-quarter rolling payout would actually eliminate the volatility problem entirely by ensuring that bonuses always reflect a year's performance. In effect, the plan benefits from the smoothing effect of an annual payout while maintaining the reinforcement of a quarterly payout.

The disadvantage of the rolling payout is that it dampens the magnitude, and therefore the reinforcing effect, of any large improvements. A period in which a substantial gain occurs will be averaged with smaller gains in previous periods and thereby diluted. The greater smoothing effect of including more periods in the averaging process therefore involves an increasing tradeoff that should be considered before making a decision to incorporate a rolling average payout in the plan.

Unlike the other smoothing alternatives, the rolling average payout presents the team with a bit of a complication at the plan startup. How should the first quarter of a quarterly payout plan be treated? Should it be averaged with prior quarters when the plan was not even in effect? This can be, and often is, done. If, however, this approach produces a result that is undesirable or does not make sense, an alternative treatment is available.

In the case of a two-quarter rolling payout provision, one-half of the employee share would be paid in the first quarter, and the rolling average arithmetic would begin in the second quarter. An analogous approach (somewhat more complicated) could be implemented for a four-quarter rolling payout. The payout in the first quarter would be one-fourth of that quarter's gain; the second-quarter payout would consist of one-fourth of the first quarter's gain plus one-fourth of the second quarter's gain; and so on.

Loss Recovery

Another alternative to the deficit reserve is *loss recovery*. This approach requires that employee payouts for future gains be reduced (or even eliminated) following a deficit. If, for example, a deficit was incurred in a gainsharing program with a 50/50 share, the employee share might be reduced to 25 percent in periods subsequent to the loss. This reduced share would remain in effect until the foregone bonuses offset the employee share of the earlier deficit, at which time the normal share would be reinstated. Unlike the deficit reserve, the loss recovery method does ensure that losses will eventually be recovered, assuming the plan remains in existence and realizes sufficient gains in the future.

The loss recovery alternative also carries a downside; when a substantial loss occurs, reinforcement and motivation may be reduced for a considerable period of time because of the reduced payout potential. For this reason, many plans with a loss recovery feature contain a provision that limits the recovery period to, for example, one year.

Year-to-Date Payout

The final alternative to the deficit reserve is a *year-to-date payout*. This method quantifies the appropriate employee payout for the year-to-date period, then subtracts the amounts that have been paid out in previous periods. With the scenario in Table 11-2, the year-to-date gain for the third quarter would be $30,000, with an associated employee share of $15,000. Since the plan has already paid out $10,000, only $5,000 would be paid in the third quarter.

As with the other methods, the year-to-date payout has a disadvantage: Its effectiveness is reduced when deficits occur later in the year. It would have no impact at all on a fourth-quarter deficit in a quarterly payout plan, as there are no future periods remaining against which the deficit can be offset.

Choosing a Smoothing Mechanism

As with other design components, there is no right or wrong choice with respect to the mechanisms used to smooth volatility or recover deficits. Each of the alternatives has advantages and disadvantages, as summarized in Table 11-6. The decision should be based on the dynamics of the formula, an evaluation of the tradeoffs, and the needs of the business.

While smoothing mechanisms are very common in profit-sharing and gain-sharing programs, they are far less prevalent in goal-sharing systems. Since goal-sharing plans, by their very nature, reward the achievement of objectives that generally represent improvements over past performance, there is considerably less risk to the company that bonuses will be paid when performance over the course of the year does not justify doing so. The fact that a goal was not achieved on an annual basis does not necessarily mean that performance on that variable declined. All it means is that performance did not increase enough to meet the goal. The same can be said for gain-sharing programs that employ target baselines, such as those based on budget or business plan assumptions rather than historical baselines.

The company's risk is even less if certain conditions exist in a goal-sharing program (or a gain-sharing plan with target baselines):

- The goals or targets represent considerable improvements from current performance levels.
- The payouts represent a relatively small share of the gains associated with achieving the goals or exceeding the targets.

Table 11-6. Advantages and disadvantages of smoothing mechanism alternatives.

Method	Advantages	Disadvantages
• Deficit reserve	Withholds only part of bonus.	Ineffective where defects are large or frequent.
• Rolling average payout	Achieves smoothing effect of less frequent payout.	Reduces reinforcement for high-gain periods.
• Loss recovery	Eliminates/reduces payouts until deficit is recovered.	Reduces motivation after deficit has occurred.
• Year-to-date payout	Payouts cannot exceed year-to-date gain.	Ineffective when deficits occur late in year.

In sum, a smoothing mechanism is not an absolute requirement for a variable pay program, but it probably makes sense more often than not for gain-sharing and profit-sharing programs. The critical determinant of the need for such a feature is the volatility of the plan's measures, within the context of the payout frequency. A measure that is quite volatile on a monthly basis may be very stable on a quarterly or semiannual basis.

The charts that were developed by the team at Step 5 (see Chapter 7) will again prove invaluable here, as a measure's volatility will be apparent at a glance.

Step 14. Establish the Method of Distribution of Bonuses to Employees

With the design team's completion of the previous step, the amount of money that is available to be distributed to participating employees can now be established. The next logical step is to distribute that money.

At first glance, this may appear to be a simple and straightforward step. Nothing, however, could be further from the truth. Decisions made here may have a major impact on the perceived fairness of the variable pay plan, and the design team's ability to deal constructively with conflict and frustration may be sorely tested in the process. And the difficulties associated with these decisions are exacerbated by a legal constraint that severely limits the team's flexibility to develop creative alternatives.

There are three basic methods for distributing bonuses to individual employees, which are discussed in the following sections. There are also several variations on the basic methods.

Percent of Income Distribution

Under the *percent-of-income* distribution method, bonuses are expressed as a percentage of the individual's total compensation. For those plans in which a pool is established (profit sharing and gain sharing), the percentage is obtained by dividing the amount of money to be distributed by the total payroll dollars for the participating employees. For goal-sharing plans, the payout for achieving each goal is simply stated as a percentage, such as 2 percent.

There are two arguments to support the percent-of-income approach. The first is based on the assumption that an individual's value to the organization is reflected by that person's level of compensation. If one individual earns higher pay than another, the differential presumably exists because of differences in the contributions those individuals make to the business. The logical extension of this line of thinking is that the higher-earning employee also contributes more to any improvement that may take place in the variable pay measures. Distributing bonuses as a percent of income simply recognizes these differences by paying larger bonuses to higher-paid employees.

The second argument for the percent-of-income distribution is that it provides for an equal relative level of reinforcement for all plan participants. An individual earning $40,000 would, theoretically, require twice the bonus of an individual earning $20,000 in order to experience the same level of gratification and motivation.

The disadvantage of the percent-of-income method is that the differentials in payments may be incongruent with the fact that variable pay is a team reward. It does not necessarily follow that higher-paid employees are better team members, and bonus differentials may aggravate any perceptions of inequity in the base compensation system. This may lead to dissatisfaction among lower-paid employees and work against the establishment of a team-oriented culture.

Equal-Shares Distribution

These concerns lead many design teams to favor the *equal-shares* distribution method. This alternative produces equal dollar bonuses for all employees. To obtain the equal-share amount, the amount of money to be distributed is divided by the number of participating employees.

The major problem with equal shares is the existence of a legal constraint that complicates matters considerably. (The legal requirements will be discussed below, following a review of the third distribution alternative.) The equal-shares approach also fails to provide an automatic proration method for those employees who do not work a full bonus period. The percent-of-income and the hours-worked (see next section) alternatives, on the other hand, provide reduced bonuses for those employees who were not on the job throughout the period.

Hours-Worked Distribution

The *hours-worked* distribution method allocates the bonus pool to the individual participants based on the number of hours worked (or, alternatively, hours paid). Like the other basic options, the arithmetic is simple: The money to be distributed is divided by the total hours worked or paid. The result is a dollars-per-hour payout figure. This amount is then multiplied by each individual's qualifying hours to accomplish the distribution.

Advocates of the hours-worked approach like the fact that the highest bonus payments go to those employees who spent the most time on the job. Another perspective is that it penalizes employees whose attendance is deficient (although the percent-of-income method will also have this characteristic for an hourly paid employee).

The biggest problem with the hours-worked method is that it is not relevant for exempt employees. The only way to incorporate these people into the plan is to pay them for a fixed number of hours, such as the standard forty hours per week. This presents a potential problem, as salaried employees are now receiving lower bonuses than many, if not most, of the hourly employees. This may not sit well with the salaried employees, who often do work additional hours without receiving overtime compensation. It may be particularly annoying for the first-line supervisor, whose bonus may well be less than that paid to each of his subordinates. For this reason, some plans credit salaried employees for a greater number of hours, such as forty-five or fifty. Whatever number is chosen, it will, by necessity, be arbitrary and seen as inequitable by at least some people in the organization.

Another concern commonly expressed about the hours-worked distribution method stems from the fact that overtime opportunities are not equal for all employees. Some individuals will be put at a disadvantage relative to other employees because of the nature of their jobs. Those employees also will likely view this distribution approach as inequitable.

Legal Issues

The legal constraint mentioned earlier complicates the decision regarding payout distribution. The Fair Labor Standards Act requires that bonuses be treated as regular compensation for the purposes of calculating the overtime premium for nonexempt employees. By paying a bonus, the company has, in effect, increased the employee's hourly pay rate and, since hours worked in excess of forty per week must be compensated at a 50 percent premium, the individual's overtime rate as well. To meet these legal requirements, the company, after paying a bonus, must make a retroactive overtime adjustment covering the overtime hours worked during the period covered by the bonus. This requirement is not greeted with enthusiasm by most companies.

Fortunately, the law does recognize some exceptions to this rule. There are four major ones:

1. *Profit-sharing bonuses.* The law clearly states that bonuses must be paid from a bona fide profit-sharing plan in order to qualify for this exclusion from the rule. That is, they must indeed represent a share of the organization's profits. Bonuses resulting from gain-sharing and goal-sharing plans clearly do not meet this requirement.
2. This exclusion applies only to those *bonuses that are paid at management's discretion* and are not tied to any performance requirements or measures that have been established in advance.
3. *Gifts.* Variable pay plans clearly do not meet the test for this exception.
4. *Bonuses paid as a percent of the employees' total compensation.* The rationale for this exemption is that the additional compensation due the overtime worker is contained in the bonus itself. This is true only if the overtime premium is included in the compensation figure against which the bonus percentage is applied. Paying the bonus as a percent of each individual's base pay therefore would not be in compliance with the law.

That final point provides the way out for the company. Adopting the percent-of-income distribution method allows bonuses to be paid without

Table 11-7.   Hours with overtime adjustment.

	Total	Individual
Straight-time hours	42,400	170
Overtime hours	7,600	30
Overtime premium hours (50%)	3,800	15
Total variable pay hours	53,000	215

retroactive overtime adjustments. It is not surprising that this method is the most commonly employed.

Unfortunately, the percent-of-income alternative tends to be unpopular with many employees in many companies. Debate over this issue has brought more than one design team almost to an impasse. The only solution one design team could find was to pay half the bonus as a percent of income and the other half in equal shares! The company was obligated, of course, to adjust overtime pay for the equal-share half of the bonus.

The equal-share distribution method is actually quite common, accounting for perhaps 25 percent of existing plans.[2] A great many, if not the majority, of these plans, however, do not provide for overtime adjustments and are therefore in conflict with the law. In most cases, this situation reflects an ignorance of the law rather than an intentional violation.

More and more companies, on the other hand, are adopting the equal-share approach and making the overtime adjustments because of a desire to ensure that the plan is viewed as equitable by most employees. Since the information required to make these adjustments resides in computers in most companies, the administrative burden is generally not as great as might be initially feared.

In addition to the administrative complications, companies are often concerned about the cost of the added overtime payments. This can be addressed, however, by subtracting an estimate of the incremental overtime payments from the pool before calculating the distribution amount.

It should be noted that there is a variation on the hours-worked distribution method that complies with the intent of the law, but not the letter of the law. This variation involves paying bonuses on the overtime premium hours as well as the straight-time hours. Overtime hours, in other words, would earn one and one-half hours' worth of bonus, as shown in Table 11-7. When this is done, the worker receives additional overtime compensation, in the form of a higher bonus, just as that individual would under the percent-of-income distribution method. Unfortunately this ap-

Table 11-8. Segmented pool.

	Total	Non-Exempt	Exempt
Employees			
Number	200	150	50
Percent	100%	75%	25%
Variable pay pool	$60,000	$45,000	$15,000
Payroll	$1,200,000	$940,000	$520,000
Percent payout		4.8%	2.9%
Average bonus		$300	$300

proach is not cited by the law as one of the acceptable exclusions from the overtime rule, so its legality is questionable. An attorney should therefore be consulted by any design team seeking to adopt this distribution method.

There are also some variations on the percent-of-income distribution method that provide the design team some additional flexibility. A number of variable pay plans place a cap on the amount of a bonus that can be received by an exempt employee. This cap is usually established at the level of the bonus paid to the highest earning nonexempt employee during the period. The feature serves to reduce the bonuses paid to the highest paid management participants and thus assuages, to some degree, the fairness concerns of the hourly employees.

Another variation on the percent-of-income approach is the *segmented pool*. While the law exempts percent-of-income payouts from the overtime rule, it does not require that all employees receive the same percentage. This opens up many possibilities for creating multiple pools in an effort to lessen the differentials in payout amounts.

As one example, the employee share of the pool could be subdivided into separate pools for exempt and nonexempt employees, as shown in Table 11-8. The basis for the division would be the number of employees in each category; if, for example, 75 percent of the participants were nonexempt, their subpool would receive 75 percent of the available dollars. The distribution of the nonexempt pool would be accomplished through the percent-of-income method to meet the legal requirements, while the exempt pool could be distributed by any method desired.

Segmenting the pool in this manner achieves an outcome that equal-

Table 11-9. Advantages and disadvantages of distribution alternatives.

Method	Advantages	Disadvantages
• Percent of income	Reflects pay differentials. Equal reinforcement.	Incongruent with team concept.
• Equal shares	Supports team orientation.	Requires overtime adjustments. Lacks automatic proration.
• Hours worked	Reflects time contribution.	Unequal bonus opportunity. Exempt employee complication.

share advocates would deem to be an improvement over the traditional percent-of-income method using a single pool: Exempt and nonexempt employees would, on average, receive equal bonuses.

Other variations on the segmented pool are possible as well. The pool could be divided, for example, into high-income and low-income pools, again based on the number of participants in each group. Both pools would then be distributed by the percent-of-income method. The lower earners would thus receive a higher percentage bonus than would the higher earners. This variation, like the previous one, provides a payout scheme that is at least closer to the equal-share idea.

It should be noted that the segmented pool cannot be carried to its logical extreme: segmenting the pool by individual. This, of course, achieves the desired outcome of equal dollar payouts, but has been ruled by the authorities to be an obvious and unacceptable attempt to circumvent the law.

It would be advisable to thoroughly analyze any segmented pool scheme, as these approaches can produce some other inequities that may damage the credibility of the variable pay system. In the exempt/nonexempt scheme, for example, some supervisors may receive lower bonuses than some of their subordinates. In the case of the high-income/low-income scheme, about half of the higher-paid employees will receive a lower dollar bonus than half of the lower-paid employees. The advantages and disadvantages of the three basic distribution methods are summarized in Table 11-9.

For this component of the variable pay plan, there is probably no alternative that everyone involved will feel good about. Whatever the design team chooses to do, a sizable number of people will not like it. The team needs to set its expectations accordingly, make the best decision it can make within the constraints of the law, and move on down the road.

References

1. Jerry L. McAdams and Elizabeth J. Hawk, *Organizational Performance and Rewards* (Scottsdale, Ariz.: American Compensation Association, 1994).
2. Ibid.

12

Completing the System Design

Having completed the steps that enable bonuses to be distributed to the participating employees, the design team has largely finished the design of the variable pay system. What remains are a few peripheral issues.

Step 15. Define Procedures for Capital Investment Adjustments

Investments in plant and equipment are a normal and continuous activity in most businesses. These capital investments are made with shareholder money or borrowed funds, and they are justified on the basis of an anticipated return that will be earned on the investment. (We will ignore those investments that are made for nonfinancial reasons, such as complying with environmental regulations.) This return comes about through lower labor costs, reduced waste of materials, higher quality, or other forms of performance improvement. Most companies, in fact, have an established *hurdle rate*, or minimum level of return, that must be earned in order for the investment to be justified and approved by management.

Very often, the improvements generated by capital investments are reflected in the variable pay measures. A capital investment that reduced the labor hours required to produce outputs, for example, would be expected to increase any measure of labor productivity. As a result, many of the improvements associated with capital investments would be shared with the participants in the variable pay plan, and the return earned by the company would therefore be correspondingly reduced. It would be incumbent upon management to take this into account before making the investment, and, as a consequence, many proposed capital investments would fail to achieve the hurdle rate of return and would not be approved.

The net effect of all this is that the variable pay plan has distorted capital investment decisions.

This is not a desirable outcome, as competitors whose capital investment decision-making process is not encumbered by a variable pay plan would be making these investments and potentially gaining a competitive advantage. To avoid this problem, most variable pay plans contain a provision that requires the plan to be adjusted when major capital investments are made so that the gain attributable to the investment is not shared with employees.

The mechanics of this adjustment are relatively straightforward in theory. The baseline or goal for the affected variable pay measure is simply adjusted, or tightened, by an amount equal to the amount of improvement brought about by the capital investment. Take, for example, a units-per-hour productivity measure with a baseline of 50 and current performance level of 55. Assume that a new piece of machinery is installed, and, as a direct result, productivity improves to 58 units per hour. The adjustment is made by adding the gain that is attributable to the capital investment—3 units per hour—to the baseline. The new baseline is 53 and the new performance level is 58; the gain for variable pay purposes (5 units per hour) has not changed.

Reality does not always cooperate with theory, however, and capital investment adjustments are rarely this simple to execute. The true impact of a capital investment is often difficult, if not impossible, to ascertain. In many companies, there is no attempt made to measure the true impact after new capital equipment is installed. Even where there is a process for tracking the results, it may be very difficult to isolate the investment's impact from other factors. The only data available in many cases are those used in making the estimate of the savings as part of the capital investment approval process. The credibility of these estimates in many companies, unfortunately, is low.

In addition, computation of the baseline adjustment may be quite complex and little understood by the plan participants. This may lead to skepticism and suspicions that the plan is being manipulated in some way.

Limiting the Number of Adjustments

In view of these difficulties, it is generally advisable to minimize the number of capital investment adjustments. This is typically accomplished by requiring these adjustments only when a capital investment of major proportions is implemented. The amount of investment required to qualify as "major" will, of course, vary from one organization to another.

The design team should review the capital investments made in previous years, as well as those planned for the future, and establish an appropriate threshold investment level that can serve to trigger an adjustment to the variable pay plan. This threshold level might be as low as $10,000 for a small organization or as high as several million dollars for a large capital-intensive facility. Ideally, the level selected should be such that it is not likely to be exceeded more than once or twice a year. An alternative to limiting the number of adjustments is to implement all the necessary adjustments at one time, such as at the end of the plan year.

Rather than define the threshold in terms of a dollar value, a few plans establish as the threshold *the amount of improvement* brought about by the capital investment. One well-known company, for example, implements a baseline adjustment for any investment that improves the variable pay formula by 2 percent or more.

Where there is a reluctance to establish a specific investment threshold, the decision to make an adjustment can be left to management or, preferably, an employee-management committee that has been charged with managing the variable pay process on an ongoing basis (see Chapter 13).

Timing and Other Considerations

The design team should also address the *timing of the adjustments* (assuming they are made individually rather than all at once at year-end). Generally, there should be a time lag between implementation of the capital investment and execution of the plan adjustment. There are two reasons for delaying the adjustment:

1. *The expected performance improvement does not normally occur instantaneously with the installation of new capital equipment.* In fact, there may even be an initial deterioration in performance owing to disruption of the production process or normal problems associated with the startup of new equipment. Under these circumstances, it would be patently unfair to adjust the baselines for improvements that have yet to occur.

2. *Lagging the adjustment would encourage employees to bring the new equipment up to its full operating potential as quickly as possible.* Thus they would have the opportunity to share in the resulting performance improvement prior to the adjustment date.

A typical plan provision would require that all capital investment adjustments be made three months following the installation of the equipment. Some plans leave the timing of the adjustment to the discretion of the committee, referenced above, that is managing the variable pay plan.

A variation on this design element is *partial adjustment*. With this alternative, gains related to capital investments are only partly eliminated from the system, typically by an adjustment amounting to 80 percent of the realized improvement. This option is designed to increase employee support for capital investments by sharing at least a portion of the related improvements. As teams take on ever greater responsibilities for managing their work areas, the likelihood of the team generating capital investment ideas increases proportionally. Because of concerns that full, or even partial, adjustments might discourage these activities, some plans exempt *employee-generated ideas* from the adjustment requirement. Alternatively, a smaller partial adjustment, such as 50 percent, might be made for these team-generated capital investments.

A company in the defense industry went even further to support employee involvement in capital investment initiatives. Ten percent of the gains recorded by a plant gain-sharing program are allocated to a special account that is used to fund improvement ideas generated by employees. This account is administered by an employee committee that is empowered to invest this money in any way that it believes will best contribute to further improvements in performance. The only management input is provided by the plant controller, who serves the committee in an advisory capacity.

When Capital Investment Adjustments May Be Unnecessary

Certain plan design features may reduce, or even eliminate entirely, the need for capital investment adjustments. In a goal-sharing program, the level of the goals established each year could reflect the impact of recent past, as well as anticipated, capital investments. Only an unplanned or unanticipated capital expenditure would create a need to adjust the goals.

This provision may also be unnecessary for a gain-sharing plan in which the baselines are reset annually to a level that is equal to the prior year's performance. In this situation, the impact of any capital investments that occurred in the prior year would be automatically reflected, at least to some degree, in the new year's baseline.

Capital investment adjustments might also be deemed to be unnecessary for a cost formula that includes depreciation as one of the cost elements; higher depreciation costs would offset, at least to some degree, the performance improvements generated by capital investments.

Finally, some gain-sharing design teams, wishing to avoid the complications of capital investment adjustments, adopt a lower employee share than would otherwise be appropriate on the basis that employees will receive "windfall" gains from capital investments. A mining company and their unions, as an example, agreed philosophically that gains should be shared 50/50, but implemented a plan with a 40 percent employee share in order to avoid the complications of capital investment adjustments.

In summary, capital investment adjustments represent a complication for a variable pay plan, but one that is necessary in most cases in order to avoid distorting capital investment decisions. To minimize the complications, the design team should write into the plan a provision that requires these adjustments be made only for major capital investments.

Step 16. Establish a Cap on Bonus Payments, If Appropriate

Some variable pay plans place a cap, or upper limit, on payouts. The caps generally range from 5 to 10 percent of pay, although examples outside of this range can certainly be found.

This issue is meaningful only for gain-sharing and profit-sharing plans. Goal-sharing plans, by their very nature, contain a built-in cap: Bonuses cannot exceed the amount that would be paid if all the plan's goals are achieved. This built-in limit on payouts is, in fact, one of the attractions of goal sharing, as discussed in Chapter 4.

In theory, there should be no need for a cap, at least for those plans that are self-funding. There would be no reason, presumably, to limit the improvement potential by capping the payout when the company is receiving a share of the gains. Caps, nonetheless, are not uncommon, and the justification for them tends to fall into one or more of the following categories:

- *The variable pay plan is new and management feels the need for protection against the possibility that a flawed plan design will produce bonuses that are larger than is justified by the improvements realized.* In these situations, management is often willing to remove the cap after the plan has proved over time to be reliable.
- *There is a possibility that external or extraordinary events could produce large "windfall" bonuses.* This might be the case for a producer or buyer of a commodity with extremely volatile pricing characteristics (assuming, of course, that the commodity's price affects the variable pay formula).
- *Base pay levels are high relative to competition.* The payment of high bonuses could bring total compensation to a level that is untenable in the marketplace.

One company used a cap as a limiting mechanism during times of poor financial results. Its plan contained a provision that allowed the company to limit payouts to 10 percent of compensation if the company was unprofitable on a year-to-date basis.

Plans that provide for regularly changing baselines or goals (see Chapter 9) have less need for a cap than those with fixed baselines. It is unlikely that excessively large bonuses would be earned where the baseline is continuously tightening, and any "windfall" bonuses would work their way out of the system over time. This does not mean, however, that caps are unheard of in these systems.

As might be expected, caps generally are not received with enthusiasm by the participants in a variable pay plan. And they can limit the amount of improvement that will be effected by the employees. Management should give careful consideration to these realities before concluding that a cap is a necessary element of the plan.

Step 17. Establish a Minimum Payout Provision, If Appropriate

While capping the payout may be appropriate only under certain conditions, placing a floor on the amount of bonus paid almost always makes sense. There has been more than one occasion where checks of a few dollars (or, in at least one case, less than a dollar) were distributed to plan participants. These occurrences generally are not positive experiences, for either the company or the employees.

To avoid paying out very small amounts, the design team should incorporate a minimum payout provision in most variable pay plans, with the possible exception of goal-sharing plans. Just as a goal-sharing plan has a built-in cap, so does it have a built-in minimum; it cannot pay out an amount less than that associated with achieving a single goal. And it would not make sense in any event to establish a very small payout for any of the plan's goals, as there would be little motivational value as a result.

Minimum payouts are usually expressed as a *dollar amount,* typically ranging between $10 and $50. If the percent-of-income or hours-worked distribution method is employed (see Chapter 11), a minimum dollar amount would normally be stated as an average payout rather than an absolute dollar minimum. If this were not done, a situation could arise where some employees receive bonuses (because their payout is above the minimum) while others do not. Alternatively, the minimum payout provision could be triggered if any employee's bonus fell below the minimum. One design team, for example, established that payouts would be deferred if any participant's bonus was less than $75.

Another alternative is to establish the minimum payout in *terms that are consistent with the distribution mechanism,* such as ½ percent or 5 cents per hour. Any bonus that is not paid because of the minimum payout provision should not be forfeited by employees, but should be carried over and added to the next payout that takes place.

In communicating this provision, the design team should take care that it not be assumed that the plan will always pay out at least the minimum amount. It is not a guarantee; the sole purpose of the minimum payment is to avoid the negative reactions that would result from distribution of very small bonuses.

Step 18. Define Eligibility Rules for Individuals

Most variable pay plans provide that certain individuals, though they are members of the participating group, are not eligible to receive a bonus from the plan under certain circumstances. It is important that the design team clearly define these eligibility rules in order to avoid conflict and problems after the plan has been implemented.

Some Common Reasons for Ineligibility

The most common reason for ineligibility is that the individual is *no longer in the company's employ.* The majority of plans state that a participant must be on the company's payroll at the end of the bonus period in order to receive a bonus. This provision effectively excludes any individual who is terminated from the company, voluntarily or otherwise, during the variable pay period. A few plans even go so far as to require that the individual be on the payroll on the day the bonus is paid.

Exceptions to this rule are generally allowed, however, for those individuals whose termination is the result of retirement or death. Most people would agree that it is inappropriate to penalize a retiree who, after giving many years of service to the company, happened to retire in the middle of a payout period. Similar sentiments apply to the beneficiary of any individual who suffers the misfortune of dying during a bonus period. In these situations, the affected employees are generally paid a bonus for the time worked during the period.

Many plans also require a *waiting period* for new employees. A common provision is that the employee must be on the payroll on the first day, as well as the last day, of the bonus period. Any new hires during the period are therefore excluded from receiving a bonus. Alternatively, the plan may require a fixed waiting period—for example, an employee must be employed for six months or one year before he is eligible to participate in the variable pay plan. These waiting periods are generally justified on the basis that a new employee is not contributing to (and may even be impeding) performance improvement efforts.

The design team should also consider the treatment of employees who go on, or return from, a *leave of absence* during the bonus period. These would include medical leaves, family leaves, military leaves, and sabbaticals. Individuals in this category could be subject to the same rules that apply to new hires or terminated employees—that is, they are not eligible for a bonus for the periods in which they go on and return from the leave. More commonly, however, employees in these situations receive a bonus for the amount of time that they are on active status during these periods.

Similarly, rules should be provided for employees *transferring in from or out to other units of the company*. Generally, these individuals are treated the same as those on a leave of absence.

Many plans exclude individuals who have not met some *attendance* standard. This type of provision was discussed in detail in Chapter 8.

A few plans, in order to reinforce safety, exclude any employee who has *suffered an injury* during the payout period. This practice is not widespread, however, and is of questionable appropriateness. Injuries are sometimes caused by another person's unsafe practices, and many would argue that this exclusion simply magnifies the misfortune of the injured individual.

Variable pay plans will occasionally exclude individuals based on some *performance* criterion. One plan, for example, excludes any employee who does not receive a favorable performance review during the plan year. Others exclude any employee who is under some kind of disciplinary status.

Finally, the eligibility of *part-time and temporary employees* must be established. While temporary employees, such as those provided by an agency, are almost always excluded, part-timers are another matter. Where part-time employees are permanent employees who just happen to work fewer than forty hours per week, there can be little justification for excluding them from the variable pay plan. This is especially true where part-time employees represent a significant and integral element of the workforce, such as in some retailing organizations.

In some cases, there are other possible employment situations that will need to be addressed by the design team to ensure that there is no confusion regarding eligibility. These might include temporary transfers to or from other company units, extended absences for training or some special project, and persons who support and are physically located within the organization but report to another company entity (such as a plant accounting department that reports to the corporate controller).

Proration

The design team may have to develop a method of prorationing bonuses for those employees, such as retirees or individuals going on leave of absence, who are entitled to a bonus for only part of the payout period. Whether or not this matter must be addressed depends upon the method of bonus distribution (see Chapter 11). If bonuses are distributed by the percent-of-income or hours-worked method, the proration is automatic: The bonus paid to an individual will be determined by the earnings or hours for the period in question. If, on the other hand, the equal-shares distribution method is adopted, there is no automatic proration mechanism. And if the design team fails to define one, an employee who works but one day during the bonus period could expect to receive a full share!

Clearly, a proration formula must be established by the design team for any plan using the equal-share distribution method. The most commonly adopted proration methods are based on hours or days worked during the period.

It is imperative that the design team give careful thought to all eligibility issues. Without a clear set of rules, needless time and energy will be spent resolving these issues after the variable pay plan is in place.

Step 19. Document the System

At this point, the design team has completed the design of the variable pay system—at least from a technical point of view. The team must attend, however, to one final design task: It must produce a plan document.

This job may be viewed as an onerous task, but it cannot be avoided. Any pay system, variable or otherwise, must have its rules and procedures clearly set down in writing in order to avoid misunderstandings, differences in interpretation, and variations in application from one period to another. Problems brought about by the lack of a detailed document can cause friction, discord, and ultimately loss of confidence in the plan by the participants.

The plan document is more than just a summary of the plan's features. It is a detailed description of every element of the plan. It defines precisely each of the plan's measures, including the sources of all the data used in their calculation. It specifies the methods used to establish baselines, as well as the mechanics of future baseline changes. It defines the company-employee sharing ratio, the frequency of payouts, and the distribution method. It lays out the mechanics of the smoothing mechanism and the procedures for capital investment adjustments. It specifies when and how employees will receive bonus checks. It defines the circum-stances that will cause the plan design to be modified, and how these modifications will be made (see Chapter 13).

This document, it should be noted, will not be effective as a vehicle for communicating the plan to the workforce. It will be far too detailed and lengthy, and general communication is not its purpose. Its purposes are to ensure consistent application of the plan provisions over time and to serve as a reference when there are questions or disputes that need to be resolved.

With the plan document finalized, the design team will have com-pleted the design process. Before the team can ride off into the sunset, however, it must see to the effective implementation of the plan.

13

Preparing for the Launch

Crafting a variable pay plan of sound design is one-half the battle; the other is making it work. Even the best-designed plan in the world will not meet expectations if it is poorly implemented and maintained. The design team therefore needs to complete one of its most important tasks: *preparing for the plan's launch and ongoing maintenance.*

The design team should plan for four processes, all of which affect the execution of any variable pay system:

1. Communicating the plan
2. Handling employee improvement ideas
3. Ensuring continuing readiness improvement
4. Implementing a process for managing and maintaining the plan

Failure to devote the proper amount of time and effort to these processes is a major mistake. Because they have put so much time and effort into the design process, it would be a tragedy for the design team to blow it on the implementation.

Communicating the Plan

Developing an effective plan for communicating the variable pay program is one of the most important things a design team does. According to one company participating in a benchmarking study conducted by the American Productivity & Quality Center, the three most important success factors for a group reward system are "Communications, communications, communications."

If the participating employees lack a basic understanding of the plan, little behavioral change will occur. Management cannot expect people to take the initiative to improve various performance variables if they do not understand what those variables are and how they can be impacted on the job.

In addition, employees are likely to distrust a plan that they do not understand. This is particularly true if the organization is in the early stages of its cultural-change process. When employees have spent their entire working lives in an environment of autocratic management, closed communications, and adversarial labor relations, they will be suspicious of any program that offers them an opportunity to increase their compensation without giving something up.

While communicating the mechanics of the plan (measures, baselines) is an obvious need, the communications process should go beyond the technical design issues and include three additional elements:

1. *The purpose of the plan.* A key aspect of any organizational change process is building awareness of the nature of the change. Variable pay can be an effective vehicle to communicate management's vision, lend credibility to the change process, and demonstrate management's commitment to change. If employees do not perceive variable pay to be an element of the change process, its effectiveness, as well as the effectiveness of the change process itself, will be diminished.

2. *How the participants can impact the measures.* An intellectual understanding of the variable pay measures is not enough; the plan participants must also be able to relate these measures to their on-the-job activities. While this may not be a particular problem with some of the measures, it could be a real issue with others. For example, what can an employee do to improve on-time delivery, reduce inventories, conserve supplies, or avoid environmental incidents? Don't assume that everyone can make a connection between these measures and their job activities, particularly if there has been little sharing of business information in the past. If employees do not know how to improve the measures, there will be no behavior change.

3. *The likelihood that the plan will change.* Employees tend to view pay systems as fixed and immutable objects, a view that has a basis in fact, as modifications to traditional compensation plans in most organizations are rare events (with the obvious exception of changes brought about by a union contract negotiation). However, any plan that is designed to support cultural change in a turbulent business environment will almost certainly have to be modified periodically if it is to continue to meet the needs of the business. It is imperative, therefore, that expectations for change be established at the outset. This issue will be discussed further later in this chapter.

There are a variety of communication vehicles available, and most companies utilize several to educate employees on the variable pay plan.

- *A brochure or other written instrument* is basic to the communication process. This document should be simple, conveying only the basic facts of the plan. The plan document developed by the design team at Step 19 will not meet this need, as it is far too lengthy and detailed to serve as an effective communications device.

- *Face-to-face meetings* in which the plan is presented to groups of employees may be the most effective communications vehicle. These meetings enable the design team to explain the plan in some detail while affording the employees the opportunity to ask questions and raise any concerns they may have. These meetings are best conducted by the design team, rather than management, to increase the credibility of the presentations. Management, however, should participate in the meetings, or at least be in attendance, to demonstrate its commitment to the variable pay process.

- *Presentation of the plan by supervisors to their work groups or crews,* especially if the organization is large and it would be impractical to educate the entire workforce through small group meetings. If this avenue is selected, it is vital that supervisors receive adequate training to enable them to make a knowledgeable presentation and effectively respond to questions. Supervisory crew meetings are sometimes used to supplement, rather than substitute for, organizationwide presentations. The supervisory meetings are structured to provide more detailed information and to generate discussion about the plan.

- *Video presentations* represent another communications vehicle. This option tends to be used in large, geographically diverse organizations where face-to-face presentations by design team members are not feasible.

The design team should not conclude that once the employees have been educated on the particulars of the variable pay plan all communication requirements have been met. Another critical element of implementation—the ongoing communication of results—must be planned as well.

Simply reporting the final numbers and level of bonus payments is grossly inadequate; the participants must receive analytical or explanatory information as well. They need to know what went well and how improvements were made so that they can continue to do the right things. They also need to know what did not go well so that they can problem-solve and overcome the obstacles to improvement.

Regardless of the plan's payout frequency, this ongoing information should be disseminated at least monthly. The knowledge that improvements are being made, and that the bonus pool is building, provides some degree of reinforcement for the participants and sustains interest where the payout period is infrequent, such as semiannual or annual. These interim reports also enable employees to address problems before the entire period has passed. Without this information, they are operating in the dark.

The vehicles used for the initial communications, such as presentations to the workforce and supervisory crew meetings, are options for ongoing communications as well. And there are additional possibilities. Large displays can be posted in the work area to communicate the latest data on the plan measures. Some organizations publish a newsletter devoted to the variable pay plan. Others report results on monitors in the cafeteria or other locations where employees congregate. One utility even enters results into the company's computer network, where they can be accessed by any employee with a desktop computer.

It would be difficult to understate the importance of the communications process for a variable pay plan, and the design team should devote an appropriate amount of time and effort to developing an effective communications plan. Shortchanging this process will almost surely have a detrimental impact on plan results.

Handling Employee Improvement Ideas

By itself, variable pay is not an improvement process; it does not directly produce improvements in the measures around which it is constructed. It can only reinforce and reward the behaviors that bring about the improvements. To some extent, therefore, the effectiveness of variable pay will depend on the existence of effective vehicles or processes to empower employees to effect changes and bring about improvements.

In an autocratic environment, employees have little opportunity to change the way things are done in their work areas. Their only real opportunity to improve performance in such an environment is to work faster or harder. While working harder may bring about some improvements in some areas (primarily labor productivity), the real potential usually lies in doing things differently. And for some variables, such as quality and safety, working harder may have no impact at all.

For this reason the existence of an employee involvement process represents a readiness issue (see Chapter 2). Without any involvement vehicles, the participants in the variable pay plan will lack the means to bring about changes that will increase their compensation, and frustration will be the predictable result.

Even where some basic involvement structures exist, there may well be a need to develop an additional vehicle to process employee improvement ideas. Many companies have experienced a major influx of ideas following implementation of a variable pay plan. Should this occur, traditional suggestion systems and problem-solving teams will probably be inadequate to handle all the ideas that will surface.

A commonly used vehicle to support variable pay systems is the *suggestion committee*, which traces its origin back to the original 1930s Scanlon Plan, generally regarded as the first gain-sharing program. Despite this technique's advanced age, it remains today a useful approach for evaluating employee ideas in support of variable pay.

In a sizable organization, suggestion committees might be organized in each of the major departments or functional groups. Each committee would typically consist of the departmental supervisor and two or three nonmanagement employees. These committees generally meet on a monthly basis to review ideas submitted by members of the department.

The suggestion committees are generally empowered to approve and implement ideas that fall within two boundaries:

1. The idea affects the committee's work area and no other.
2. The cost of implementing the idea is below some maximum, generally in the $200 to $1,000 range.

While these are generally the minimum limits on the suggestion committee's authority, some plans add additional requirements as well. One organization, for example, also requires that the suggestion:

1. Have a payback of six months or less.
2. Will not cause the work area involved to exceed its operating budget.

Ideas that do not fall within these bounds (or are beyond the departmental committee's ability to evaluate) are forwarded to a higher-level team, which consists of some management staff members and selected nonmanagement members of the departmental committees. This group approves or rejects the ideas submitted to it and provides feedback to the departmental committee and the individual who submitted the idea.

Smaller organizations that do not require this amount of structure may have a single team that handles all ideas submitted by employees throughout the organization. The idea-handling role may even be combined with the plan-maintenance role (discussed later in this chapter) in a single group. A typical example of suggestion committee procedures is presented in Appendix A.

Absent an advanced involvement and empowerment process, such as self-directed work teams, the design team should give serious thought to the issue of idea handling. Processing employee improvement ideas effectively and efficiently may prove to be a key success factor.

Improving Readiness

Readiness for variable pay was discussed in detail in Chapter 2. The point was made that readiness is not an absolute, and that few organizations are as ready as they ideally should be. Nonetheless, business imperatives often require that cultural change, along with the associated changes in reward systems, be pursued under less than ideal circumstances.

The organization's leaders, on both management and labor sides, should not cease to be concerned about readiness once the decision is made to proceed with design of a variable pay system. There will be ample opportunity to work toward improved readiness during the lengthy design process and thus increase the probability of a successful launch. Even after the plan is operational, initiatives to improve readiness should be ongoing in order to continually improve the environment within which the plan functions.

There are a variety of strategies that can be adopted to address each of the readiness issues that were discussed in Chapter 2.

Management Commitment to Change

The single most important readiness issue, as was suggested in Chapter 2, is *management commitment to change*. How does one go about increasing management commitment to change—or commitment to anything else, for that matter? The key is to convince management that cultural change and variable pay can produce significantly better business results and may even be critical to the long-term viability of the organization. In other words, a business case must be made. This can be accomplished only through education. Management must learn about the nature of the cultural transformation initiatives being pursued throughout industry today and the results that are being achieved. It helps if a number of companies in the industry are well along the way to creating high-involvement work systems and alternative reward programs; nothing energizes management more than the fear of being left behind by competitors. Management awareness can also be increased through such vehicles as books and periodical articles, seminars, conferences, and visits with counterparts at leading companies.

Another aspect of the management commitment issue that should be addressed as part of the readiness improvement initiatives is *visibility of commitment.* Having a commitment is not enough; if that commitment is not apparent to the rest of the organization, skepticism and resistance will be as great as if the commitment did not exist.

Management can make its commitment visible in a variety of ways:

1. Establish and communicate organizational goals relative to the change process.
2. Commit resources for training, consulting, and other support activities.
3. Ensure that the status of the change process is on the agenda for every staff meeting.
4. Display a personal interest in the process, through such activities as seeking feedback from employees at all levels.
5. Promptly and decisively address impediments to change that are clear to the rest of the organization.
6. Modify other organizational systems to ensure that they reinforce the desired culture. These include selection systems, job descriptions, appraisal systems, promotional practices, training systems, and planning and budgeting systems.

Employee Involvement

The existence of effective employee involvement vehicles was another readiness issue discussed in Chapter 2. This issue was explored in the previous section in this chapter.

Information Sharing

Information sharing was noted in Chapter 2 as a readiness issue because of its effect on trust and because of the need for employees to have business information to make good decisions. There are a number of vehicles through which business information can be conveyed to employees. Some of the more common ones include:

- *Quarterly (or even monthly) meetings with employees* to report on business results. The information conveyed should include operating information, such as output, quality, productivity, and other performance variables, and can also include financial data, such as costs and profits.
- *Departmental or crew meetings, led by supervisors,* to discuss departmental business issues and performance.
- *Newsletters or other written material* containing articles on business issues, such as new product introductions, feedback from custom-

ers, competitive challenges, and progress on major change initiatives.
- *Television screens,* located in lunchrooms or other areas where employees congregate, displaying current company news.
- *Distribution of annual and quarterly reports* to all employees in publicly owned companies.
- *Product displays,* including those of competitors as well as those of the company.

A Feeling of Trust

Low *trust* is a readiness problem that is a legacy of autocratic management, little information sharing, and adversarial labor relations. When employees 'are treated as adversaries rather than valued contributors to the business, it should not be surprising that the outcome is an environment of mistrust. A lack of trust is generally a deep-seated problem and is not susceptible to a quick fix. This should not be taken to mean, however, that nothing can or should be done about increasing feelings of trust.

On the contrary, low trust is such an insidious and damaging organizational attribute that no effort should be spared to improve it. Strategies to improve trust do not necessarily address trust directly, but rather deal with the organizational conditions that reduce trust. Thus, initiatives described here around information sharing, employee involvement, and collaborative labor-management relationships should also serve to raise the trust level over time. In addition, an employee-management team might be brought together to identify and address causes of low trust.

Increased Teamwork

Readiness relative to *teamwork* can be improved through several initiatives:

- *Employee problem-solving teams* can be organized to identify the root causes of poor teamwork and develop solutions.
- *A cascading goal-setting process,* in which each organizational entity develops goals that support the goals developed at the next higher level, can focus employees on broad organizational objectives that require teamwork to achieve.
- *An internal-customer process,* based on the premise that each department or team serves another internal entity, can be developed. Each unit would identify its internal customer, work with that customer to define the customer's requirements, and strive to eliminate shortfalls in meeting those requirements.

Employment Stability

Employment stability was cited as a readiness issue because of the incongruity of job insecurity with a high-commitment, high-involvement philosophy. While absolute job security may not be realistic in a rapidly changing, global business environment, there are definite strategies that can be adopted to improve employment stability. These include:

- Maintaining a policy of lean staffing so that layoffs are minimized during business downturns.
- Using part-time or temporary employees, rather than adding regular employees, during times of peak workload.
- Retraining excess employees to fill open positions in other parts of the organization, even if relocation is necessary.
- Relying on attrition to bring the workforce into balance with the business level.
- Work sharing or reducing the hours of all employees rather than eliminating jobs.
- Offering retirement incentives when workforce reductions are needed.

While some of these approaches would appear to involve increased costs for the corporation, they may in fact be cost-effective. There are many indirect costs associated with workforce reductions, not the least of which is the dampening effect on the morale and commitment of the survivors. And if the economic condition that led to the workforce reduction is temporary, the costs of recalling people or hiring new and inexperienced employees can be considerable.

Supervisory Support

A key readiness issue, *supervisory support* almost certainly should receive continuing attention during the design process and after the variable pay system is launched. An entire program can be developed to improve supervisory commitment to participative management and to variable pay.
This program might include:

- *Education and awareness building about the purpose of variable pay and the associated cultural change process.* While some degree of variable pay education must be provided to all members of the organization, special attention should be given to supervisors and middle managers because of their crucial role as the interface between senior management and the working level. Supervisors must understand the importance of variable pay to the viability of the business, and they must accept a change in role to support the involvement process that variable pay is designed to support. They should also be thoroughly educated on the design of the variable pay system in order to increase their understanding and their ability to answer questions of their subordinates.

■ *Integration into the supervisors' appraisal and reward systems.* The premise that rewards influence behaviors is one of the foundations of variable pay. There exists an excellent opportunity to apply this principle to other reward systems as well in pursuit of supervisory behavior change. The willingness and ability of the supervisor to adapt to participative management and support the variable pay process should be an element of those individuals' performance appraisals and a key determinant of any merit increase that they might be eligible to receive. In addition, it should be made clear to supervisors that their opportunities for advancement in the company will be contingent on their developing a management style that is congruent with a high-involvement, team-oriented workplace.

■ *Involvement in the change process.* Supervisors, unfortunately, are sometimes the least involved people in the organization. Change is often forced upon them without affording them any opportunity to influence the course of the change process. Is it any wonder, then, that they resist initiatives that would substantially change their status and role in the organization?

There are a variety of ways that supervisory involvement in the change process can be achieved. Focus groups can be conducted with supervisors to identify their issues and concerns. Senior management can hold regular meetings with supervisors to seek their input on decisions that affect them. A committee of supervisors can be formed and charged with planning for and managing the supervisory role transformation process. A supervisor could even serve on any steering committee that is managing the overall cultural-change process. And there certainly should be a first-line supervisor on the variable pay design team and the variable pay steering committee.

■ *Employment security commitments.* A natural outcome of any employee involvement process is less management in the long run. And it may appear to first-line supervisors that they will be the first to go. With their livelihood perceived to be in jeopardy, they have a vested interest in maintaining the status quo.

Management can lessen considerably this apprehension, and thus reduce supervisory resistance to change, by assuring supervisors that their employment is secure. Their roles will change, and they may even be assigned to a different job, but supervisors who support the change process need not worry about their continued employment.

Union Support

The final readiness issue identified in Chapter 2 was *union support*. One strategy here is the same as that suggested above relative to building management commitment: awareness and education.

Just as management must understand the purpose and benefits of variable pay for the company, so must union leadership gain an appreciation of how variable pay can support union objectives (such as higher pay, more satisfying jobs, and greater job security) and advance the well-being of the union's members. The entire learning process, in fact, offers an excellent opportunity for management and union leadership to advance the cause of labor-management cooperation by obtaining their education jointly. Many companies today invite union leaders and members to attend seminars and in-house educational programs along with management.

Union support for variable pay can also be advanced through some of the strategies adopted to increase supervisory support. These include the involvement of union leaders in the design process and commitments from management that no employee will lose his or her job as a result of the variable pay process.

Maintaining the Plan

If one thing can be said with certainty about a variable pay plan, it is this: Sooner or later, the plan will have to be changed.

Management and employees today must deal with a dynamic and rapidly changing business environment. New competitors, perhaps from another part of the world, may enter the marketplace. Customer requirements may shift. New technologies may make existing processes obsolete. Product lines may be added or dropped in an effort to maintain growth and increase profitability. Restructurings and reengineering initiatives may alter the company's cost structure and work processes. The company's fundamental business strategy may even change.

Any of these occurrences could invalidate an existing variable pay plan. Should this happen, the plan must be modified if it is to remain viable. It makes no sense to maintain a plan that is inequitable, for either the company or its employees, or no longer meets the needs of the business.

And other circumstances, apart from changes in the business environment, may also necessitate a modification to the plan. The plan may have a design flaw, or erroneous data may have been used in calculating baselines or actual results. Or improvements may occur to such a degree that there is little or no potential for further gains.

That last point seems to concern management more than any other when it comes to maintaining the viability of the plan. In some cases, management has even chosen *not to implement* variable pay for fear that improvement opportunities will eventually run out, employees will become disgruntled, and performance will deteriorate back to levels before variable pay.

Should this eventuality occur, there are several options available for modifying the plan:

1. *The measures with little improvement opportunity could be dropped and replaced with other measures where significant opportunities exist.* The risk, of course, is that performance will deteriorate on the measures that are no longer part of the plan. One possible solution to this problem is to treat the original measure as a gate; the performance level must be maintained if there is to be a full payout from the other measures.

2. *The baseline for the measures in question could be frozen.* In the case of goal sharing, goals could be set at levels equal to that of current performance so that employees could continue earning bonuses for maintaining this very high level of performance.

One could certainly make a case for rewarding the members of an organization that operates at an industry-leading or near-perfect level of performance. One company even defined in advance the point at which the baseline for its unit-cost measure would become frozen. Above a certain unit cost, the plan paid out 50 percent of the cost savings versus an eight-quarter rolling average baseline; below that unit cost level, the baseline remained at that defined level.

3. *The system could be converted to one that rewards the achievement of broader business goals.* These goals might include gaining market share, improving customer satisfaction or retention, introducing new products on time, or achieving preferred-supplier status with customers.

4. *The system could be converted to a profit-sharing plan.* This might make eminent sense in a situation where employees have improved every controllable variable to the greatest degree possible. Employees in this situation are truly behaving as businesspeople and should therefore be rewarded as businesspeople by sharing in the profits of the enterprise.

It is questionable whether management should even be worrying about this issue. A lack of improvement opportunities is a problem that most companies in the world would love to have. In any event, the organization will, sooner or later, face a need to change the plan for one reason or another. It is a virtual inevitability. If the required modifications cannot be made in a timely and effective fashion, with the buy-in by participating employees, the plan's very existence will be threatened.

Ensuring the Plan's Long Life

To ensure the long-term viability of the variable pay plan, the design team must do two things:

1. *As suggested earlier, it must create an expectation among the participants that the plan will change over time.* This expectation should be clearly established through the initial education process and then reinforced through ongoing communications.

More than one organization has faced a crisis when employees resisted changes to the variable pay plan that badly needed to be made. Management in some cases shoots itself in the foot by assuring employees at the time of the plan launch that no changes will be made.

2. *The design team should create a clearly defined process to modify the plan when required.* This process should be effective not only at developing sound plan modifications but also at obtaining employee buy-in to these modifications. The obvious way to achieve these outcomes is to apply the same involvement philosophy that was used to design the plan in the first place. A team of management and nonmanagement people can be established to manage and maintain the variable pay plan on an ongoing basis.

The makeup of this team, which we will call a steering committee, would be much like that of the design team. It would be a cross-functional team, with different skills and points of view represented. Unlike the design team, however, the steering committee would be a permanent group. While its membership will probably change, the group itself exists for the life of the variable pay plan.

When circumstances dictate a need to change the plan, the steering committee would identify options, evaluate alternatives, and reach consensus decisions just as the original design team did. To do so, the team might seek input from management, technical specialists, consultants, and other plan participants. The team would also develop a plan to effectively communicate the changes to the rest of the organization.

The steering committee would perform other responsibilities as well. It would, for example, do the following:

1. Thoroughly review and understand the results after the close of each payout period. The team would, in effect, "certify" the data in order to allay any suspicions or skepticism on the part of the plan participants.

2. Prepare a communication to convey each period's results, along with explanatory information, to the rest of the organization.
3. Interpret the plan rules, through consensus decision making, when situations arise that are not clearly defined in the plan document. There may be a question about an individual's eligibility, for example, or the appropriate treatment of an unusual occurrence that may not be clearly defined in the plan document.
4. Evaluate employee improvement suggestions if no other group exists for that purpose.
5. Conduct a thorough evaluation of the plan's effectiveness at least annually. This would include obtaining feedback from plan participants through surveys, focus groups, or some other vehicle.

In general, the committee would deal with any problems or concerns that may arise relative to the plan.

In most cases, the original design team, or at least a substantial part of it, remains together and becomes the initial steering committee. This makes eminent sense, as no one else in the organization understands all the details of the plan or has a high degree of ownership for the plan. Over time, new members rotate in and replace the original members. The options for selecting these new members are much the same as those for the original team: They may be chosen from a pool of volunteers, for example, or each work area may select its own representative.

The variable pay steering committee is a powerful concept, as it enables the company to continue to model participative management practices with respect to the variable pay plan. It also provides a credible vehicle for implementing the inevitable changes to the plan and avoids many of the problems that would exist if management implemented these changes unilaterally.

Attention to these implementation issues—communications, idea handling, ongoing readiness improvement, and plan maintenance—may well prove to be as important as the plan design itself. If the design team effectively attends to these issues, it will have done an exemplary job and will have reason to feel good about the result.

14

Lessons Learned

In any field of endeavor, people must learn from the experiences of others in order to advance the state of the art and enjoy a straighter and smoother path to success than that followed by the field's pioneers. Fortunately, variable pay is now at the stage of development where an enormous knowledge base of experiences has been accumulated. Some of the lessons learned will be discussed in this chapter.

Wandering in the Wilderness

A top executive of a company with a successful variable pay system once remarked, "We wandered in the wilderness for two years, but we finally got it together." His company had a rough start. No one understood the plan, behaviors did not change appreciably, and initial results did not meet expectations. But the commitment was there, and management believed in the variable pay concept. Management rolled up its sleeves, identified and attacked the problems, and even redesigned the system. Today, this company represents a variable pay success story.

This gentleman's experience was far from unique. While some variable pay plans take off and soar from day one, many more have a rocky beginning. Variable pay represents change, and the forces arrayed against change in any organization are formidable. Change almost never comes easy.

What ultimately separates the winners from the losers is commitment and persistence. People in leadership positions, whether they be management, union, or otherwise, must be prepared to commit personal time and effort to the care and feeding of a new variable pay plan. When problems arise or expectations aren't met, they must take the initiative to find solutions.

A high level of commitment and leadership can overcome almost any impediment to the success of variable pay. It is probably the single most important success factor.

Is There Life After Gain Sharing or Goal Sharing?

Lurking in the hearts of many executives in many companies that have implemented variable pay is a great fear: Someday, all the possible improvements will have been harvested, the tightening baselines will eventually eliminate all possibility of further bonuses, and the whole system will collapse. There will be no more payouts, and everybody will revert to pre-variable-pay behaviors. Hopefully, all this will happen after the executive retires.

As suggested in the previous chapter, the possibility that this scenario will come to pass is probably remote. If any company has ever reached the point where no more improvement opportunities exist, it has managed to keep this a secret thus far. And if any organization should reach this happy state, management can (and should) reward its employees for maintaining this exemplary level of performance.

But no one can accurately predict the future, and there can be no assurances that the variable pay plan will last forever. The reality is, however, that there are now many plans that continue to function effectively after ten to fifteen years in operation. There are even a few that go back thirty years and more. One company, in fact, marked the fortieth anniversary of its gain-sharing program by organizing an employee team to consider some fundamental changes to the plan design—for the first time!

Where a variable pay plan (and the associated cultural change) has established a record of success and enjoys the commitment of management and employees, the plan's failure will not be an issue. The stakeholders in the success of the plan will come together to do whatever is needed to maintain its viability. It's been done over and over again. So those worried executives need to do all that they can to ensure their plans' success in the early years and then trust the maintenance process to find a way to modify the plans as needed over time.

Conventional Wisdom and Other Myths

There is much conventional wisdom about variable pay. This conventional wisdom arose in the late 1970s, when interest in variable pay was growing but there was little practical experience to guide interested parties in developing and implementing these systems. There was, accordingly, a tendency to rely on academic theory or management's personal beliefs for guidance.

Unfortunately, much of the conventional wisdom is wrong. There are many successful plans in existence today that should not, by theoretical standards, have succeeded.

Some examples of the conventional wisdom include the following:

1. *Variable pay works only in small organizations.* Whether or not this is true depends on your definition of *small*. The purveyors of the conventional wisdom usually consider organizations larger than two or three hundred people to be beyond the size that will enable variable pay to succeed.

The fact is that a number of organizations with employee populations of between one and two thousand have enjoyed considerable success with variable pay. Consider, for example, the following:

- An automotive plant with 1,350 employees was uncompetitive and on the verge of being closed by its parent company. Management and union leadership joined together to develop a "shared destiny" strategy to try to save the plant. A key element of this strategy was variable pay. Seven years later, considerable bonuses had been paid and the plan was still going strong. As for the future of the plant, it is no longer on the block; it fact, it has been expanded.
- A tire plant with 1,800 employees developed a variable pay plan in 1977. The plan is still alive and well today.
- Variable pay plans at an industrial equipment plant with 1,750 employees and an aerospace electronics plant with 1,500 employees have been effectively rewarding improvements for ten years and five years, respectively.

This is not to suggest that an organization of any size whatsoever can expect variable pay to significantly change employee behaviors. Certainly a company with tens of thousands of employees will have difficulty making a companywide variable pay plan meaningful to all its employees. Such a company can, however, gain the advantages of smallness by implementing variable pay plans at the division, operating unit, or department level. Alternatively, it could adopt the financially funded goal-sharing approach (see Chapter 5), with individual units required to achieve relevant goals in order to earn their share of the companywide payout. The benefits of smallness can thus be obtained in any size organization.

Clearly, the smaller the organization, the easier it will be to motivate employees and change behaviors through variable pay. But whatever constitutes "too large" with respect to variable pay effectiveness, it is not two hundred employees. It is probably not even a thousand employees, as the examples above suggest.

2. *The plan must be simple, or it will not succeed.* This is one of the most enduring and widely held beliefs about variable pay. And it would seem to be entirely logical: How could employees be expected to respond to something they do not understand?

Like some other elements of the conventional wisdom, this assumption has a kernel of truth but is vastly overstated. The reality is that there are many very complicated, yet very successful, variable pay programs in existence today.

As a practical matter, it is probably impossible to design a truly simple plan in a complex business. Most organizations today produce a variety of products or services and employ complicated accounting and costing systems. Quantifying productivity accurately is usually not as simple as adding up the number of widgets produced and dividing by the number of hours worked. A truly simple formula would likely be subject to so many distortions that it would be impractical, if not dangerous, for use in determining compensation.

Expecting all employees to thoroughly understand the mechanics of a variable pay plan, particularly when they have been provided little business information in the past, is simply too high an expectation. All that is required is that they have a basic conceptual understanding of what is being measured ("Improving productivity means producing more widgets per hour") and an ability to relate the plan measures to their jobs.

The latter requirement is particularly important and is often overlooked in the communication process. A perfect understanding of the arithmetic underlying the formula will be useless if employees do not comprehend what they can do on the job to improve the measures.

The formula must provide an accurate and meaningful indicator of performance. If it fails to do so, the plan will not be supported by management. Simpler is definitely better, but the design team should not accord simplicity a higher priority than accuracy and reliability.

3. *Variable pay should be implemented only after a well-developed cultural change process is in place.* This particular assumption was more widely believed, and probably more legitimate, in the days when variable pay was still an innovation in the compensation arena. In the 1970s, attitudes among managers, employees, and unions were quite different from how they are today. There was little information sharing and employee involvement, and the very suggestion that management and union might join in a collaborative venture to develop a compensation system away from the bargaining table would have been met with derisive laughter in most companies. In this environment, the only companies that had a high probabil-

ity of succeeding with variable pay were those that had made major progress in changing the organizational culture. The impediments to change were otherwise too great.

Today, things are quite different. There are few companies that are not at least experimenting with employee involvement and team processes, and management and union leaders generally are much more willing to work together to improve the viability of the business. Even where the change processes have not yet advanced very far, there is greater receptivity to change than there was twenty years ago.

The point was made in Chapter 2 that the general consensus in the field today is that variable pay can lead an organizational change as well as support an existing change process. The logic for this idea stems from the power of compensation to serve as a communications or signaling device. The behaviors or outcomes that management is willing to reward speaks volumes for management's vision and priorities. Implementing variable pay early in a change process can, therefore, signal management's commitment to change more eloquently than can any words.

This does not mean that readiness need not be considered, or that variable pay should be the very first step in an organizational change initiative. The organization that scores very low on most of the readiness criteria (see Chapter 2) should probably pursue some information-sharing activities and simple involvement structures first, in order to build trust and unfreeze the organization. The installation of variable pay at a later time can then signal an acceleration of the change process to a more receptive organization.

In reality, the organization that is serious about creating a high-involvement, team-oriented culture probably cannot wait until the desired culture has become established, for the lack of a congruent reward system will likely become a barrier to further progress before that point is ever reached.

4. *The number of measures in a plan should be limited.* In the great majority of organizationwide plans having multiple measures, the number of measures falls in the range of three to seven. A greater number presumably would be difficult for employees to remember and would cause improvement efforts to become unfocused and overly diffused.

What, then, can explain the success enjoyed by a chemical plant that employs nineteen measures in its plan? Or the financial services company that has a hundred measures? These organizations certainly do not expect that all of the measures will be meaningful to all the plan participants. Rather, their objective is to ensure that all employees will relate to at least some of the measures, and that each employee will then focus individual improvement efforts on the few that can be directly affected. These companies thus gain some of the motivational benefits of small-group incentives while minimizing the risk of suboptimizing behaviors and perceptions of inequity that often accompany the small-group approach (see Chapter 2).

5. *Large payouts are required to motivate people and change behaviors.* This belief does not really qualify as conventional wisdom, as it is not generally advanced in the literature on variable pay. However, many managers contemplating variable pay believe it to be true.

Depending upon which survey you choose to cite, the average payout from variable pay plans falls somewhere in the 3 to 6 percent range. A substantial majority of survey participants also report that their plans have been successful in meeting their objectives. It is not hard, in fact, to find examples of plans that are highly successful by any standards, yet never pay out more than 3 or 4 percent of pay.

What is often overlooked is the recognition aspect of bonus payments. For people who have spent years working in a traditional organization, the variable pay bonus may represent the first time that they have received a tangible reward for contributing to the success of the business. Furthermore, the reward legitimizes and sanctions behaviors that bring more satisfaction to the individual—performing at a high level and being part of a winning team. There is more to the payout, in other words, than the financial value of the bonus. The money represents a form of recognition that may be more powerful than the money itself. When viewed in this way, the magnitude of the bonus becomes much less important.

The lesson here is that you should not let the conventional wisdom limit your flexibility to design and implement a variable pay system that effectively supports the business and organizational strategy. The conventional wisdom provides (in some cases) some useful guidance, but no design team should allow the conventional wisdom to dictate its actions. There are virtually no absolutes with respect to variable pay.

Variable Pay Does Work

Variable pay plans have been around long enough in significant numbers that there is now a substantial body of knowledge with respect to their efficacy. And the evidence is clear: Variable pay, when properly designed and well supported, does produce business results.

Success stories are not hard to find. Consider the following examples:

- A plant that was (apparently) operating at capacity implemented a gain-sharing plan that effectively resulted in a doubling of the plant's capacity. The company canceled plans to build a new plant and saved millions of dollars in capital. This startling improvement was, according to the plant manager, due entirely to the gain-sharing program.

- A chemical plant reported savings exceeding $3 million over three years and paid bonuses averaging $7,000 per employee in one year.[1]
- An aerospace plant reported a 22 percent decline in costs in the plan's first quarter, resulting in $1.5 million in savings. After three years, cumulative cost savings totaled $12.5 million.[2]
- A telecommunications equipment manufacturer reported $50 million in savings over seven years from employee ideas generated by the variable pay program.[3]
- A variable pay plan at a division of a struggling company resulted in a 100 percent improvement in labor productivity. The plan, according to one executive, "saved the company."

The evidence is not just anecdotal. Virtually all survey results also support the contention that variable pay works:

- In a survey of 110 companies in six midwestern states, 38 percent of the respondents reported productivity gains of 10 to 18 percent annually, while another 36 percent reported productivity gains of 18 to 23 percent annually.[4]
- In a 382-company survey by The Conference Board, 86 percent of the respondents reported that gain-sharing plans were either "successful" or "very successful" (other response options were "partially successful" and "not successful"). Comparable responses for organizationwide incentives, small-group incentives, and profit sharing were 70 percent, 68 percent, and 70 percent, respectively.[5]
- An American Compensation Association study of 663 variable pay plans found that the median return earned on the money paid out in bonuses was 134 percent.[6]

The Keys to Success

While the success rate for variable pay is reasonably high, success is not, by any means, assured. Along with the success stories, there are plenty of glaring failures. The good news is that the keys to success are clear. Anyone who has observed a sizable number of these efforts will recognize the conditions that lead to success.

Management Commitment to Change

The single most important success factor, as suggested earlier, is management commitment to change. This may sound trite to those managers who have heard about management commitment and change more times than they can count. The fact remains, however, that leadership and commitment are absolutely vital to the success of a variable pay plan.

Changing the way employees are compensated presents plenty of challenges under the best of circumstances. But variable pay is not just a pay vehicle; it is a support system for a transformation in organizational culture. If that cultural change does not have the full support and attention of management, it will fail. And if the cultural-change initiative fails, the variable pay system will have nothing to support.

Support From Managers and Supervisors

The support of middle management and first-line supervisors is also a key success factor. The management people who are closest to the working level have a major influence on employee behaviors and can therefore make or break a variable pay process. All too often, the middle layers of the organization are left out of the planning for change, and their commitment to senior management's initiatives are taken for granted. The result is resistance and an undermining of the entire change process. A strategy to build supervisory commitment to variable pay, as well as to the change process itself, will pay off by negating a major impediment to success.

Empowerment of Employees

Continuous attention to the involvement process is another important component of a variable pay process. Involvement and empowerment are the drivers for improvement activities, and if employees are frustrated in their efforts to improve the performance of their work areas, their interest in and support for variable pay will be greatly diminished. Improvements will fail to meet the expectations of both management and the plan participants, and the life of the plan will likely be limited.

A Solid Design

A good system design is another prerequisite for a successful variable pay program. It is imperative that those charged with the design of a variable pay plan be given ample time and all the support and technical resources needed. Variable-pay professionals cringe and look for the nearest exit whenever they hear the dreaded words, "We have to have a variable pay system implemented in six weeks." A poor system design will almost certainly produce an undesirable outcome from either a company or an employee point of view. It will then lose the support of a key constituency and will not survive.

Effective Communications

While virtually everyone professes to know it is important, effective communications is probably more consequential, and less often accomplished, than most people realize. If employees do not have at least a rudimentary understanding of what they need to do on their jobs to generate bonuses, the necessary behavioral changes will not occur. In addition, they will likely mistrust the system. A lack of ongoing information regarding results, and why they occurred, will further feed this mistrust and lack of interest.

Most organizations overestimate the effectiveness of their communications efforts, and the result is an underinformed workforce and a variable pay plan that does not live up to its potential. It may not be much of an exaggeration to say that management cannot overcommunicate when it comes to a variable pay plan.

Willingness to Adapt

Another key success factor is the willingness and ability to adapt to a changing business environment. Variable pay must be viewed as a dynamic system that can be modified as the business needs dictate. A rigid system that cannot readily be modified will probably not last more than a few years. If the plan is not meeting the needs of the business, it no longer has value to the company. Those plans that stand the test of time invariably go through periodic modifications and even a major redesign or two.

While the success of variable pay, like any organizational-change initiative, can never be taken for granted, attention to these keys to success dramatically increase the probability of a positive outcome.

The Bottom Line

While variable pay is not a new idea, its widespread use in recent years signals a fundamental shift in management's view of the purpose of compensation. It represents, in fact, a dawning recognition by American industry that compensation can be used to support strategic business initiatives.

This reorientation has come about for the right reason: It meets a business need. The growth of variable pay has paralleled the fundamental change in management philosophy that has, in turn, accompanied the growth of a global economy. When done right, it effectively supports the transformation of an organization to a high-involvement, team-oriented work system. And the attainment of this high-involvement culture is nothing less than a survival issue for many companies today.

In addition to serving a different purpose, variable pay also differs from traditional approaches to compensation in that it offers enormous flexibility. There is no set of rules; nor are there only a limited number of generic approaches to choose from. Variable pay offers any organization the opportunity to develop a creative compensation system that uniquely meets its business and cultural needs.

Variable pay makes eminent sense for any enterprise facing a high level of competition or other forces that call for an organizational focus on performance improvement. Variable pay is a system whose time has come.

References

1. Michael A. Bennett, "Gainsharing—Company Uses Technique to Enhance Safety, Cost-Cutting, Customer Service," *ACA News*, March 1994.
2. Steve Scheffler, *Case 82: Gainsharing, PEP, and PAID Lead LTV-Camden Into the Future* (Houston: American Productivity & Quality Center, 1991).
3. Bob Filipczak, "Ericsson General Electric: The Evolution of Empowerment," *Training*, September 1993.
4. Woodruf Imberman, "Principles of Gain-Sharing," *Papermaker*, December 1994.
5. Conference Board, *Variable Pay: Nontraditional Programs for Motivation and Reward* (New York: Conference Board, 1993).
6. Jerry L. McAdams and Elizabeth J. Hawk, *Organizational Performance and Rewards: 663 Experiences in Making the Link* (Phoenix: American Compensation Association, 1994).

Appendix

Suggestion Committee Procedures

Departmental Team Structure

- The idea-handling teams will be made up of elected representatives from each department and a supervisor.
- Employee representatives will be elected by the group they represent. There should be a posting to solicit volunteers and nominations, followed by a secret ballot.
- Terms of team members will be one year. In order to stagger the terms of team members, elections will be held every six months. Team members can serve two consecutive terms.
- An alternate team member will also be elected and will attend the team meetings when a regular member is absent or unable to attend. Any permanent vacancy will be filled by the alternate team member. The alternate member will be the person receiving the next highest number of votes.
- The management representative for each Departmental Team will be appointed by the Variable Pay Plan Coordinator with input from department managers.
- A chairperson will be elected by each team. The length of the chairperson's term will be at the discretion of the team members.
- Suggestions will be submitted to the suggestor's departmental representative or supervisor for presentation to the Departmental Team. Suggestions may include, but are not limited to, the following areas:

  A. Improving methods by:
     1. Eliminating unnecessary operations
     2. Simplifying jobs

3. Simplifying methods
4. Reducing material handling

B. Improving utilization of equipment:

1. Increasing output
2. Improving design or construction
3. Reducing setup time and downtime
4. Practicing preventive maintenance

C. Building better products:

1. Improving quality
2. Improving design
3. Simplifying manufacturing
4. Improving procurement of materials and services
5. Improving delivery
6. Reducing scrap and rework

D. More efficient planning:

1. Eliminating unnecessary reports and forms
2. Simplifying reports and forms
3. Reducing phone, postage, shipping, and other costs

E. Attitudes of employees:

1. Improving communications and cooperation between employees and all departments

- The Departmental Teams will meet at least once a month to act on new suggestions, review old suggestions, and discuss ways of reducing costs and improving productivity, quality, and service. Each team will elect a recorder to record all suggestions and to keep accurate minutes of their meetings.
- The Departmental Teams are responsible for reviewing all suggestions submitted and should take one of the following actions:

A. Accept and act to initiate the implementation of all suggestions that fall within the guidelines (see below).

B. Hold the suggestion for future investigation.

C. Refer the suggestion to the Review Team.

D. Reject the suggestion, stating the reasons for rejection, and forward to the Review Team for final review.

- The guidelines for accepting suggestions are as follows:

  A. The cost of implementation is not more than $500.

  B. The suggestion affects no other department or shift. A suggestion affecting another department or shift can be shared with the other teams and implemented if both teams agree.

- Team members should encourage people to submit ideas, help people develop and write up their ideas, give good feedback to those who submit ideas, and keep coworkers informed of team activities.
- Each Departmental Team will elect an employee to represent the Departmental Team on the Review Team.
- The Review Team representative will be responsible for:

  A. Discussing Review Team minutes with the team supervisor

  B. Filing a copy of the Review Team minutes in the Review Team file

  C. Report to the Review Team all suggestions generated by the Department Team he represents

  D. Providing feedback on all Review Team activities to the Departmental Team

Review Team Structure

- The Review Team membership will consist of the facility manager, the facility controller, the quality manager, and two additional staff members, as selected by the Variable Pay Plan Coordinator in consultation with the facility manager.
- The chairperson will be the Variable Pay Plan Coordinator. The Plan Coordinator will record and distribute meeting minutes.
- The Review Team will evaluate and implement suggestions that are beyond the authority of the Departmental Teams. The Review Team will report to the Departmental Teams the disposition of all suggestions submitted to it.
- The Review Team will also review the Variable Pay Plan results, discuss business conditions or major business changes that might affect the plan, review suggestions implemented or rejected by the Departmental Teams, and resolve any issues that arise relative to the Variable Pay Plan.

- All decisions made by the Review Team will be by consensus.
- Each Departmental Team should be represented at Review Team meetings. If an elected member to the Review Team cannot attend the meeting, another elected member of the Departmental Team should attend in his place.
- Suggestion forms will be made available to the Departmental Team members and supervisors.

Suggested Readings

Books

Belcher, John G., Jr. *Gain Sharing: The New Path to Profits and Productivity.* Houston: Gulf Publishing Company, 1991. An overview of gain-sharing design components and issues.

Blinder, Alan S., ed. *Paying for Productivity.* Washington, D.C.: The Brookings Institution, 1990. A collection of academic papers examining the relationship between various alternative reward systems and firm performance.

Gomez-Mejia, Luis R., and David B. Balkin. *Compensation, Organizational Strategy, and Firm Performance.* Cincinnati: South-Western Publishing Company, 1992. Research-oriented work on the impact of compensation on firm performance.

Lawler, Edward E., III. *The Ultimate Advantage: Creating the High-Involvement Organization.* San Francisco: Jossey-Bass, 1992. Creating a high-involvement organization to gain a competitive advantage.

———. *Strategic Pay.* San Francisco: Jossey-Bass, 1990. How to use pay as a strategic tool for improving organizational performance.

Risher, Howard, and Charles Fay, eds. *The Performance Imperative: Strategies for Enhancing Workforce Effectiveness.* San Francisco: Jossey-Bass, 1995. A comprehensive collection of articles on approaches to improving workforce effectiveness, including compensation approaches.

Schuster, Jay R., and Patricia K. Zingheim. *The New Pay: Linking Employee and Organizational Performance.* New York: Lexington Books, 1992. Discussion of the failures of traditional pay and the need for alternative approaches to all forms of pay—base pay, variable pay, and benefits.

Articles and Research Reports

Beck, David. "Implementing a Gainsharing Plan: What Companies Need to Know." *Compensation & Benefits Review,* January-February 1992.

Belcher, John G., Jr. "Gainsharing and Variable Pay: The State of the Art." *Compensation & Benefits Review*, May-June 1994.

———. "Brief 85: The Family of Measures." Houston: American Productivity & Quality Center, October 1991.

———. "Case 82: Reward Systems: Time for Change." Houston: American Productivity & Quality Center, November 1989.

Berman, Steven, Beverly L. Little, Steven E. Markham, and K. Dow Scott. "Gainsharing Experiments in Health Care." *Compensation & Benefits Review*, March-April 1992.

Conference Board, "Variable Pay: Nontraditional Programs for Motivation and Reward," 1993.

———. "Small Group Incentives: Goal-Based Pay," 1992.

Filipczak, Bob. "Ericsson General Electric: The Evolution of Empowerment." *Training*, September 1993.

Greene, Robert J. "Effective Compensation Strategies for Project-Focused Personnel." *ACA Journal*, Summer 1994.

Gross, Steven E., and Jeffrey P. Bacher. "The New Variable Pay Programs: How Some Succeed, Why Some Don't." *Compensation & Benefits Review*, January-February 1993.

Guthrie, James P., and Edward P. Cunningham. "Pay for Performance: The Quaker Oats Alternative." *Compensation & Benefits Review*, March-April 1992.

Lawler, Edward E., III, and Susan G. Cohen. "Designing Pay Systems for Teams." *ACA Journal*, Autumn 1992.

Mack, Toby. "Putting Incentive Compensation to Work." *Association Management*, December 1993.

Markham, Steven E., et al. "Gainsharing Experiments in Health Care." *Compensation & Benefits Review*, March-April 1992.

Masternack, Robert L. "Gainsharing Programs at Two Fortune 500 Facilities: Why One Worked Better." *National Productivity Review*, Winter 1991/92.

McAdams, Jerry L., and Elizabeth J. Hawk. *Organizational Performance and Rewards*. Scottsdale, Ariz.: American Compensation Association, 1994.

O'Neill, Darlene. "Blending the Best of Profit Sharing and Gainsharing." *HRMagazine*, March 1994.

Saunier, Anne. M., and Elizabeth J. Hawk. "Realizing the Potential of Teams Through Team-Based Rewards." *Compensation & Benefits Review*, July-August 1994.

Scheffler, Steve. "SeaPay at SeaPak." *Continuous Journey*, October/November 1993.

———. "Case 82: Gainsharing, PEP, and PAID Lead LTV-Camden Into the Future." Houston: American Productivity & Quality Center, June 1991.

Schuster, Jay R., and Patricia K. Zingheim. "The New Variable Pay: Key Design Issues." *Compensation & Benefits Review,* March-April 1993.

Sisco, Rebecca. "Put Your Money Where Your Teams Are." *Training,* July 1992.

Tucker, Sharon A., and Donald E. Strickland. *Perspectives in Total Compensation: Role of Compensation in High-Commitment Organizations.* Phoenix: American Compensation Association, June 1991.

Turnasella, Ted. "Aligning Pay With Business Strategies and Cultural Values." *Compensation & Benefits Review,* September-October 1994.

Wallace, Marc J. *Rewards and Renewal: America's Search for Competitive Advantage Through Alternative Pay Strategies.* Phoenix: American Compensation Association, 1990.

Wilkinson, Janis G. "Duke Power Integrates Employee Rewards with Its Business Vision of Excellence." *National Productivity Review,* Summer 1993.

Zingheim, Patricia K., and Jay R. Schuster. "Linking Quality and Pay." *HR-Magazine,* December 1992.

Zitaner, Eric D. "Variable Pay Programs: Tracking Their Direction." *Compensation & Benefits Review,* November-December 1992.

Index